The Works of William Robertson: Historical Disquisition Concerning the Knowledge Which the Ancients Had of India; and the Progress of Trade with That Country Prior to Discovery of the Passage to It by the Cape of Good Hope

Alexander Stewart, William Robertson

Nabu Public Domain Reprints:

You are holding a reproduction of an original work published before 1923 that is in the public domain in the United States of America, and possibly other countries. You may freely copy and distribute this work as no entity (individual or corporate) has a copyright on the body of the work. This book may contain prior copyright references, and library stamps (as most of these works were scanned from library copies). These have been scanned and retained as part of the historical artifact.

This book may have occasional imperfections such as missing or blurred pages, poor pictures, errant marks, etc. that were either part of the original artifact, or were introduced by the scanning process. We believe this work is culturally important, and despite the imperfections, have elected to bring it back into print as part of our continuing commitment to the preservation of printed works worldwide. We appreciate your understanding of the imperfections in the preservation process, and hope you enjoy this valuable book.

1820.

100 110

THE WORKS

OF

WILLIAM ROBERTSON, D.D.

PRINCIPAL OF THE UNIVERSITY OF EDINBURGH,
HISTORIOGRAPHER TO HIS MAJESTY FOR SCOTLAND,

AND

MEMBER OF THE ROYAL ACADEMY OF HISTORY
AT MADRID.

TO WHICH IS PREFIXED

AN ACCOUNT OF HIS LIFE AND WRITINGS,

BY THE REV. ALEX. STEWART.

IN TWELVE VOLUMES.

VOL. XII.

LONDON:

PRINTED FOR W. SHARPE & SON, W. ALLASON, C. CHAPPLE, W. ROBINSON & SONS, J. MOLLISON, T. FISHER, J. BUMPUS, G. & J. OFFOR, J. CRANWELL, J. EVANS & SONS, J. MAYNARD, E. WILSON, W. BAYNES & SON, T. MASON, J. ROBINS & CO. AND W. HARWOOD, LONDON; ALSO W. STEWART & CO. AND J. CARFRAE, EDINBURGH; AND W. TURNBULL, GLASGOW.

1820.

Printed by Walker and Greig,
Edinburgh.

AN HISTORICAL DISQUISITION

CONCERNING

THE KNOWLEDGE WHICH THE ANCIENTS HAD OF

INDIA;

AND THE

PROGRESS OF TRADE WITH THAT COUNTRY

PRIOR TO THE DISCOVERY OF THE PASSAGE TO IT

BY THE CAPE OF GOOD HOPE.

WITH AN APPENDIX,

CONTAINING

OBSERVATIONS ON THE CIVIL POLITY—THE LAWS AND JUDICIAL PROCEEDINGS—
THE ARTS AND SCIENCES—AND RELIGIOUS INSTITUTIONS OF THE

INDIANS.

NEW YORK
PUBLIC
LIBRARY

PREFACE.

THE perusal of Major RENNELL's Memoir for illustrating his Map of Indostan, one of the most valuable geographical treatises that has appeared in any age or country, gave rise to the following Work. It suggested to me the idea of examining more fully than I had done in the Introductory Book to my History of America, into the knowledge which the Ancients had of India, and of considering what is certain, what is obscure, and what is fabulous, in the accounts of that country which they have handed down to us. In undertaking this inquiry, I had originally no other object than my own amusement and instruction: But in carrying it on, and consulting with diligence the authors of antiquity, some facts, hitherto unobserved, and many which had not been examined with proper attention, occurred; new views opened; my ideas gradually extended and became more interesting; until, at length, I imagined that the result of my researches might prove amusing and instructive to others, by exhibiting such a view of the various modes in which intercourse with India had been carried on from the earliest times, as might shew how much that great branch of commerce has contributed, in every age, to increase the wealth and power of the nations which possessed it.

Thus the Historical Disquisition which I now lay before the Reader was begun and completed. What degree of merit it possesses, the Public must determine. My grateful recollection of the favourable manner in which my other Works have been received, naturally increases the solicitude with which I wait for its decision concerning this which I now publish.

When I first turned my thoughts to this subject, I was so fully aware of the disadvantage under which I laboured in undertaking to describe countries of which I had not any local knowledge, that I have been at the utmost pains to guard against any errors which this might occasion. I have consulted, with persevering industry, the works of all the authors I could procure, who have given any account of India; I have never formed any decided opinion, which was not supported by respectable authority; and as I have the good fortune to reckon among the number of my friends, some Gentlemen who have filled important stations, civil and military, in India, and who have visited many different parts of it, I had recourse frequently to them, and from their conversation learned things which I could not have found in books. Were it proper to mention their names, the Public would allow, that, by their discernment and abilities, they are fully entitled to the confidence which I have placed in them.

In the progress of the Work, I became sensible of my own deficiency with respect to another point. In order to give an accurate idea of the imperfection both of the theory and practice of navigation among the Ancients, and to explain, with scientific precision, the manner in which they ascertained the position of places, and calculated their longitude and latitude, a greater portion of mathematical knowledge was requisite, than my attention to other studies had permitted me to acquire. What I wanted, the friendship of my ingenious and respectable Colleague, Mr Playfair, Professor of Mathematics, has supplied; and I have been enabled by him to elucidate all the points I have mentioned, in a manner which, I am confident, will afford my readers complete satisfaction. To him, likewise, I am indebted for the construction of two maps necessary for illustrating this Disquisition, which without his assistance I could not have undertaken.

I HAVE adhered, in this Work, to an arrangement I followed in my former compositions, and to which the Public has been long accustomed. I have kept historical narrative as much separate as possible from scientific and critical discussions, by reserving the latter for Notes and Illustrations. I flatter myself that I may claim, without presumption, the merit of having examined with diligence what I submit to public inspection, and of having referred, with scrupulous accuracy, to the authors from whom I have derived information.

COLLEGE OF EDINBURGH,
May 10. 1791.

CONTENTS.

SECTION I.

INTERCOURSE with India, from the earliest Times until the conquest of Egypt by the Romans, - - - - - 1

SECTION II.

Intercourse with India, from the Establishment of the Roman Dominion in Egypt, to the Conquest of that Kingdom by the Mahomedans, - - - - 47

SECTION III.

Intercourse with India, from the Conquest of Egypt by the Mahomedans, to the Discovery of the Passage by the Cape of Good Hope, and the Establishment of the Portuguese Dominion in the East, - - 99

SECTION IV.

General Observations, - - - - 163

Appendix, - - - - - 195
Notes and Illustrations, - - - 289

AN HISTORICAL DISQUISITION CONCERNING ANCIENT INDIA.

SECTION I.

Intercourse with India, from the earliest Times until the Conquest of Egypt by the Romans.

WHOEVER attempts to trace the operations of men in remote times, and to mark the various steps of their progress in any line of exertion, will soon have the mortification to find, that the period of authentic history is extremely limited. It is little more than three thousand years since the Books of Moses, the most ancient and only genuine record of what passed in the early ages of the world, were composed. Herodotus, the most ancient Heathen historian whose works have reached us, flourished a thousand years later. If we push our inquiries concerning any point beyond the era where written history commences, we enter upon the region of conjecture, of fable, and of uncertainty. Upon that ground I will neither venture myself, nor endeavour to conduct my readers. In my researches concerning the

SECT. I. intercourse between the Eastern and Western regions of the earth, and concerning the progress of that great branch of trade, which, in every age, has contributed so conspicuously towards raising the people who carried it on to wealth and power, I shall confine myself within the precincts I have marked out. Wherever the inspired writers, intent upon higher objects, mention occasionally any circumstance that tends to illustrate the subject of my inquiries, I shall attend to it with reverence. Whatever other writers relate, I shall examine with freedom, and endeavour to ascertain the degree of credit to which they are entitled.

The original station allotted to man by his Creator, was in the mild and fertile regions of the East. There the human race began its career of improvement; and from the remains of sciences which were anciently cultivated, as well as of arts which were anciently exercised in India, we may conclude it to be one of the first countries in which men made any considerable progress in that career. The wisdom of the East was early celebrated,[*] and its productions were early in request among distant nations.[†] The intercourse, however, between different countries was carried on at first entirely by land. As the people of the East appear soon to have acquired complete dominion over the useful animals,[‡] they could early

---

[*] 1 Kings, iv. 30.   [†] Gen. xxxvii. 25.
[‡] Gen. xii. 16. xxiv. 10, 11.

undertake the long and toilsome journies which it was necessary to make, in order to maintain this intercourse; and by the provident bounty of Heaven, they were furnished with a beast of burden, without whose aid it would have been impossible to accomplish them. The camel, by its persevering strength, by its moderation in the use of food, and the singularity of its internal structure, which enables it to lay in a stock of water sufficient for several days, put it in their power to convey bulky commodities through those deserts which must be traversed by all who travel from any of the countries west of the Euphrates towards India. Trade was carried on in this manner, particularly by the nations near to the Arabian Gulf, from the earliest period to which historical information reaches. Distant journies, however, would be undertaken at first only occasionally, and by a few adventurers. But by degrees, from attention to their mutual safety and comfort, numerous bodies of merchants assembled at stated times, and forming a temporary association, (known afterwards by the name of a Caravan), governed by officers of their own choice, and subject to regulations of which experience had taught them the utility, they performed journies of such extent and duration, as appear astonishing to nations not accustomed to this mode of carrying on commerce.

But, notwithstanding every improvement that could be made in the manner of conveying the productions of one country to another by land, the inconveniences which attended it were obvious and unavoidable. It was often dangerous; always expensive, and tedious, and fatiguing. A method of communication more easy and expeditious was sought, and the ingenuity of man gradually discovered, that the rivers, the arms of the sea, and even the ocean itself, were destined to open and facilitate intercourse with the various regions of the earth, between which they appear, at first view, to be placed as insuperable barriers. Navigation, however, and ship-building, (as I have observed in another work),* are arts so nice and complicated, that they require the talents as well as experience of many successive ages, to bring them to any degree of perfection. From the raft or canoe, which first served to carry a savage over the river that obstructed him in the chase, to the construction of a vessel capable of conveying a numerous crew, or a considerable cargo of goods, to a distant coast, the progress of improvement is immense. Many efforts would be made, many experiments would be tried, and much labour as well as ingenuity would be employed, before this arduous and important undertaking could be accomplished.

EVEN after some improvement was made in ship-building, the intercourse of nations with each other by sea was far from being extensive. From the accounts of the earliest historians we learn, that navigation made its first efforts in the Medi-

---

* Hist. of America, vol. i. p. 2.

terranean and the Arabian Gulf, and in them the first active operations of commerce were carried on. From an attentive inspection of the position and form of these two great inland seas, these accounts appear to be highly probable. These seas lay open the continents of Europe, Asia, and Africa, and spreading to a great extent along the coasts of the most fertile and most early civilized countries in each, seem to have been destined by nature to facilitate their communication with one another. We find, accordingly, that the first voyages of the Egyptians and Phœnicians, the most ancient navigators mentioned in history, were made in the Mediterranean. Their trade, however, was not long confined to the countries bordering upon it. By acquiring early possession of ports on the Arabian Gulf, they extended the sphere of their commerce, and are represented as the first people of the West who opened a communication by sea with India.

In that account of the progress of navigation and discovery which I prefixed to the History of America, I considered with attention the maritime operations of the Egyptians and Phœnicians: a brief review of them here, as far as they relate to their connexion with India, is all that is requisite for illustrating the subject of my present inquiries. With respect to the former of these people, the information which history affords is slender, and of doubtful authority. The fertile soil and mild climate of Egypt produced the necessaries and comforts of life in such profusion, as to render its inhabitants so independent of other countries, that it became early an established maxim in their policy, to renounce all intercourse with foreigners. In consequence of this, they held all seafaring persons in detestation, as impious and profane; and fortifying their harbours, they denied strangers admission into them.*

The enterprising ambition of Sesostris, disdaining the restraints imposed upon it by these contracted ideas of his subjects, prompted him to render the Egyptians a commercial people; and in the course of his reign he so completely accomplished this, that (if we may give credit to some historians) he was able to fit out a fleet of four hundred ships in the Arabian Gulf, which conquered all the countries stretching along the Erythræan Sea to India. At the same time his army, led by himself, marched through Asia, and subjected to his dominion every part of it as far as to the banks of the Ganges; and crossing that river, advanced to the Eastern Ocean.† But these efforts produced no permanent effect, and appear to have been so contrary to the genius and habits of the Egyptians, that, on the death of Sesostris, they resumed their ancient maxims, and many ages elapsed before the commercial connexion of Egypt with India came to be of

---

* Diodor. Sicul. lib. i. p. 78. edit. Wesselingi. Amst. 1746. Strab. Geog. lib. xvii. p. 1142. A. edit. Casaub. Amst. 1707.
† Diod. Sic. lib. i. p. 64.

such importance as to merit any notice in this Disquisition.*

The history of the early maritime operations of Phœnicia is not involved in the same obscurity with those of Egypt. Every circumstance in the character and situation of the Phœnicians was favourable to the commercial spirit. The territory which they possessed was neither large nor fertile. It was from commerce only that they could derive either opulence or power. Accordingly, the trade carried on by the Phœnicians of Sidon and Tyre was extensive and adventurous; and, both in their manners and policy, they resemble the great commercial states of modern times, more than any people in the ancient world. Among the various branches of their commerce, that with India may be regarded as one of the most considerable and most lucrative. As by their situation on the Mediterranean, and the imperfect state of navigation, they could not attempt to open a direct communication with India by sea; the enterprising spirit of commerce prompted them to wrest from the Idumæans some commodious harbours towards the bottom of the Arabian Gulf. From these they held a regular intercourse with India on the one hand, and with the eastern and southern coasts of Africa on the other. The distance, however, from the Arabian Gulf to Tyre was considerable, and rendered the conveyance of goods to it by land car-

---

* See Note I. Page 289.

riage so tedious and expensive, that it became necessary for them to take possession of Rhinocolura, the nearest port in the Mediterranean to the Arabian Gulf. Thither all the commodities brought from India were conveyed over land, by a route much shorter, and more practicable, than that by which the productions of the East were carried at a subsequent period from the opposite shore of the Arabian Gulf to the Nile.* At Rhinocolura they were re-shipped, and transported by an easy navigation to Tyre, and distributed through the world. This, as it is the earliest route of communication with India, of which we have any authentic description, had so many advantages over any ever known before the modern discovery of a new course of navigation to the East, that the Phœnicians could supply other nations with the productions of India in greater abundance, and at a cheaper rate, than any people of antiquity. To this circumstance, which, for a considerable time, secured to them a monopoly of that trade, was owing, not only the extraordinary wealth of individuals, which rendered the " merchants of Tyre princes, and her traffickers the honourable of the earth,"† but the extensive power of the State itself, which first taught mankind to conceive what vast resources a commercial people possess, and what great exertions they are capable of making.‡

---

* Diod. Sic. lib. i. p. 70.   Strab. lib. xvi. p. 1128. A.
† Isaiah, xxiii. 8.   ‡ See NOTE II. Page 292.

The Jews, by their vicinity to Tyre, had such an opportunity of observing the wealth which flowed into that city from the lucrative commerce carried on by the Phœnicians from their settlements on the Arabian Gulf, as incited them to aim at obtaining some share of it. This they effected under the prosperous reigns of David and Solomon, partly by the conquests which they made of a small district in the land of Edom, that gave them possession of the harbours of Elath and Esiongeber on the Red Sea, and partly by the friendship of Hiram, King of Tyre, who enabled Solomon to fit out fleets, which, under the direction of Phœnician pilots, sailed to Tarshish and Ophir.* In what region of the earth we should search for these famous ports, which furnished the navy of Solomon with the various commodities enumerated by the sacred historians, is an inquiry that has long exercised the industry of learned men. They were early supposed to be situated in some part of India, and the Jews were held to be one of the nations which traded with that country. But the opinion more generally adopted is, that Solomon's fleets, after passing the straits of Babelmandeb, held their course along the south-west coast of Africa, as far as the kingdom of Sofala, a country celebrated for its rich mines of gold and silver, (from which it has been denominated the Golden Sofala by oriental writers),† and abounding in all the

---

* 1 Kings, ix. 26. x. 22.
† Notices des MSS. du Roi, tom. ii. p. 40.

other articles which composed the cargoes of the Jewish ships. This opinion, which the accurate researches of M. D'Anville rendered highly probable,* seems now to be established with the utmost certainty by a late learned traveller; who, by his knowledge of the monsoons in the Arabian Gulf, and his attention to the ancient mode of navigation, both in that sea and along the African coast, has not only accounted for the extraordinary length of time which the fleets of Solomon took in going and returning, but has shewn, from circumstances mentioned concerning the voyage, that it was not made to any place in India.† The Jews, then, we may conclude, have no title to be reckoned among the nations which carried on intercourse with India by sea; and if, from deference to the sentiments of some respectable authors, their claim were to be admitted, we know with certainty, that the commercial effort which they made in the reign of Solomon was merely a transient one, and that they quickly returned to their former state of unsocial seclusion from the rest of mankind.

From collecting the scanty information which history affords, concerning the most early attempts to open a commercial intercourse with India, I now proceed, with more certainty and greater confidence, to trace the progress of com-

---

* Dissert. sur le Pays d'Ophir, Mem. de Litterat. tom. xxx. p. 83, &c.
† Bruce's Travels, book ii. ch. 4.

munication with that country, under the guidance of authors who recorded events nearer to their own times, and with respect to which they had received more full and accurate intelligence.

The first establishment of any foreign power in India, which can be ascertained by evidence meriting any degree of credit, is that of the Persians; and even of this we have only a very general and doubtful account. Darius the son of Hystaspes, though raised to the throne of Persia by chance or by artifice, possessed such active and enterprising talents as rendered him worthy of that high station. He examined the different provinces of his kingdom more diligently than any of his predecessors, and explored regions of Asia formerly little known.* Having subjected to his dominion many of the countries which stretched south-east from the Caspian Sea towards the river Oxus, his curiosity was excited to acquire a more extensive and accurate knowledge of India, on which they bordered. With this view he appointed Scylax of Caryandra to take the command of a squadron fitted out at Caspatyrus, in the country of Pactya, (the modern Pehkely), towards the upper part of the navigable course of the river Indus, and to fall down its stream until he should reach the ocean. This Scylax performed, though it should seem with much difficulty, and notwithstanding many obstacles; for he spent no less than two years

---

* Herodot. lib. iv. c. 44.

and six months in conducting his squadron from the place where he embarked, to the Arabian Gulf.* The account which he gave of the populousness, fertility, and high cultivation of that region of India through which his course lay, rendered Darius impatient to become master of a country so valuable. This he soon accomplished; and though his conquests in India seem not to have extended beyond the district watered by the Indus, we are led to form an high idea of its opulence, as well as of the number of its inhabitants, in ancient times, when we learn that the tribute which he levied from it was near a third part of the whole revenue of the Persian monarchy.† But neither this voyage of Scylax, nor the conquests of Darius, to which it gave rise, diffused any general knowledge of India. The Greeks, who were the only enlightened race of men at that time in Europe, paid but little attention to the transactions of the people whom they considered as Barbarians, especially in countries far remote from their own; and Scylax had embellished the narrative of his voyage with so many circumstances manifestly fabulous,‡ that he seems to have met with the just punishment to which persons who have a notorious propensity to what is marvellous are often subjected, of being listened to with distrust, even when they relate what is exactly true.

---

* Herodot. lib. iv. c. 42. 44.
† Id. lib. iii. c. 90—96. See NOTE III. Page 293.
‡ Philostr. Vita Apoll. lib. iii. c. 47. and Note 3d of Olearius Tzetzet. Chiliad. vii. vers. 680.

About an hundred and sixty years after the reign of Darius Hystaspes, Alexander the Great undertook his expedition into India. The wild sallies of passion, the indecent excesses of intemperance, and the ostentatious displays of vanity too frequent in the conduct of this extraordinary man, have so degraded his character, that the pre-eminence of his merit, either as a conqueror, a politician, or a legislator, has seldom been justly estimated. The subject of my present inquiry leads me to consider his operations only in one light, but it will enable me to exhibit a striking view of the grandeur and extent of his plans. He seems, soon after his first successes in Asia, to have formed the idea of establishing an universal monarchy, and aspired to the dominion of the sea as well as of the land. From the wonderful efforts of the Tyrians in their own defence, when left without any ally or protector, he conceived an high opinion of the resources of maritime power, and of the wealth to be derived from commerce, especially that with India, which he found engrossed by the citizens of Tyre. With a view to secure this commerce, and to establish a station for it preferable in many respects to that of Tyre, as soon as he completed the conquest of Egypt he founded a city near one of the mouths of the Nile, which he honoured with his own name; and with such admirable discernment was the situation of it chosen, that Alexandria soon became the greatest trading city in the ancient world; and notwithstanding many successive revolutions in empire, continued, during eighteen

SECT.
I.

centuries, to be the chief seat of commerce with India.* Amidst the military operations to which Alexander was soon obliged to turn his attention, the desire of acquiring the lucrative commerce which the Tyrians had carried on with India, was not relinquished. Events soon occurred, that not only confirmed and added strength to this desire, but opened to him a prospect of obtaining the sovereignty of those regions which supplied the rest of mankind with so many precious commodities.

After his final victory over the Persians, he was led in pursuit of the last Darius, and of Bessus, the murderer of that unfortunate monarch, to traverse that part of Asia which stretches from the Caspian Sea beyond the river Oxus. He advanced towards the east as far as Maracanda,† then a city of some note, and destined in a future period, under the modern name of Samarcand, to be the capital of an empire not inferior to his own, either in extent or in power. In a progress of several months through provinces hitherto unknown to the Greeks, in a line of march often approaching near to India, and among people accustomed to much intercourse with it, he learned many things concerning the state of a country‡ that had been long the object of his thoughts and wishes,§ which increased his desire of invading it. Decisive and prompt in all his resolutions, he set out from Bactria, and cross-

---

* Hist. of America, vol. i. p. 21. † Arrian, iii. c. 30.
‡ Strabo, xv. p. 1021. A. § Arrian, iv. c. 15.

ed that ridge of mountains, which, under various denominations, forms the Stony Girdle (if I may use an expression of the oriental geographers) which encircles Asia, and constitutes the northern barrier of India.

SECT. I.

The most practicable avenue to every country, it is obvious, must be formed by circumstances in its natural situation, such as the defiles which lead through mountains, the course of rivers, and the places where they may be passed with the greatest ease and safety. In no place of the earth is this line of approach marked and defined more conspicuously, than on the northern frontier of India; insomuch that the three great invaders of this country, Alexander, Tamerlane, and Nadir Shah, in three distant ages, and with views and talents extremely different, advanced by the same route, with very little deviation. Alexander had the merit of having first discovered the way. After passing the mountains, he encamped at Alexandria Paropamisana, not far from the mountains denominated the Indian Caucasus by his historians, now known by the name of Hindoo Kho;* and having subdued or conciliated the nations seated on the north-west bank of the Indus, he crossed the river at Taxila, now Attock,† where its stream is so tranquil

---

* In the second edition of his Memoir, Major Rennel gives the modern names of the Hydaspes, with some variation in their orthography, *Behut* and *Jhylam*.

† Rennell, Mem. p. 92. See Note IV. Page 298.

that a bridge can be thrown over it with greater ease than at any other place.

AFTER passing the Indus, Alexander marched forward in the road which leads directly to the Ganges, and the opulent provinces to the south-east, now comprehended under the general name of Indostan. But, on the banks of the Hydaspes, known in modern times by the name of the Betah or Chelum, he was opposed by Porus, a powerful monarch of the country, at the head of a numerous army. The war with Porus, and the hostilities in which he was successively engaged with other Indian princes, led him to deviate from his original route, and to turn more towards the south-west. In carrying on these operations, Alexander marched through one of the richest and best peopled countries of India, now called the Panjab, from the five great rivers by which it is watered; and as we know that this march was performed in the rainy season, when even Indian armies cannot keep the field, it gives an high idea both of Alexander's persevering spirit, and of the extraordinary vigour and hardiness of constitution which soldiers, in ancient times, derived from the united effects of gymnastic exercise and military discipline. In every step of his progress, objects no less striking than new presented themselves to Alexander. The magnitude of the Indus,[*] even after he had seen the Nile, the Euphrates, and the Tigris, must have

---

[*] Strabo, lib. xv. p. 1027. C. and note 5. Casaub.

filled him with surprise. No country he had hitherto visited was so populous and well cultivated, or abounded in so many valuable productions of nature and of art, as that part of India through which he had led his army. But when he was informed in every place, and probably with exaggerated description, how much the Indus was inferior to the Ganges, and how far all that he had hitherto beheld was surpassed in the happy regions through which that great river flows, it is not wonderful that his eagerness to view and to take possession of them should have prompted him to assemble his soldiers, and to propose that they should resume their march towards that quarter, where wealth, dominion, and fame awaited them. But they had already done so much, and had suffered so greatly, especially from incessant rains and extensive inundations, that their patience as well as strength were exhausted,* and with one voice they refused to advance farther. In this resolution they persisted with such sullen obstinacy, that Alexander, though possessed in the highest degree of every quality that gains an ascendant over the minds of military men, was obliged to yield, and to issue orders for marching back to Persia.†

The scene of this memorable transaction was on the banks of the Hyphasis, the modern Beyah, which was the utmost limit of Alexander's pro-

---

* See Note V. Page 295. † Arrian, v. c. 24, 25.

gress in India. From this it is manifest, that he did not traverse the whole extent of the Panjab. Its south-west boundary is formed by a river anciently known by the name of Hysudrus, and now by that of the Setlege, to which Alexander never approached nearer than the southern bank of the Hyphasis, where he erected twelve stupendous altars, which he intended as a monument of his exploits, and which (if we may believe the biographer of Apollonius Tyanæus) were still remaining, with legible inscriptions, when that fantastic sophist visited India, three hundred and seventy-three years after Alexander's expedition.* The breadth of the Panjab, from Ludhana on the Setlege to Attock on the Indus, is computed to be two hundred and fifty-nine geographical miles, in a straight line; and Alexander's march, computed in the same manner, did not extend above two hundred miles. But, both as he advanced and returned, his troops were so spread over the country, and often acted in so many separate divisions, and all his movements were so exactly measured and delineated by men of science, whom he kept in pay for the purpose, that he acquired a very extensive and accurate knowledge of that part of India.†

When, upon his return, he reached the banks of the Hydaspes, he found that the officers to

---

* Philostr. Vita Apollon. lib. ii. c. 43. edit. Olear. Lips.. 1709.

† Plin. Nat. Hist. lib. vi. c. 17.

whom he had given it in charge to build and collect as many vessels as possible, had executed his orders with such activity and success, that they had assembled a numerous fleet. As, amidst the hurry of war, and the rage of conquest, he never lost sight of his pacific and commercial schemes, the destination of his fleet was to sail down the Indus to the ocean, and from its mouth to proceed to the Persian Gulf, that a communication by sea might be opened with India and the centre of his dominions.

The conduct of this expedition was committed to Nearchus, an officer equal to that important trust. But as Alexander was ambitious to acquire fame of every kind, and fond of engaging in new and splendid undertakings, he himself accompanied Nearchus in his navigation down the river. The armament was indeed so great and magnificent, as deserved to be commanded by the conqueror of Asia. It was composed of an army of a hundred and twenty thousand men, and two hundred elephants, and of a fleet of near two thousand vessels, various in burden and form;* on board of which one-third of the troops embarked, while the remainder marching in two divisions, one on the right, and the other on the left of the river, accompanied them in their progress. As they advanced, the nations on each side were either compelled or persuaded to submit. Retarded by the various operations in

---

* See Note VI. Page 296.

which this engaged him, as well as by the slow navigation of such a fleet as he conducted, Alexander was above nine months before he reached the ocean.*

ALEXANDER's progress in India, in this line of direction, was far more considerable than that which he made by the route we formerly traced; and when we attend to the various movements of his troops, the number of cities which they took, and the different states which they subdued, he may be said not only to have viewed, but to have explored, the countries through which he passed. This part of India has been so little frequented by Europeans in later times, that neither the position of places, nor their distances, can be ascertained with the same accuracy as in the interior provinces, or even in the Panjab. But from the researches of Major Rennell, carried on with no less discernment than industry, the distance of that place on the Hydaspes where Alexander fitted out his fleet from the ocean, cannot be less than a thousand British miles. Of this extensive region a considerable portion, particularly the upper Delta, stretching from the capital of the ancient Malli, now Moultan, to Patala, the modern Tatta, is distinguished for its fertility and population.†

SOON after he reached the ocean, Alexander, satisfied with having accomplished this arduous

---

* Strabo, lib. xv. p. 1014.   † Rennell, Mem. 68, &c.

undertaking, led his army by land back to Persia. The command of the fleet, with a considerable body of troops on board of it, he left to Nearchus, who, after a coasting voyage of seven months, conducted it safely up the Persian Gulf into the Euphrates.*

In this manner did Alexander first open the knowledge of India to the people of Europe, and an extensive district of it was surveyed with greater accuracy than could have been expected from the short time he remained in that country. Fortunately an exact account, not only of his military operations, but of every thing worthy of notice in the countries where they were carried on, was recorded in the Memoirs or Journals of three of his principal officers, Ptolemy, the son of Lagus, Aristobulus, and Nearchus. The two former have not, indeed, reached our times; but it is probable that the most important facts which they contained are preserved, as Arrian professes to have followed them as his guides in his History of the Expedition of Alexander;† a work which, though composed long after Greece had lost its liberty, and in an age when genius and taste were on the decline, is not unworthy the purest times of Attic literature.

With respect to the general state of India, we learn from these writers, that, in the age of Alex-

---

* Plin. Nat. Hist. lib. vi. c. 23.   See Note VII. Page 297.
† Arrian, lib. i. in proëmio.

ander, though there was not established in it any powerful empire, resembling that which in modern times stretched its dominion from the Indus almost to Cape Comorin, it was, even then, formed into monarchies of considerable extent. The King of the Prasij was prepared, on the banks of the Ganges, to oppose the Macedonians, with an army of twenty thousand cavalry, two hundred thousand infantry, two thousand armed chariots, and a great number of elephants.* The territory of which Alexander constituted Porus the sovereign, is said to have contained seven distinct nations, and no fewer than two thousand towns.† Even in the most restricted sense that can be given to the vague indefinite appellations of *nations* and *towns*, an idea is conveyed of a very great degree of population. As the fleet sailed down the river, the country on each side was found to be in no respect inferior to that of which the government was committed to Porus.

It was likewise from the Memoirs of the same officers that Europe derived its first authentic information concerning the climate, the soil, the productions, and the inhabitants of India; and in a country where the manners, the customs, and even the dress of the people, are almost as permanent and invariable as the face of nature itself, it is wonderful how exactly the descrip-

---

* Diod. Sicul. lib. xvii. p. 292.
† Arrian, lib. vi. c. 2.

tions given by Alexander's officers delineate what we now behold in India, at the distance of two thousand years. The stated change of seasons, now known by the name of *Monsoons*; the periodical rains; the swelling of the rivers; the inundations which these occasion; the appearance of the country during their continuance, are particularly mentioned and described. No less accurate are the accounts which they have given of the inhabitants; their delicate and slender form, their dark complexion, their black uncurled hair, their garments of cotton, their living entirely upon vegetable food, their division into seperate tribes or *casts*, the members of which never intermarry, the custom of wives burning themselves with their deceased husbands, and many other particulars, in all which they perfectly resemble the modern Hindoos. To enter into any detail with respect to these in this place would be premature; but as the subject, though curious and interesting, will lead unavoidably into discussions not well suited to the nature of an historical work, I shall reserve my ideas concerning it for an Appendix, to be annexed to this Disquisition; and hope they may contribute to throw some additional light upon the origin and nature of the commerce with India.

Much as the western world was indebted for its knowledge of India to the expedition of Alexander, it was only a small portion of that vast continent which he explored. His operations did not extend beyond the modern province of

Lahore, and the countries on the banks of the Indus from Moultan to the sea. These, however, were surveyed with that degree of accuracy which I have already described; and it is a circumstance not unworthy of notice, that this district of India which Europeans first entered, and with which they were best acquainted in ancient times, is now less known than almost any part of that continent;* neither commerce nor war, to which, in every age, geography is chiefly indebted for its improvement, having led any nation of Europe to frequent or explore it.

If an untimely death had not put a period to the reign of the Macedonian hero, India, we have reason to think, would have been more fully explored by the ancients, and the European dominion would have been established there two thousand years sooner. When Alexander invaded India, he had something more in view than a transient incursion. It was his object to annex that extensive and opulent country to his empire; and though the refractory spirit of his army obliged him, at that time, to suspend the prosecution of his plan, he was far from relinquishing it. To exhibit a general view of the measures which he adopted for this purpose, and to point out their propriety and probable success, is not foreign from the subject of this Disquisition, and will convey a more just idea than is usually entertained, of the original genius and

---

* Rennell's Mem. 144.

extent of political wisdom which distinguished this illustrious man.

WHEN Alexander became master of the Persian empire, he early perceived, that with all the power of his hereditary dominions, reinforced by the troops which the ascendant he had acquired over the various states of Greece might enable him to raise there, he could not hope to retain in subjection territories so extensive and populous; that, to render his authority secure and permanent, it must be established in the affection of the nations which he had subdued, and maintained by their arms; and that, in order to acquire this advantage, all distinctions between the victors and the vanquished must be abolished, and his European and Asiatic subjects must be incorporated and become one people, by obeying the same laws, and by adopting the same manners, institutions, and discipline.

LIBERAL as this plan of policy was, and well adapted to accomplish what he had in view, nothing could be more repugnant to the ideas and prejudices of his countrymen. The Greeks had such an high opinion of the pre-eminence to which they were raised by civilization and science, that they seem hardly to have acknowledged the rest of mankind to be of the same species with themselves. To every other people they gave the degrading appellation of Barbarians, and, in consequence of their own boasted superiority, they asserted a right of dominion over them, in the same manner (to use their own expression) as the soul has over the body, and men have over irrational animals. Extravagant as this pretension may now appear, it found admission, to the disgrace of ancient philosophy, into all the schools. Aristotle, full of this opinion, in support of which he employs arguments more subtle than solid,* advised Alexander to govern the Greeks like subjects, and the Barbarians as slaves; to consider the former as companions, the latter as creatures of an inferior nature.† But the sentiments of the pupil were more enlarged than those of his master, and his experience in governing men taught the monarch what the speculative science of the philosopher did not discover. Soon after the victory at Arbela, Alexander himself, and, by his persuasion, many of his officers, assumed the Persian dress, and conformed to several of their customs. At the same time he encouraged the Persian nobles to imitate the manners of the Macedonians, to learn the Greek language, and to acquire a relish for the beauties of the elegant writers in that tongue, which were then universally studied and admired. In order to render the union more complete, he resolved to marry one of the daughters of Darius, and chose wives for a hundred of his principal officers in the most illustrious Persian families. Their nuptials were celebrated

---

* Aristot. Polit. i. c. 3—7.
† Plut. de Fortuna Alex. Orat. i. p. 502. vol. vii. edit. Reiske. Strabo, lib. i. p. 116. A.

with great pomp and festivity, and with high exultation of the conquered people. In imitation of them, above ten thousand Macedonians, of inferior rank, married Persian women, to each of whom Alexander gave nuptial presents, as a testimony of his approbation of their conduct.*

But assiduously as Alexander laboured to unite his European and Asiatic subjects by the most indissoluble ties, he did not trust entirely to the success of that measure for the security of his new conquests. In every province which he subdued, he made choice of proper stations, where he built and fortified cities, in which he placed garrisons composed partly of such of the natives as conformed to the Grecian manners and discipline, and partly of such of his European subjects as were worn out with the fatigues of service, and wished for repose and a permanent establishment. These cities were numerous, and served not only as a chain of posts to keep open the communication between the different provinces of his dominions, but as places of strength to overawe and curb the conquered people. Thirty thousand of his new subjects, who had been disciplined in these cities, and armed after the European fashion, appeared before Alexander in Susa, and were formed by him into that compact solid body of infantry, known by the name of the Phalanx, which constituted the strength of a

---

* Arrian, lib. vii. c. 4. Plut. de Fort. Alex. p. 304. See Note VIII. Page 301.

Macedonian army. But in order to secure entire authority over this new corps, as well as to render it more effective, he appointed that every officer in it intrusted with command, either superior or subaltern, should be European. As the ingenuity of mankind naturally has recourse in similar situations to the same expedients, the European powers, who now in their Indian territories employ numerous bodies of the natives in their service, have, in forming the establishment of these troops, adopted the same maxims; and, probably without knowing it, have modelled their battalions of Sepoys upon the same principles as Alexander did his phalanx of Persians.

The farther Alexander pushed his conquests from the banks of the Euphrates, which may be considered as the centre of his dominions, he found it necessary to build and to fortify a greater number of cities. Several of these to the east and south of the Caspian Sea, are mentioned by ancient authors; and in India itself he founded two cities on the banks of the Hydaspes, and a third on the Acesines, both navigable rivers, which, after uniting their streams, fall into the Indus.*
From the choice of such situations it is obvious, that he intended, by means of these cities, to keep open a communication with India, not only by land, but by sea. It was chiefly with a view to the latter of these objects, (as I have already observed), that he examined the navigation of

---

* See Note IX. Page 303.

the Indus with so much attention. With the same view, on his return to Susa, he in person surveyed the course of the Euphrates and Tigris, and gave directions to remove the cataracts or dams, which the ancient monarchs of Persia, induced by a peculiar precept of their religion, which enjoined them to guard with the utmost care against defiling any of the elements, had constructed near the mouths of these rivers, in order to shut out their subjects from any access to the ocean.* By opening the navigation in this manner, he proposed, that the valuable commodities of India should be conveyed from the Persian Gulf into the interior parts of his Asiatic dominions, while by the Arabian Gulf they should be carried to Alexandria, and distributed to the rest of the world.

GRAND and extensive as these schemes were, the precautions employed, and the arrangements made for carrying them into execution, were so various and so proper, that Alexander had good reason to entertain sanguine hopes of their proving successful. At the time when the mutinous spirit of his soldiers obliged him to relinquish his operations in India, he was not thirty years of age complete. At this enterprising period of life, a Prince of a spirit so active, persevering, and indefatigable, must have soon found means to resume a favourite measure on which he had

---

* Arrian, lib. vi. c. 7. Strabo, lib. xvi. p. 1074, &c. See NOTE X. Page 303.

SECT. I.

been long intent. If he had invaded India a second time, he would not, as formerly, have been obliged to force his way through hostile and unexplored regions, opposed at every step by nations and tribes of Barbarians whose names had never reached Greece. All Asia, from the shores of the Ionian Sea to the banks of the Hyphasis, would then have been subject to his dominion; and through that immense stretch of country he had established such a chain of cities, or fortified stations,* that his armies might have continued their march with safety, and have found a regular succession of magazines provided for their subsistence. Nor would it have been difficult for him to bring into the field forces sufficient to have achieved the conquest of a country so populous and extensive as India. Having armed and disciplined his subjects in the East like Europeans, they would have been ambitious to imitate and to equal their instructors; and Alexander might have drawn recruits, not from his scanty domains in Macedonia and Greece, but from the vast regions of Asia, which, in every age, has covered the earth, and astonished mankind with its numerous armies. When at the head of such a formidable power he had reached the confines of India, he might have entered it under circumstances very different from those in his first expedition. He had secured a firm footing there, partly by means of the garrisons that he left in the three cities which he had built and fortified,

---

* See Note XI. Page 304.

and partly by his alliance with Taxiles and Porus. These two Indian Princes, won by Alexander's humanity and beneficence, which, as they were virtues seldom displayed in the ancient mode of carrying on war, excited of course an higher degree of admiration and gratitude, had continued steady in their attachment to the Macedonians. Reinforced by their troops, and guided by their information as well as by the experience which he had acquired in his former compaigns, Alexander must have made rapid progress in a country, where every invader, from his time to the present age, has proved successful.

SECT. I.

But this and all his other splendid schemes were terminated at once by his untimely death. In consequence of that, however, events took place, which illustrate and confirm the justness of the preceding speculations and conjectures by evidence the most striking and satisfactory. When that great empire which the superior genius of Alexander had kept united and in subjection, no longer felt his superintending controul, it broke into pieces, and its various provinces were seized by his principal officers, and parcelled out among them. From ambition, emulation, and personal animosity, they soon turned their arms against one another; and as several of the leaders were equally eminent for political abilities and for military skill, the contest was maintained long, and carried on with frequent vicissitudes of fortune. Amidst the various convulsions and revolutions which these occasioned, it was found that the measures of Alexander for the preservation of his conquests had been concerted with such sagacity, that, upon the final restoration of tranquillity, the Macedonian dominion continued to be established in every part of Asia, and not one province had shaken off the yoke. Even India, the most remote of Alexander's conquests, quietly submitted to Pytho the son of Agenor, and afterwards to Seleucus, who successively obtained dominion over that part of Asia. Porus and Taxiles, notwithstanding the death of their benefactor, neither declined submission to the authority of the Macedonians, nor made any attempt to recover independence.

During the contests for power and superiority among the successors of Alexander, Seleucus, who, in every effort of enterprising ambition, was inferior to none of them, having rendered himself master of all the provinces of the Persian empire comprehended under the name of Upper Asia, considered those countries of India which had been subdued by Alexander, as belonging to that portion of the Macedonian empire of which he was now the sovereign. Seleucus, like all the officers formed under Alexander, entertained such high ideas of the advantages which might be derived from a commercial intercourse with India, as induced him to march into that country, partly with a view of establishing his own authority there, and party in order to curb Sandracottus, who having lately acquired the sovereignty of the

Prasij, a powerful nation on the banks of the Ganges, threatened to attack the Macedonians, whose Indian territories bordered on his dominions. Unfortunately no account of this expedition, which seems to have been splendid and successful, has reached our times. All we know of it is, that he advanced considerably beyond the utmost boundary of Alexander's progress in India,* and would probably have proceeded much farther, if he had not been constrained to stop short in his career, in order to oppose Antigonus, who was preparing to invade his dominions at the head of a formidable army. Before he began his march towards the Euphrates, he concluded a treaty with Sandracottus; in consequence of which, that monarch quietly retained the kingdom he had acquired. But the powers and possessions of the Macedonians seem to have remained unimpaired during the reign of Seleucus, which terminated forty-two years after the death of Alexander.

WITH a view of cultivating a friendly intercourse with Sandracottus, Seleucus made choice of Megasthenes, an officer who, from his having accompanied Alexander in his expedition into India, had some knowledge of the state of the country and the manners of its inhabitants, and sent him as his ambassador to Palibothra.† In this famous capital of the Prasij, situated on the

---

* See Note XII. Page 305.
† Strabo, lib. ii. p. 121, &c. Arrian. Hist. Ind. passim.

SECT. I.

banks of the Ganges, Megasthenes resided several years, and was probably the first European who ever beheld that mighty river, far superior to any of the ancient continent in magnitude,* and no less distinguished by the fertility of the countries through which it flows. This journey of Megasthenes to Palibothra made Europeans acquainted with a large extent of country, of which they had not hitherto any knowledge; for Alexander did not advance farther towards the south-east than that part of the river Hydraotes or Raûvee, where the modern city of Lahore is situated; and Palibothra, the site of which, as it is a capital position in the geography of ancient India, I have investigated with the utmost attention, appears to me the same with that of the modern city of Allahabad, at the confluence of the two great rivers, Jumna and Ganges.† As the road from Lahore to Allahabad runs through some of the most cultivated and opulent provinces of India, the more the country was explored, the idea of its value rose higher. Accordingly, what Megasthenes observed during his progress to Palibothra, and his residence there, made such an impression upon his own mind, as induced him to publish an ample account of India, in order to make his countrymen more thoroughly acquainted with its importance. From his writings the ancients seem to have derived almost all their knowledge of the interior state of India, and from comparing the three most ample accounts of it, by Diodorus Si-

---

* See NOTE XIII. Page 306. † See NOTE XIV. Page 307.

culus, Strabo, and Arrian, they appear manifestly, from their near resemblance, to be a transcript of his words. But, unfortunately, Megasthenes was so fond of the marvellous, that he mingled with the truths which he related many extravagant fictions; and to him may be traced up the fabulous tales of men with ears so large that they could wrap themselves up in them, of others with a single eye, without mouths, without noses, with long feet, and toes turned backwards; of people only three spans in height, of wild men with heads in the shape of a wedge, of ants as large as foxes that dug up gold, and many other things no less wonderful.* The extracts from his narrative which have been transmitted to us by Strabo, Arrian, and other writers, seem not to be entitled to credit, unless when they are supported by internal evidence, and confirmed by the testimony of other ancient authors, or when they coincide with the experience of modern times. His account, however, of the dimensions and geography of India, is curious and accurate. His description of the power and opulence of the Prasij perfectly resembles that which might have been given of some of the greater states in the modern Indostan, before the establishment of the Mahomedan or European power in India, and is consonant to the accounts which Alexander had received concerning that people. He was informed, as has been already mentioned, that they were prepared to oppose him on the banks of the Gan-

---

* Strabo, lib. xx. 1032. A. 1037. C.

ges, with an army consisting of twenty thousand cavalry, two hundred thousand infantry, and two thousand armed chariots;* and Megasthenes relates, that he had an audience of Sandracottus in a place where he was encamped with an army of four hundred thousand men.† The enormous dimensions which he assigns to Palibothra, of no less than ten miles in length, and two in breadth, and surrounded by walls in which there were five hundred and seventy towers, and sixty-four gates, would probably have been ranked by Europeans among the wonders which he delighted to relate, if they were not now well acquainted with the rambling manner in which the cities of India were built, and did not know with certainty, that both in former and in the present times, it might boast of cities still more extensive.‡

This embassy of Megasthenes to Sandracottus, and another of Diamachus to his son and successor Allitrochidas, are the last transactions of the Syrian monarchs with India, of which we have any account.‖ Nor can we either fix with accuracy the time, or describe the manner in which their possessions in India were wrested from them. It is probable that they were obliged to abandon that country soon after the death of Seleucus.§

But though the great monarchs of Syria lost, about this period, those provinces in India which

---

* Diod. Sicul. lib. xvii. p. 232. Q. Curt. lib. ix. c. 2.
† Strabo, lib. xv. p. 1035. C.   ‡ Rennell, Mem. 49, 50.
‖ See Note XV. Page 309.   § Justin. lib. xv. c. 4.

had been subject to their dominion, the Greeks in a smaller kingdom, composed of some fragments of Alexander's empire, still maintained an intercourse with India, and even made some considerable acquisition of territory there. This was the kingdom of Bactria, originally subject to Seleucus, but wrested from his son or grandson, and rendered an independent state, about sixty-nine years after the death of Alexander. Concerning the transactions of this kingdom, we must rest satisfied with gleaning a few imperfect hints in ancient authors. From them we learn, that its commerce with India was great; that the conquests of the Bactrian kings in that country were more extensive than those of Alexander himself, and particularly that they recovered possession of the district near the mouth of the Indus, which he had subdued.* Each of the six princes who reigned in Bactria carried on military operations in India with such success, that they penetrated far into the interior part of the country, and, proud of the conquests which they had made, as well as of the extensive dominions over which they reigned, some of them assumed the lofty title of *Great King*, which distinguished the Persian monarchs in the days of their highest splendour. But we should not have known how long this kingdom of Bactria subsisted, or in what manner it terminated, if M. de Guignes had not called in the historians of China to supply the defects

---

* Strabo, lib. xi. 785. D. lib. xv. 1006. B. Justin. lib. xli. c. 4. Bayer, Hist. Regni Græcor. Bactriani, passim.

of the Greek and Roman writers. By them we are informed, that about one hundred and twenty-six years before the Christian era, a powerful horde of Tartars, pushed from their native seats on the confines of China, and obliged to move towards the west by the pressure of a more numerous body that rolled on behind them, passed the Jaxartes, and pouring in upon Bactria, like an irresistible torrent, overwhelmed that kingdom, and put an end to the dominion of the Greeks* there, after it had been established near one hundred and thirty years.†

From this time until the close of the fifteenth century, when the Portuguese, by doubling the Cape of Good Hope, opened a new communication with the East, and carried their victorious arms into every part of India, no European power acquired territory, or established its dominion there. During this long period, of more than sixteen hundred years, all schemes of conquest in India seem to have been totally relinquished, and nothing more was aimed at by any nation, than to secure an intercourse of trade with that opulent country.

It was in Egypt that the seat of this intercourse was established; and it is not without surprise that we observe how soon and how regularly the commerce with the East came to be carried

---

* Mem. de Litterat. tom. xxv. p. 17, &c.
† See Note XVI. Page 309.

on by that channel in which the sagacity of Alexander destined it to flow. Ptolemy, the son of Lagus, as soon as he took possession of Egypt, established the seat of government in Alexandria. By some exertions of authority, and many acts of liberality, but chiefly by the fame of his mild and equal administration, he drew such a number of inhabitants to this favourite residence, that it soon became a populous and wealthy city. As Ptolemy deserved and had possessed the confidence of Alexander more perfectly than any of his officers, he knew well that his chief object in founding Alexandria was to secure the advantages arising from the trade with India. A long and prosperous reign was favourable to the prosecution of that object; and though ancient authors have not enabled us to trace the steps which the first Ptolemy took for this purpose, we have a striking evidence of his extraordinary attention to naval affairs, in his erecting a light-house on the island of Pharos, at the mouth of the harbour of Alexandria,[*] a work of such magnificence as to be reckoned one of the seven wonders of the world. With respect to the commercial arrangements of his son Ptolemy Philadelphus, we have more perfect information. In order to bring the trade with India (which began to revive at Tyre, its ancient station) to centre in Alexandria,[†] he set about forming a canal, an hundred cubits in breadth, and thirty cubits in depth, between Ar-

---

[*] Strabo, lib. xvii. p. 1140. C.
[†] Ibid. lib. xvi. 1089. A.

sinoe on the Red Sea, not far from the situation of the modern Suez, and the Peleusica or eastern branch of the Nile, by means of which the productions of India might have been conveyed to that capital wholly by water. But either on account of some danger apprehended from completing it, that work was never finished; or from the slow and dangerous navigation towards the northern extremity of the Red Sea, this canal was found to be of so little use, that in order to facilitate the communication with India, he built a city on the west coast of that sea, almost under the Tropic, to which he gave the name of Berenice.* This new city soon became the staple of the trade with India.† From Berenice the goods were transported by land to Coptos, a city three miles distant from the Nile, but which had a communication with that river by a navigable canal, of which there are still some remains,‡ and thence carried down the stream to Alexandria. The distance between Berenice and Coptos was, according to Pliny, two hundred and fifty-eight Roman miles, and the road lay through the desert of Thebais, almost entirely destitute of water. But the attention of a powerful monarch made provision for supplying this want, by searching for springs; and wherever these were found he built inns, or more probably in the eastern style caravanseras, for the accommodation of merchants.§

---

* Strabo, lib. xvii. 1156. D.   Plin. Nat. Hist. lib. vi. c. 29.
† See Note XVII. Page 310.
‡ D'Anville, Mem. de l'Egypte, p. 21.
§ Strabo, lib. xvii. p. 1157. D. 1169.

In this channel the intercourse between the East and West continued to be carried on during two hundred and fifty years, as long as Egypt remained an independent kingdom.

The ships destined for India took their departure from Berenice, and sailing, according to the ancient mode of navigation, along the Arabian shore to the promontory Syagrus, (now Cape Rasalgate,) held their course along the coast of Persia, either directly to Pattala, (now Tatta,) at the head of the lower Delta of the Indus, or to some other emporium on the west coast of India. To this part of India, which Alexander had visited and subdued, the commerce under the protection of the Egyptian monarchs seems to have been confined for a considerable time. Afterwards a more convenient course was followed, and from Cape Rasalgate vessels sailed in a direct course to Zizerus. This, according to M. de Montesquieu,* was the kingdom of Sigertis, on the seacoast adjacent to the mouth of the Indus, conquered by the Greek monarchs of Bactria; according to Major Rennell,† it was a port on the northern part of the Malabar coast. Ancient authors have not conveyed such information as will enable us to pronounce with certainty which of these two opposite opinions is best founded. Nor can we point out with accuracy, what were the other ports in India which the merchants

---

* L'Esprit des Loix, lib. xxi. c. 7.
† Introduct. p. xxxvii.

from Berenice frequented, when that trade was first opened. As they sailed in vessels of small burden, which crept timidly along the coast, it is probable that their voyages were circumscribed within very narrow limits, and that, under the Ptolemies, no considerable progress was made in the discovery of India.*

FROM this monopoly of the commerce by sea between the East and West, which Egypt long enjoyed, it derived that extraordinary degree of opulence and power for which it was conspicuous. In modern times, acquainted with the vigilant and enterprising activity of commercial rivalship, there is hardly any circumstance in ancient story which appears more surprising, than that the sovereigns of Egypt should have been permitted to engross this lucrative trade without competition, or any attempt to wrest it out of their hands; especially as the powerful monarchs of Syria might, from the Persian Gulf, have carried on an intercourse with the same parts of India, by a shorter and safer course of navigation. Different considerations seem to have induced them so tamely to relinquish all the obvious advantages of this commerce. The Kings of Egypt, by their attention to maritime affairs, had formed a powerful fleet, which gave them such decided command of the sea, that they could have crushed with ease any rival in trade. No commercial intercourse seems ever to have been

---

* See NOTE XVIII. Page 312.

carried on by sea between Persia and India. The Persians had such an insuperable aversion to that element, or were so much afraid of foreign invasion, that their monarchs (as I have already observed) obstructed the navigation of the great rivers, which gave access to the interior parts of the country, by artificial works. As their subjects, however, were no less desirous than the people around them to possess the valuable productions and elegant manufactures of India, these were conveyed to all the parts of their extensive dominions by land carriage. The commodities destined for the supply of the northern provinces, were transported on camels from the banks of the Indus to those of the Oxus, down the stream of which they were carried to the Caspian Sea, and distributed, partly by land carriage, and partly by navigable rivers, through the different countries, bounded on one hand by the Caspian, and on the other by the Euxine Sea.* The commodities of India intended for the southern and interior provinces, proceeded by land from the Caspian Gates to some of the great rivers, by which they were circulated through every part of the country. This was the ancient mode of intercourse with India, while the Persian empire was governed by its native Princes; and it has been observed in every age, that when any branch of commerce has got into a certain channel, although it may be neither the most proper nor the most commodious one, it requires long time,

---

* Strabo, lib. xii. 776. D. Plin. Nat. Hist. lib. vi. c. 17.

and considerable efforts, to give it a different direction.*

To all these reasons for suffering the monarchs of Egypt to continue in the undisturbed possession of the trade with India by sea, another may be added. Many of the ancients, by an error in geography extremely unaccountable, and in which they persisted, notwithstanding repeated opportunities of obtaining more accurate information, believed the Caspian Sea to be a branch of the great Northern Ocean; and the Kings of Syria might hope by that means to open a communication with Europe, and to circulate through it the valuable productions of the East, without intruding into those seas, the navigation of which the Egyptian monarchs seemed to consider as their exclusive right. This idea had been early formed by the Greeks, when they became masters of Asia. Seleucus Nicator, the first and most sagacious of the Syrian Kings, at the time when he was assassinated, entertained thoughts of forming a junction between the Caspian and Euxine Seas by a canal;† and if this could have been effected, his subjects, besides the extension of their trade in Europe, might have supplied all the countries in the north of Asia, on the coast of the Euxine Sea, as well as many of those which stretch eastward from the Caspian, with the productions of India. As those countries, though now thinly inhabited by a miserable race of men,

---

* See NOTE XIX. Page 313. † Plin. Nat. Hist. lib. vi. c. 11.

destitute of industry and of wealth, were in ancient times extremely populous, and filled with great and opulent cities, this must have been considered as a branch of commerce of such magnitude and value, as to render the securing of it an object worthy the attention of the most powerful monarch.

But while the monarchs of Egypt and Syria laboured with emulation and ardour to secure to their subjects all the advantages of the Indian trade, a power arose in the West which proved fatal to both. The Romans, by the vigour of their military institutions, and the wisdom of their political conduct, having rendered themselves masters of all Italy and Sicily, soon overturned the rival republic of Carthage, subjected Macedonia and Greece, extended their dominion over Syria, and at last turned their victorious arms against Egypt, the only kingdom remaining of those established by the successors of Alexander the Great. After a series of events, which belong not to the subject of this Disquisition, Egypt was annexed to the Roman empire, and reduced into the form of a Roman province by Augustus. Aware of its great importance, he, with that provident sagacity which distinguishes his character, not only reserved it as one of the provinces subject immediately to imperial authority, but by various precautions, well known to every scholar, provided for its security. This extraordinary solicitude seems to have proceeded, not only from considering Egypt as one of the chief granaries

SECT. on which the capital depended for subsistence,
I. but as the seat of that lucrative commerce which had enabled its ancient monarchs to amass such enormous wealth, as excited the admiration and envy of other princes, and produced, when brought into the treasury of the empire, a considerable alteration, both in the value of property and the state of manners, in Rome itself.

AN HISTORICAL DISQUISITION CONCERNING ANCIENT INDIA.

SECTION II.

Intercourse with India, from the Establishment of the Roman Dominion in Egypt, to the Conquest of that Kingdom by the Mahomedans.

UPON the conquest of Egypt by the Romans, and the reduction of that kingdom to a province of their empire, the trade with India continued to be carried on in the same mode under their powerful protection: Rome, enriched with the spoils and the tribute of almost all the known world, had acquired a taste for luxuries of every kind. Among people of this description, the productions of India have always been held in the highest estimation. The capital of the greatest empire ever established in Europe, filled with citizens who had now no occupation but to enjoy and dissipate the wealth accumulated by their ancestors, demanded every thing elegant, rare, or costly, which that remote region could furnish, in order to support its pomp, or heighten its pleasures. To supply this demand, new and extraordinary efforts became requisite, and the commerce with India increased to a degree which (as I have observed in another place*) will appear astonishing even to the present age, in which that branch of trade has been extended far beyond the practice or conception of any former period.

BESIDES the Indian commodities imported into the capital of the empire from Egypt, the Romans received an additional supply of them by another mode of conveyance. From the earliest times, there seems to have been some communication between Mesopotamia and other provinces on the banks of the Euphrates, and those parts of Syria and Palestine which lay near the Mediterranean. The migration of Abram from Ur of the Chaldees to Sichem in the land of Canaan, is an instance of this.† The journey through the desert which separated these countries, was much facilitated by its affording one station abounding with water, and capable of cultivation. As the intercourse increased, the possession of this station became an object of so much importance, that Solomon, when he turned his attention towards the extension of commerce among his subjects, built a fenced city there.‡ Its Syrian name of *Tadmor in the wilderness,* and its Greek one of *Palmyra,* are both descriptive of its situation in a spot adorned with palm-trees. This is not

---

* Hist. of America, vol. i. p. 28. † Gen. xi. xii.
‡ 1 Kings, ix. 18. 2 Chron. viii. 4.

only plentifully supplied with water, but surrounded by a portion of fertile land, which (though of no great extent) renders it a delightful habitation in the midst of barren sands and an inhospitable desert. Its happy position, at the distance of eighty-five miles from the river Euphrates, and about one hundred and seventeen miles from the nearest coast of the Mediterranean,* induced its inhabitants to enter with ardour into the trade of conveying commodities from one of these to the other. As the most valuable productions of India, brought up the Euphrates from the Persian Gulf, are of such small bulk as to bear the expense of a long land carriage, this trade soon became so considerable that the opulence and power of Palmyra increased rapidly. Its government was of the form which is best suited to the genius of a commercial city, republican; and from the peculiar advantages of its situation, as well as the spirit of its inhabitants, it long maintained its independence, though surrounded by powerful and ambitious neighbours. Under the Syrian monarchs descended from Seleucus it attained to its highest degree of splendour and wealth; one great source of which seems to have been, the supplying their

---

* In a former edition, I stated the distance of Palmyra from the Euphrates at sixty miles, and from the Mediterranean at two hundred and three miles. Into these errors I was led by M. D'Anville, who, in his Memoire sur l'Euphrate et le Tigris, a work published in old age, did not retain his wonted accuracy. From information communicated by Major Rennell, I have substituted the true distances.

subjects with Indian commodities. When Syria submitted to the irresistible arms of Rome, Palmyra continued upwards of two centuries a free state, and its friendship was courted with emulation and solicitude by the Romans, and their rivals for empire, the Parthians. That it traded with both, and particularly that from it Rome, as well as other parts of the empire, received the productions of India, we learn from Appian, an author of good credit.* But in tracing the progress of the commerce of the ancients with the East, I should not have ventured, upon his single testimony, to mention this among the channels of note in which it was carried on, if a singular discovery, for which we are indebted to the liberal curiosity and enterprising spirit of our own countrymen, did not confirm and illustrate what he relates. Towards the close of the last century, some gentlemen of the English factory at Aleppo, incited by what they heard in the East concerning the wonderful ruins of Palmyra, ventured, notwithstanding the fatigue and danger of a journey through the desert, to visit them. To their astonishment they beheld a fertile spot of some miles in extent arising like an island out of a vast plain of sand, covered with the remains of temples, porticoes, aqueducts, and other public works, which, in magnificence and splendour, and some of them in elegance, were not unworthy of Athens or of Rome in their most prosperous state. Allured by their description of them, about sixty

---

* Appian. de Bello Civil. lib. v. p. 1076. edit. Tollii.

years thereafter, a party of more enlightened travellers, having reviewed the ruins of Palmyra with greater attention and more scientific skill, declared that what they beheld there exceeded the most exalted ideas which they had formed concerning it.*

From both these accounts, as well as from recollecting the extraordinary degree of power to which Palmyra had attained, when Egypt, Syria, Mesopotamia, and a considerable part of Asia Minor were conquered by its arms; when Odenatus, its chief magistrate, was decorated with the imperial purple, and Zenobia contended for the dominion of the East with Rome under one of its most warlike Emperors, it is evident that a state which could derive little importance from its original territory, must have owed its aggrandizement to the opulence acquired by extensive commerce. Of this the Indian trade was undoubtedly the most considerable, and most lucrative branch. But it is a cruel mortification, in searching for what is instructive in the history of past times, to find that the exploits of conquerors who have desolated the earth, and the freaks of tyrants who have rendered nations unhappy, are recorded with minute and often disgusting accuracy, while the discovery of useful arts, and the progress of the most beneficial branches of commerce, are passed over in silence, and suffered to sink into oblivion.

---

* Wood's Ruins of Palmyra, p. 37.

AFTER the conquest of Palmyra by Aurelian, trade never revived there. At present a few miserable huts of beggarly Arabs are scattered in the courts of its stately temples, or deform its elegant porticoes; and exhibit an humiliating contrast to its ancient magnificence.

BUT while the merchants of Egypt and Syria exerted their activity in order to supply the increasing demands of Rome for Indian commodities, and vied with each other in their efforts, the eagerness of gain (as Pliny observes) brought India itself nearer to the rest of the world. In the course of their voyages to that country, the Greek and Egyptian pilots could not fail to observe the regular shifting of the periodical winds or monsoons, and how steadily they continued to blow during one part of the year from the east, and during the other from the west. Encouraged by attending to this circumstance, Hippalus, the commander of a ship engaged in the Indian trade, ventured, about fourscore years after Egypt was annexed to the Roman empire, to relinquish the slow and circuitous course which I have described, and stretching boldly from the mouth of the Arabian Gulf across the ocean, was carried by the western monsoon to Musiris, a harbour in that part of India now known by the name of the Malabar Coast.

THIS route to India was held to be a discovery of such importance, that in order to perpetuate the memory of the inventor, the name of Hippalus was given to the wind which enabled him to perform the voyage.* As this was one of the greatest efforts of navigation in the ancient world, and opened the best communication by sea between the East and West that was known for fourteen hundred years, it merits a particular description. Fortunately Pliny has enabled us to give it with a degree of accuracy, which can seldom be attained in tracing the naval or commercial operations of the ancients. From Alexandria (he observes) to Juliopolis is two miles; there the cargo destined for India is embarked on the Nile, and is carried to Coptos, which is distant three hundred and three miles, and the voyage is usually accomplished in twelve days. From Coptos goods are conveyed by land carriage to Berenice on the Arabian Gulf, halting at different stations, regulated according to the conveniency of watering. The distance between these cities is two hundred and fifty-eight miles. On account of the heat the caravan travels only during the night, and the journey is finished on the twelfth day. From Berenice ships take their departure about midsummer, and in thirty days reach Ocelis (Gella) at the mouth of the Arabian Gulf, or Cane (Cape Fartaque) on the coast of Arabia Felix. Thence they sail, in forty days, to Musiris, the first emporium in India. They begin their voyage homewards early in the Egyptian month Thibi, which answers to our December; they sail with a north-east wind, and, when

---

* Perip. Mar. Erythr. p. 32.

they enter the Arabian Gulf, meet with a south or south-west wind, and thus complete the voyage in less than a year.*

THE account which Pliny gives of Musiris, and of Barace, another harbour not far distant, which was likewise frequented by the ships from Berenice, as being both so incommodious for trade, on account of the shallowness of the ports, that it became necessary to discharge and take in the cargoes in small boats, does not enable us to fix their position with perfect accuracy. This description applies to many ports on the Malabar Coast; but, from two circumstances mentioned by him, one, that they are not far distant from Cottonara, the country which produces pepper in great abundance; and the other, that in sailing towards them, the course lay near Nitrias, the station of the pirates; I adopt the opinion of Major Rennell, that they were situated somewhere between Goa and Tellicherry, and that probably the modern Meerzaw or Merjee is the Musiris of the ancients, and Barcelore their Barace.†

As in these two ports was the principal staple of the trade between Egypt and India, when in its most flourishing state, this seems to be the proper place for inquiring into the nature of the commerce which the ancients, particularly the

---

* Plin. Nat. Hist. lib. vi. c. 23. See NOTE XX. Page 310.
† Introd. p. xxxvii.

Romans, carried on with that country, and for enumerating the commodities most in request which they imported from it. But as the operations of commerce, and the mode of regulating it, were little attended to in those states of antiquity of whose transactions we have any accurate knowledge, their historians hardly enter into any detail concerning a subject of such subordinate importance in their political system; and it is mostly from brief hints, detached facts, and incidental observations, that we can gather information concerning it.*

In every age it has been a commerce of luxury, rather than of necessity, which has been carried on between Europe and India. Its elegant manufactures, spices, and precious stones, are neither objects of desire to nations of simple manners, nor are such nations possessed of wealth sufficient to purchase them. But at the time the Romans became masters of the Indian trade, they were not only (as has already been observed) in that stage of society when men are eager to obtain every thing that can render the enjoyment of life more exquisite, or add to its splendour, but they had acquired all the fantastic tastes formed by the caprice and extravagance of wealth. They were, of consequence, highly delighted with those new objects of gratification with which India supplied them in such abundance. The productions of that country, natural as well as arti-

---

* See Note XXI, Page 317.

SECT. II. ficial, seem to have been much the same in that age as in the present. But the taste of the Romans in luxury differed, in many respects, from that of modern times; and, of course, their demands from India differed considerably from ours.

In order to convey an idea of their demands as complete as possible, I shall, in the first place, make some observations on the three great articles of general importation from India; 1. Spices and aromatics; 2. Precious stones and pearls; 3. Silk; And then I shall give some account (as far as I can venture to do it from authentic information) of the assortment of cargoes, both outward and homeward bound, for the vessels fitted out at Berenice to different ports of India.

I. Spices and aromatics. From the mode of religious worship in the heathen world; from the incredible number of their deities, and of the temples consecrated to them; the consumption of frankincense and other aromatics, which were used in every sacred function, must have been very great. But the vanity of men occasioned a greater consumption of these fragrant substances than their piety. It was the custom of the Romans to burn the bodies of their dead; and they deemed it a display of magnificence to cover, not only the body, but the funeral pile on which it was laid, with the most costly spices. At the funeral of Sylla, two hundred and ten burdens of spices were strewed upon the pile. Nero is reported to have burnt a quantity of cinnamon and cassia at the funeral of Poppœa, greater than the countries from which it was imported produced in one year. " We consume in heaps these precious substances with the carcases of the dead, (says Pliny): We offer them to the gods only in grains."* It was not from India, I am aware, but from Arabia, that aromatics were first imported into Europe; and some of them, particularly frankincense, were productions of that country. But the Arabians were accustomed, together with spices of native growth, to furnish foreign merchants with others of higher value, which they brought from India, and the regions beyond it. The commercial intercourse of the Arabians with the eastern parts of Asia, was not only early, but considerable. By means of their trading caravans, they conveyed into their own country all the valuable productions of the East, among which spices held a chief place. In every ancient account of Indian commodities, spices and aromatics of various kinds form a principal article.† Some authors assert, that the greater part of those purchased in Arabia were not the growth of that country, but brought from India.‡ That this assertion was well founded, appears from what has been observed in modern times. The frankincense of Arabia, though reckoned the peculiar and most precious production of the coun-

---

* Nat. Hist. lib. xii. c. 18.
† Peripl. Mar. Eryth. p. 22. 28. Strabo, lib. ii. p. 156. A. lib. xv. p. 1018. A.
‡ Strabo, lib. xvii. p. 1129. C.

try, is much inferior in quality to that imported into it from the East; and it is chiefly with the latter that the Arabians at present supply the extensive demands of various provinces of Asia for this commodity.* It is upon good authority, then, that I have mentioned the importation of spices as one of the most considerable branches of ancient commerce with India. In the Augustan age, an entire street in Rome seems to have been occupied by those who sold frankincense, pepper, and other aromatics.†

II. Precious stones, together with which pearls may be classed, seem to be the article next in value imported by the Romans from the East. As these have no pretension to be of any real use, their value arises entirely from their beauty and their rarity, and even when estimated most moderately, is always high. But among nations far advanced in luxury, when they are deemed not only ornaments but marks of distinction, the vain and the opulent vie so eagerly with one another for the possession of them, that they rise in price to an exorbitant and almost incredible height. Diamonds, though the art of cutting them was imperfectly known to the ancients, held an high place in estimation among them, as well as among us. The comparative value of other precious stones varied according to the diversity of tastes and the caprice of fashion. The im-

---

* Neibuhr, Descript. de l'Arabie, tom. i. p. 126.
† Hor. lib. ii. epist. 1.

nense number of them mentioned by Pliny, and the laborious care with which he describes and arranges them,* will astonish, I should suppose, the most skilful lapidary or jeweller of modern times, and shews the high request in which they were held by the Romans.

But among all the articles of luxury, the Romans seem to have given the preference to pearls.† Persons of every rank purchased them with eagerness; they were worn on every part of dress; and there is such a difference, both in size and in value, among pearls, that while such as were large and of superior lustre adorned the wealthy and the great, smaller ones and of inferior quality gratified the vanity of persons in more humble stations of life. Julius Cæsar presented Servilia, the mother of Brutus, with a pearl, for which he paid forty-eight thousand four hundred and fifty-seven pounds. The famous pearl ear-rings of Cleopatra were in value one hundred and sixty-one thousand four hundred and fifty-eight pounds.‡ Precious stones, it is true, as well as pearls, were found not only in India, but in many different countries, and all were ransacked in order to gratify the pride of Rome. India, however, furnished the chief part, and its productions were allowed to be most abundant, diversified, and valuable.

III. Another production of India in great demand at Rome, was silk; and when we recollect

---

* Nat. Hist. lib. xxxvii.   † See Note XXII. Page 317.
‡ Plin. Nat. Hist. lib. ix. c. 35. See Note XXIII. Page 318.

the variety of elegant fabrics into which it may be formed, and how much these have added to the splendour of dress and furniture, we cannot wonder at its being held in such estimation by luxurious people. The price it bore was exorbitant; but it was deemed a dress too expensive and too delicate for men,[*] and was appropriated wholly to women of eminent rank and opulence. This, however, did not render the demand for it less eager, especially after the example of the dissolute Elagabalus introduced the use of it among the other sex, and accustomed men to the disgrace (as the severity of ancient ideas accounted it) of wearing this effeminate garb. Two circumstances concerning the traffic of silk among the Romans merit observation. Contrary to what usually takes place in the operations of trade, the more general use of that commodity seems not to have increased the quantity imported, in such proportion as to answer the growing demand for it; and the price of silk was not reduced during the course of two hundred and fifty years from the time of its being first known in Rome. In the reign of Aurelian, it still continued to be valued at its weight in gold. This, it is probable, was owing to the mode in which that commodity was procured by the merchants of Alexandria. They had no direct intercourse with China, the only country in which the silk-worm was then reared, and its labour rendered an article of commerce. All the silk which they purchased in the different

---

[*] Tacit. Annal. lib. ii. c. 33.

ports of India that they frequented, was brought thither in ships of the country; and either from some defect of skill in managing the silk-worm, the produce of its ingenious industry among the Chinese was scanty, or the intermediate dealers found greater advantage in furnishing the market of Alexandria with a small quantity at an high price, than to lower its value by increasing the quantity. The other circumstance which I had in view is more extraordinary, and affords a striking proof of the imperfect communication of the ancients with remote nations, and of the slender knowledge which they had of their natural productions or arts. Much as the manufactures of silk were admired, and often as silk is mentioned by the Greek and Roman authors, they had not, for several centuries after the use of it became common, any certain knowledge either of the countries to which they were indebted for this favourite article of elegance, or of the manner in which it was produced. By some, silk was supposed to be a fine down adhering to the leaves of certain trees or flowers; others imagined it to be a delicate species of wool or cotton; and even those who had learned that it was the work of an insect, show, by their descriptions, that they had no distinct idea of the manner in which it was formed.* It was in consequence of an event that happened in the sixth century of the Christian era, of which I shall hereafter take notice, that the real nature of silk became known in Europe.

---

* See Note XXIV. Page 319.

SECT. II.

The other commodities usually imported from India will be mentioned in the account, which I now proceed to give, of the cargoes sent out and brought home in the ships employed in the trade with that country. For this we are indebted to the Circumnavigation of the Erythræan Sea, ascribed to Arrian, a curious though short treatise, less known than it deserves to be, and which enters into some details concerning commerce, to which there is nothing similar in any ancient writer. The first place in India, in which the ships from Egypt, while they followed the ancient course of navigation, were accustomed to trade, was Patala in the river Indus. They imported into it woollen cloth of a slight fabric, linen in chequer-work, some precious stones, and some aromatics unknown in India; coral, storax, glass vessels of different kinds, some wrought silver, money, and wine. In return for these, they received spices of various kinds, sapphires, and other gems, silk stuffs, silk thread, cotton cloths,* and black pepper. But a far more considerable emporium on the same coast was Barygaza, and on that account the author whom I follow here describes its situation, and the mode of approaching it, with great minuteness and accuracy. Its situation corresponds entirely with that of Baroach, on the great river Nerbuddah, down the stream of which, or by land carriage from the great city of Tagara across high mountains,† all the productions of the interior country were

---

* See Note XXV. Page 320. † See Note XXVI. Page 320.

conveyed to it. The articles of importation and exportation in this great mart were extensive and various. Besides those already mentioned, our author enumerates among the former, Italian, Greek, and Arabian wines, brass, tin, lead, girdles or sashes of curious texture, melilot, white glass, red arsenic, black lead, gold and silver coin. Among the exports he mentions the onyx, and other gems, ivory, myrrh, various fabrics of cotton, both plain and ornamented with flowers, and long pepper.* At Musiris, the next emporium of note on that coast, the articles imported were much the same as at Barygaza; but as it lay nearer to the eastern parts of India, and seems to have had much communication with them, the commodities exported from it were more numerous and more valuable. He specifies particularly pearls in great abundance and of extraordinary beauty, a variety of silk stuffs, rich perfumes, tortoise-shell, different kinds of transparent gems, especially diamonds, and pepper in large quantities, and of the best quality. †

The justness of the account given by this author of the articles imported from India, is confirmed by a Roman law, in which the Indian commodities subject to the payment of duties are enumerated.‡ By comparing these two accounts, we may form an idea tolerably exact of

---

* Peripl. Mar. Erythr. p. 28. † Ibid. 31, 32.
‡ Digest. lib. xxxix. tit. 4. §.16. De publicanis et vectigalibus.

the nature and extent of the trade with India in ancient times.

As the state of society and manners among the natives of India, in the earliest period in which they are known, nearly resembled what we observe among their descendants in the present age; their wants and demands were, of course, much the same. The ingenuity of their own artists was so able to supply these, that they stood little in need of foreign manufactures or productions, except some of the useful metals, which their own country did not furnish in sufficient quantity; and then, as now, it was mostly with gold and silver that the luxuries of the East were purchased. In two particulars, however, our importations from India differ greatly from those of the ancients. The dress, both of the Greeks and Romans, was almost entirely woollen, which, by their frequent use of the warm bath, was rendered abundantly comfortable. Their consumption of linen and cotton cloths was much inferior to that of modern times, when these are worn by persons in every rank of life. Accordingly, a great branch of modern importation from that part of India with which the ancients were acquainted, is in *piece-goods;* comprehending, under that mercantile term, the immense variety of fabrics which Indian ingenuity has formed of cotton. But as far as I have observed, we have no authority that will justify us in stating the ancient importation of these to be in any degree considerable.

In modern times, though it continues still to be chiefly a commerce of luxury that is carried on with India, yet, together with the articles that minister to it, we import, to a considerable extent, various commodities which are to be considered merely as the materials of our domestic manufactures. Such are the cotton-wool of Indostan, the silk of China, and the saltpetre of Bengal. But in the accounts of ancient importations from India, raw silk and silk-thread excepted, I find nothing mentioned that could serve as the materials of any home-manufacture. The navigation of the ancients never having extended to China, the quantity of unwrought silk with which they were supplied, by means of the Indian traders, appears to have been so scanty, that the manufacture of it could not make an addition of any moment to their domestic industry.

After this succinct account of the commerce carried on by the ancients in India, I proceed to inquire what knowledge they had of the countries beyond the ports of Musiris and Barace, the utmost boundary towards the east to which I have hitherto traced their progress. The author of the Circumnavigation of the Erythræan Sea, whose accuracy of description justifies the confidence with which I have followed him for some time, seems to have been little acquainted with that part of the coast which stretches from Barace towards the south. He mentions, indeed, cursorily, two or three different ports, but gives no intimation that any of them were staples of the commerce with Egypt. He hastens to Comar, or Cape Comorin, the southernmost point of the Indian peninsula; and his description of it is so accurate, and so conformable to its real state, as shews his information concerning it to have been perfectly authentic.* Near to this he places the pearl fishery of Colchos, the modern Kilkare, undoubtedly the same with that now carried on by the Dutch in the strait which separates the island of Ceylon from the continent; as adjacent to this he mentions three different ports, which appear to have been situated on the east side of the peninsula, now known by the name of the Coromandel Coast. He describes these as *emporia*, or stations of trade;† but from an attentive consideration of some circumstances in his account of them, I think it probable that the ships from Berenice did not sail to any of these ports, though they were supplied, as he informs us, with the commodities brought from Egypt, as well as with the productions of the opposite coast of the peninsula; but these seem to have been imported in *country ships*.‡ It was likewise in vessels of their own, varying in form and burden, and distinguished by different names, some of which he mentions, that they traded with the Golden Chersonesus, or kingdom of Malacca,

---

* Peripl. p. 33. D'Anville, Ant. de l'Inde, 118, &c.
† Peripl. p. 34. ‡ Τοπικα πλοῖα.

and the countries near the Ganges. Not far from the mouth of that river he places an island, which he describes as situated under the rising sun, and as the last region in the East that was inhabited.* Of all these parts of India, the author of the Circumnavigation appears to have had very slender knowledge, as is manifest, not only from what he mentions concerning this imaginary island, and from his not attempting to describe them, but from his relating, with the credulity and love of the marvellous which always accompany and characterize ignorance, that these remote regions were peopled with cannibals, and men of uncouth and monstrous forms.†

I HAVE been induced to bestow this attention in tracing the course delineated in the Circumnavigation of the Erythræan Sea, because the author of it is the first ancient writer to whom we are indebted for any knowledge of the eastern coast of the great peninsula of India, or of the countries which lie beyond it. To Strabo, who composed his great work on geography in the reign of Augustus, India, particularly the most eastern parts of it, was little known. He begins his description of it with requesting the indulgence of his readers, on account of the scanty information he could obtain with respect to a country so remote, which Europeans had seldom visited, and many of them transiently only, in the functions of military service. He observes, that

---

* Peripl. p. 36.   † Peripl. p. 35.

even commerce had contributed little towards an accurate investigation of the country, as few of the merchants from Egypt, and the Arabian Gulf, had ever sailed as far as the Ganges; and from men so illiterate, intelligence that merited a full degree of confidence could scarcely be expected. His descriptions of India, particularly its interior provinces, are borrowed almost entirely from the memoirs of Alexander's officers, with some slender additions from more recent accounts, and these so few in number, and sometimes so inaccurate, as to furnish a striking proof of the small progress which the ancients had made, from the time of Alexander, in exploring that country. When an author, possessed of such discernment and industry as Strabo, who visited in person several distant regions, that he might be able to describe them with greater accuracy, relates, that the Ganges enters the ocean by one mouth,* we are warranted in concluding, that in his time there was either no direct navigation carried on to that great river by the traders from the Arabian Gulf, or that this voyage was undertaken so seldom, that science had not then derived much information from it.

The next author, in order of time, from whom we receive any account of India, is the elder Pliny, who flourished about fifty years later than Strabo. As in the short description of India given in his Natural History, he follows the same guides with

---

* Strabo, lib. xv. 1011. C.

Strabo, and seems to have had no knowledge of the interior country, but what he derived from the memoirs of the officers who served under Alexander and his immediate successors, it is unnecessary to examine his description minutely. He has added, however, two valuable articles, for which he was indebted to more recent discoveries. The one is the account of the new course of navigation from the Arabian Gulf to the coast of Malabar, the nature and importance of which I have already explained. The other is a description of the island of Taprobana, which I shall consider particularly, after inquiring into what Ptolemy has contributed towards our knowledge of the ancient state of the Indian continent.

Though Ptolemy, who published his works about fourscore years after Pliny, seems to have been distinguished for his persevering industry, and talent for arrangement, rather than for an inventive genius; geography has been more indebted to him for its improvement, than to any other philosopher. Fortunately for that science, in forming his general system of geography, he adopted the ideas, and imitated the practice of Hipparchus, who lived near four hundred years before his time. That great philosopher was the first who attempted to make a catalogue of the stars. In order to ascertain their position in the heavens with accuracy, he measured their distance from certain circles of the spheres, computing it by degrees, either from east to west, or from north to south. The former was denominated the longitude of the star, the latter its latitude. This mode he found to be of such utility in his astronomical researches, that he applied it with no less happy effect to geography; and it is a circumstance worthy of notice, that it was by observing and describing the heavens, men were first taught to measure and delineate the earth with exactness. This method of fixing the position of places, invented by Hipparchus, though known to the geographers between his time and that of Ptolemy, and mentioned both by Strabo* and by Pliny,† was not employed by any of them. Of this neglect the most probable account seems to be, that as none of them were astronomers, they did not fully comprehend all the advantages geography might derive from this invention.‡ These Ptolemy, who had devoted a long life to the improvement of astronomy, theoretical as well as practical, perfectly discerned, and as in both Hipparchus was his guide, he, in his famous treatise on geography, described the different parts of the earth according to their longitude and latitude. Geography was thus established upon its proper principles, and intimately connected with astronomical observations and mathematical science. This work of Ptolemy soon rose high in estimation among the ancients.§ During the middle ages, both in Arabia and in Europe, the decisions of Ptolemy, in every thing relating to geography, were submitted to with an assent as implicit as

---

* Lib. ii.   † Nat. Hist. lib. ii. c. 12. 26. 70.
‡ Note XXVII. Page 321.   § Note XXVIII. Page 321.

was yielded to those of Aristotle in all other departments of science. On the revival of a more liberal spirit of inquiry in the sixteenth century, the merit of Ptolemy's improvements in geography was examined and recognized; that scientific language which he first rendered general, continues to be used; and the position of places is still ascertained in the same distinct and compendious manner, by specifying their longitude and latitude.

NOT satisfied with adopting the general principles of Hipparchus, Ptolemy emulated him in the application of them; and, as that philosopher had arranged all the constellations, he ventured upon what was no less arduous, to survey all the regions of the earth which were then known, and with minute and bold decision he fixed the longitude and latitude of the most remarkable places in each of them. All his determinations, however, are not to be considered as the result of actual observation, nor did Ptolemy publish them as such. Astronomical science was confined, at that time, to a few countries. A considerable part of the globe was little visited, and imperfectly described. The position of a small number of places only had been fixed with any degree of accuracy. Ptolemy was therefore obliged to consult the itineraries and surveys of the Roman empire, which the political wisdom of that great state had completed* with immense labour and

---

* See NOTE XXIX. Page 322.

SECT. II.

expense. Beyond the precincts of the empire, he had nothing on which he could rely, but the journals and reports of travellers. Upon these all his conclusions were founded; and as he resided in Alexandria at a time when the trade from that city to India was carried on to its utmost extent, this situation might have been expected to afford him the means of procuring ample information concerning it. But either from the imperfect manner in which that country was explored in his time, or from his placing too much confidence in the reports of persons who had visited it with little attention or discernment,* his general delineation of the form of the Indian continent is the most erroneous that has been transmitted to us from antiquity. By an astonishing mistake, he has made the peninsula of India stretch from the Sinus Barygazenus, or Gulf of Cambay, from west to east, instead of extending, according to its real direction, from north to south.† This error will appear the more unaccountable, when we recollect that Megasthenes had published a measurement of the Indian peninsula, which approaches near to its true dimensions; and that this had been adopted, with some variations, by Eratosthenes, Strabo, Diodorus Siculus, and Pliny, who wrote prior to the age of Ptolemy.‡

---

* Geogr. lib. i. c. 17. † See NOTE XXX. Page 323.
‡ Strabo, lib. xv. 1010. B. Arrian. Hist. Indic. c. 3, 4.
Diod. Sicul. lib. ii. 148. Plin. Nat. Hist. lib. vi. c. 21. See NOTE XXXI. Page 323.

Although Ptolemy was led to form such an erroneous opinion concerning the general dimensions of the Indian continent, his information with respect to the country in detail, and the situation of particular places, was more accurate; and he is the first author possessed of such knowledge as enabled him to trace the sea-coast, to mention the most noted places situated upon it, and to specify the longitude and latitude of each, from Cape Comorin eastward, to the utmost boundary of ancient navigation. With regard to some districts, particularly along the east side of the peninsula as far as the mouth of the Ganges, the accounts which he had received seem to have been so far exact, as to correspond more nearly perhaps with the actual state of the country, than the descriptions which he gives of any other part of India. M. D'Anville, with his usual industry and discernment, has considered the principal stations as they are fixed by him, and finds that they correspond to Kilkare, Negapatam, the mouth of the river Cauveri, Masulipatam, Point Gordeware, &c. It is foreign to the object of this Disquisition to enter into such a minute detail; but in several instances we may observe, that not only the conformity of position, but the similarity of ancient and modern names, is very striking.[*] The great river Cauveri is by Ptolemy named Chaberis; Arcot, in the interior country, is Arcati Regia; and probably the whole coast

---

[*] Ptolem. Geogr. lib. vii. c. 1. D'Anvillé, Antiq. de l'Inde, 127, &c.

has received its present name of Coromandel from *Sor Mandulam*, or the kingdom of Soræ, which is situated upon it.

In the course of one hundred and thirty-six years, which elapsed from the death of Strabo to that of Ptolemy, the commercial intercourse with India was greatly extended; the latter geographer had acquired such an accession of new information concerning the Ganges, that he mentions the names of six different mouths of that river, and describes their positions. His delineation, however, of that part of India which lies beyond the Ganges, is not less erroneous in its general form than that which he gave of the peninsula, and bears as little resemblance to the actual position of those countries. He ventures, nevertheless, upon a survey of them, similar to that which he had made of the other great division of India, which I have already examined. He mentions the places of note along the coast, some of which he distinguishes as *emporia*; but whether that name was given to them on account of their being staples of trade to the natives, in their traffic carried on from one district of India to another, or whether they were ports to which vessels from the Arabian Gulf resorted directly, is not specified. The latter I should think to be the idea which Ptolemy means to convey; but those regions of India were so remote, and, from the timid and slow course of ancient navigation, were probably so little frequented, that his information concerning them is extremely defective, and his descriptions more obscure, more inaccurate, and less conformable to the real state of the country, than in any part of his geography. That peninsula to which he gives the name of the Golden Chersonesus, he delineates as if it stretched directly from north to south, and fixes the latitude of Sabana Emporium, its southern extremity, three degrees beyond the line. To the east of this peninsula he places what he calls the Great Bay, and in the most remote part of it the station of Catigara, the utmost boundary of navigation in ancient times, to which he assigns no less than eight degrees and a half of southern latitude. Beyond this he declares the earth to be altogether unknown, and asserts that the land turns thence to the westward, and stretches in that direction until it joins the promontory of Prassum in Ethiopia, which, according to his idea, terminated the continent of Africa to the south.* In consequence of this error, no less unaccountable than enormous, he must have believed the Erythræan Sea, in its whole extent from the coast of Africa to that of Cambodia, to be a vast basin, without any communication with the ocean.†

Out of the confusion of those wild ideas, in which the accounts of ignorant or fabulous travellers have involved the geography of Ptolemy, M. D'Anville has attempted to bring order; and,

---

* Ptolem. Geogr. lib. vii. c. 3. 5. D'Anville, Ant. de l'Inde, 187.
† See Note XXXII. Page 323.

SECT. II.

with much ingenuity, he has formed opinions with respect to some capital positions, which have the appearance of being well founded. The peninsula of Malacca is, according to him, the Golden Chersonesus of Ptolemy; but instead of the direction which he has given it, we know that it bends some degrees towards the east, and that Cape de Romania, its southern extremity, is more than a degree to the north of the line. The Gulf of Siam he considers as the Great Bay of Ptolemy; but the position on the east side of that bay, corresponding to Catigara, is actually as many degrees to the north of the equator, as he supposed it to be south of it. Beyond this he mentions an inland city, to which he gives the name of Thinæ or Sinæ Metropolis. The longitude which he assigns to it, is one hundred and eighty degrees from his first meridian in the Fortunate Island, and is the utmost point towards the east to which the ancients had advanced by sea. Its latitude he calculates to be three degrees south of the line. If, with M. D'Anville, we conclude the situation of Sin-hoa, in the western part of the kingdom of Cochin-China, to be the same with Sinæ Metropolis, Ptolemy has erred in fixing its position no less than fifty degrees of longitude, and twenty degrees of latitude.*

---

* Ptolem. Geogr. lib. vii. c. 3. D'Anville, Limites du Monde connu des Anciens au-delà du Gange. Mem. de Litterat. xxxii. 604, &c. Ant. de l'Inde, Supplem. i. 161, &c. See NOTE XXXIII. Page 924.

THESE errors of Ptolemy concerning the remote parts of Asia, have been rendered more conspicuous by a mistaken opinion of modern times engrafted upon them. Sinæ, the most distant station mentioned in his geography, has such a near resemblance in sound to China, the name by which the greatest and most civilized empire in the East is known to Europeans, that, upon their first acquaintance with it, they hastily concluded them to be the same; and of consequence it was supposed that China was known to the ancients, though no point seems to be more ascertained, than that they never advanced by sea beyond that boundary which I have allotted to their navigation.

HAVING thus traced the discoveries of India which the ancients made by sea, I shall next examine what additional knowledge of that country they acquired from their progress by land. It appears (as I have formerly related) that there was a trade carried on early with India through the provinces that stretch along its northern frontier. Its various productions and manufactures were transported by land carriage into the interior parts of the Persian dominions, or were conveyed, by means of the navigable rivers which flow through the Upper Asia, to the Caspian Sea, and from that to the Euxine. While the successors of Seleucus retained the dominion of the East, this continued to be the mode of supplying their subjects with the commodities of India. When the Romans had extended their conquests so far that the Euphrates was the eastern limit of their empire, they found this trade still established; and as it opened to them a new communication with the East, by means of which they received an additional supply of luxuries, for which they had acquired the highest relish, it became an object of their policy to protect and encourage it. As the progress of the caravans or companies of merchants, which travelled towards the countries whence they received the most valuable manufactures, particularly those of silk, was often interrupted and rendered dangerous by the Parthians, who had acquired possession of all the provinces which extended from the Caspian Sea to that part of Scythia or Tartary which borders on China, the Romans endeavoured to render this intercourse more secure by a negociation with one of the monarchs of that great empire. Of this singular transaction there is, indeed, no vestige in the Greek or Roman writers; our knowledge of it is derived entirely from the Chinese historians, by whom we are informed that Antoun, (the Emperor Marcus Antonius), the King of the people of the Western Ocean, sent an embassy with this view to Oun-ti, who reigned over China in the hundred and sixty-sixth year of the Christian era.* What was the success of this attempt is not known, nor can we say whether it facilitated such an in-

---

* Memoire sur les Liaisons et le Commerce des Romains avec les Tartares et les Chinois, par M. de Guignes. Mem. de Litterat. xxxii. 355, &c.

tercourse between these two remote nations, as contributed towards the supply of their mutual wants. The design certainly was not unworthy of the enlightened Emperor of Rome to whom it is ascribed.

It is evident, however, that in prosecuting this trade with China, a considerable part of the extensive countries to the east of the Caspian Sea must have been traversed; and though the chief inducement to undertake those distant journies was gain, yet, in the course of ages, there must have mingled among the adventurers persons of curiosity and abilities, who could turn their attention from commercial objects to those of more general concern. From them such information was procured, and subjected to scientific discussion, as enabled Ptolemy to give a description of those inland and remote regions of Asia,* fully as accurate as that of several countries, of which, from their vicinity, he may have been supposed to have received more distinct accounts. The farthest point towards the east, to which his knowledge of this part of Asia extended, is Sera Metropolis, which, from various circumstances, appears to have been in the same situation with Kant-cheou, a city of some note in Chen-si, the most westerly province of the Chinese empire. This he places in the longitude of one hundred and seventy-seven degrees fifteen minutes, near three degrees to the west of Sinæ Metropolis,

---

* Lib. vi. c. 11—18.

which he had described as the utmost limit of Asia discovered by sea. Nor was Ptolemy's knowledge of this district of Asia confined only to that part of it through which the caravans may be supposed to have proceeded directly in their route eastward; he had received likewise some general information concerning various nations towards the north, which, according to the position that he gives them, occupied parts of the great plain of Tartary, extending considerably beyond Lassa, the capital of Thibet, and the residence of the Dalai Lama.

The latitudes of several places in this part of Asia are fixed by Ptolemy with such uncommon precision, that we can hardly doubt of their having been ascertained by actual observation. Out of many instances of this, I shall select three, of places situated in very different parts of the country under review. The latitude of Nagara, on the river Cophenes, (the modern Attock,) is, according to Ptolemy, thirty-two degrees and thirty minutes; which coincides precisely with the observation of an eastern geographer quoted by M. D'Anville.* The latitude of Maracanda, or Samarcand, as fixed by him, is thirty-nine degrees fifteen minutes. According to the Astronomical Tables of Ulug Beg, the grandson of Timur, whose royal residence was in that city, it is thirty-nine degrees thirty-seven minutes.†

---

* Eclaircissemens, &c. English Translation, p. 10.
† Tab. Geogr. ap. Hudson, Geogr. Minores, iii. 145.

The latitude of Sera Metropolis, in Ptolemy, is thirty-eight degrees fifteen minutes; that of Kant-cheou, as determined by the Jesuit missionaries, is thirty-nine degrees. I have enumerated these striking examples of the coincidence of his calculations with those established by modern observations, for two reasons: One, because they clearly prove that these remote parts of Asia had been examined with some considerable degree of attention; the other, because I feel great satisfaction, after having been obliged to mention several errors and defects in Ptolemy's geography, in rendering justice to a philosopher who has contributed so much towards the improvement of that science. The facts which I have produced afford the strongest evidence of the extent of his information, as well as the justness of his conclusions concerning countries, with which, from their remote situation, we might have supposed him to be least acquainted.

HITHERTO I have confined my researches concerning the knowledge which the ancients had of India, to the continent; I return now to consider the discoveries which they had made of the islands situated in various parts of the ocean with which it is surrounded, and begin, as I proposed, with Taprobane, the greatest and most valuable of them. This island lay so directly in the course of navigators who ventured beyond Cape Comorin, especially when, according to the ancient mode of sailing, they seldom ventured far from the coast, that its position, one should have thought, must have been determined with the utmost precision. There is, however, hardly any point in the geography of the ancients more undecided and uncertain. Prior to the age of Alexander the Great, the name of Taprobane was unknown in Europe. In consequence of the active curiosity with which he explored every country that he subdued or visited, some information concerning it seems to have been obtained. From his time, almost every writer on geography has mentioned it; but their accounts of it are so various, and often so contradictory, that we can scarcely believe them to be describing the same island. Strabo, the earliest writer now extant from whom we have any particular account of it, affirms that it was as large as Britain, and situated at the distance of seven days, according to some reports, and according to others, of twenty days sailing from the southern extremity of the Indian peninsula; from which, contrary to what is known to be its real position, he describes it as stretching towards the west above five hundred stadia.* Pomponius Mela, the author next in order of time, is uncertain whether he should consider Taprobane as an island, or as the beginning of another world; but as no person, he says, had ever sailed round it, he seems to incline towards the latter opinion.† Pliny gives a more ample description of Taprobane,

---

* Strabo, lib. ii. 124. B. 180. B. 192. A. lib. xv. 1012. B.
† De Situ Orbis, lib. iii. c. 7.

which, instead of bringing any accession of light, involves every thing relating to it in additional obscurity. After enumerating the various and discordant opinions of the Greek writers, he informs us, that ambassadors were sent by a King of that island to the Emperor Claudius, from whom the Romans learned several things concerning it which were formerly unknown, particularly that there were five hundred towns in the island, and that in the centre of it there was a lake three hundred and seventy-five miles in circumference. These ambassadors were astonished at the sight of the Great Bear and the Pleiades, being constellations which did not appear in their sky; and were still more amazed when they beheld their shadows point towards the north, and the sun rise on their left hand, and set on their right. They affirmed, too, that in their country the moon was never seen until the eighth day after the change, and continued to be visible only to the sixteenth.* It is surprising to find an author so intelligent as Pliny relating all these circumstances without animadversion, and particularly that he does not take notice, that what the ambassadors reported concerning the appearance of the moon could not take place in any region of the earth.

PTOLEMY, though so near to the age of Pliny, seems to have been altogether unacquainted with his description of Taprobane, or with the embassy

---

* Nat. Hist. lib. vi. c. 22.

to the Emperor Claudius. He places that island opposite to Cape Comorin, at no great distance from the continent, and delineates it as stretching from north to south no less than fifteen degrees, two of which he supposes to be south of the equator; and, if his representation of its dimensions had been just, it was well entitled, from its magnitude, to be compared with Britain.* Agathemerus, who wrote after Ptolemy, and was well acquainted with his geography, considers Taprobane as the largest of all islands, and assigns to Britain only the second place. †

From this diversity of the descriptions given by ancient writers, it is not surprising that the moderns should have entertained very different sentiments with respect to the island in the Indian Ocean, which was to be considered as the same with the Taprobane of the Greeks and Romans. As both Pliny and Ptolemy describe it as lying in part to the south of the equator, some learned men maintain Sumatra to be the island which corresponds to this description. But the great distance of Sumatra from the peninsula of India does not accord with any account which the Greek or Roman writers have given of the situation of Taprobane, and we have no evidence that the navigation of the ancients ever extended so far as Sumatra. The opinion more generally received is, that the Taprobane of the ancients

---

* Ptol. lib. vii. c. 4. D'Anville, Ant. de l'Inde, p. 142.
† Lib. ii. c. 8. apud Hudson. Geogr. Minor. vol. ii.

is the island of Ceylon; and not only its vicinity to the continent of India, but the general form of the island as delineated by Ptolemy, as well as the position of several places in it, mentioned by him, establish this opinion (notwithstanding some extraordinary mistakes, of which I shall afterwards take notice), with a great degree of certainty.

The other islands, to the east of Taprobane, mentioned by Ptolemy, might be shewn (if such a detail were necessary) to be the Andaman and Nicobar Islands in the Gulf of Bengal.

After this long, and, I am afraid, tedious investigation of the progress made by the ancients in exploring the different parts of India, and after tracing them as far as they advanced towards the east either by sea or land, I shall offer some general remarks concerning the mode in which their discoveries were conducted, and the degree of confidence with which we may rely on the accounts of them, which could not have been offered with the same advantage until this investigation was finished.

The art of delineating maps, exhibiting either the figure of the whole earth, as far as it had been explored, or that of particular countries, was known to the ancients; and without the use of them to assist the imagination, it was impossible to have formed a distinct idea either of the one or of the other. Some of these maps are mentioned by Herodotus and other early Greek writers. But no maps prior to those which were formed in order to illustrate the geography of Ptolemy, have reached our times, in consequence of which it is very difficult to conceive what was the relative situation of the different places mentioned by the ancient geographers, unless when it is precisely ascertained by measurement.* As soon, however, as the mode of marking the situation of each place, by specifying its longitude and latitude, was introduced, and came to be generally adopted, every position could be described in compendious and scientific terms. But still the accuracy of this new method, and the improvement which geography derived from it, depends upon the mode in which the ancients estimated the latitude and longitude of places.

Though the ancients proceeded in determining the latitude and longitude of places upon the same principles with the moderns, yet it was by means of instruments very inferior in their construction to those now used, and without the same minute attention to every circumstance that may affect the accuracy of an observation, an attention of which long experience only can demonstrate the necessity. In order to ascertain the latitude of any place, the ancients observed the meridian altitude of the sun, either by means of the shadow of a perpendicular gnomon, or by means of an astrolabe, from which it was easy to compute

---

* See Note XXXIV. Page 326.

how many degrees and minutes the place of observation was distant from the equator. When neither of these methods could be employed, they inferred the latitude of any place from the best accounts which they could procure of the length of its longest day.

With respect to determining the longitude of any place, they were much more at a loss, as there was only one set of celestial phenomena to which they could have recourse. These were the eclipses of the moon (for those of the sun were not then so well understood as to be subservient to the purposes of geography); the difference between the time at which an eclipse was observed to begin or to end at two different places, gave immediately the difference between the meridians of those places. But the difficulty of making those observations with accuracy, and the impossibility of repeating them often, rendered them of so little use in geography, that the ancients, in determining longitudes, were obliged, for the most part, to have recourse to actual surveys, or to the vague information which was to be obtained from the reckonings of sailors, or the itineraries of travellers.

But though the ancients, by means of the operations which I have mentioned, could determine the position of places with a considerable degree of accuracy at land, it is very uncertain whether or not they had any proper mode of determining this at sea. The navigators of antiquity seem rarely to have had recourse to astronomical observation. They had no instruments suited to a moveable and unsteady observatory; and though, by their practice of landing frequently, they might, in some measure, have supplied that defect, yet no ancient author, as far as I know, has given an account of any astronomical observation made by them during the course of their voyages. It seems to be evident from Ptolemy, who employs some chapters in shewing how geography may be improved, and its errors may be rectified, from the reports of navigators,[*] that all their calculations were founded solely upon reckoning, and were not the result of observation. Even after all the improvements which the moderns have made in the science of navigation, this mode of computing by reckoning is known to be so loose and uncertain, that, from it alone, no conclusion can be deduced with any great degree of precision. Among the ancients, this inaccuracy must have been greatly augmented, as they were accustomed in their voyages, instead of steering a direct course, which might have been more easily measured, to a circuitous navigation along the coast; and were unacquainted with the compass, or any other instrument by which its bearings might have been ascertained. We find, accordingly, the position of many places which we may suppose to have been determined at sea, fixed with little exactness. When, in consequence of an active trade, the ports of any country were

---

[*] Lib. i. c. 7—14.

much frequented, the reckonings of different navigators may have served, in some measure, to correct each other, and may have enabled geographers to form their conclusions with a nearer approximation to truth. But in remote countries, which have neither been the seat of military operations, nor explored by caravans travelling frequently through them, every thing is more vague and undefined, and the resemblance between the ancient descriptions of them, and their actual figure, is often so faint that it can hardly be traced. The latitude of places, too, as might be expected, was in general much more accurately known by the ancients than their longitude. The observations by which the former was determined are simple, made with ease, and are not liable to much error. The other cannot be ascertained precisely, without more complex operations, and the use of instruments much more perfect than any that the ancients seem to have possessed.* Among the vast number of places, the position of which is fixed by Ptolemy, I know not if he approaches as near to truth in the longitude of any one, as he has done in fixing the latitude of the three cities which I formerly mentioned as a striking, though not singular instance of his exactness.

These observations induce me to adhere to an opinion which I proposed in another place,† that the Greeks and Romans, in their commercial in-

---

* See Note XXXV. Page 327.
† Hist. of America, vol. i. p. 27.

tercourse with India, were seldom led, either by curiosity or the love of gain, to visit the more eastern parts of it. A variety of particulars occur to confirm this opinion. Though Ptolemy bestows the appellation of *Emporia* on several places situated on the coast which stretches from the eastern mouth of the Ganges to the extremity of the Golden Chersonesus, it is uncertain whether, from his having given them this name, we are to consider them as harbours frequented by ships from Egypt, or merely by vessels of the country. Beyond the Golden Chersonesus, it is remarkable that he mentions one *Emporium* only,* which plainly indicates the intercourse with this region of India to have been very inconsiderable. Had voyages from the Arabian Gulf to those countries of India been as frequent as to have entitled Ptolemy to specify so minutely the longitude and latitude of the great number of places which he mentions, he must, in consequence of this, have acquired such information as would have prevented several great errors into which he has fallen. Had it been usual to double Cape Comorin, and to sail up the Bay of Bengal to the mouth of the Ganges, some of the ancient geographers would not have been so uncertain, and others so widely mistaken, with respect to the situation and magnitude of the Island of Ceylon. If the merchants of Alexandria had often visited the ports of the Golden Chersonesus, and of the Great Bay, Ptolemy's descriptions of them must

---

* Lib. vii. c. 2.

have been rendered more correspondent to their real form, nor could he have believed several places to lie beyond the line, which are in truth some degrees on this side of it.

But though the navigation of the ancients may not have extended to the farther India, we are certain that various commodities of that country were imported into Egypt, and thence were conveyed to Rome, and to other parts of the empire. From circumstances which I have already enumerated, we are warranted in concluding, that these were brought in vessels of the country to Musiris, and to the other ports on the Malabar Coast, which were, at that period, the staples of trade with Egypt. In a country of such extent as India, where the natural productions are various, and greatly diversified by art and industry, an active domestic commerce, both by sea and by land, must have early taken place among its different provinces. Of this we have some hints in ancient authors; and where the sources of information are so few and so scanty, we must rest satisfied with hints. Among the different classes, or casts, into which the people of India were divided, merchants are mentioned as one;* from which we may conclude trade to have been one of the established occupations of men in that country. From the author of the Circumnavigation of the Erythræan Sea we learn, that the inhabitants of the Coromandel Coast

---

* Plin. Nat. Hist. lib. vi. c. 22.

traded in vessels of their own with those of Malabar; that the interior trade of Barygaza was considerable; and that there was, at all seasons, a number of country ships to be found in the harbour of Musiris.* By Strabo we are informed, that the most valuable productions of Taprobane were carried to different *Emporia* of India.† In this way the traders from Egypt might be supplied with them, and thus could finish their voyages within the year, which must have been protracted much longer if they had extended as far towards the east as is generally supposed.

From all this it appears to be probable, that Ptolemy derived the information concerning the eastern parts of India, upon which he founds his calculations, not so much from any direct and regular intercourse between Egypt and these countries, as from the reports of a few adventurers, whom an enterprising spirit, or the love of gain, prompted to proceed beyond the usual limits of navigation.

Though, from the age of Ptolemy, the trade with India continued to be carried on in its former channel, and both Rome, the ancient capital of the empire, and Constantinople, the new seat of government, were supplied with the precious commodities of that country by the merchants of Alexandria, yet, until the reign of the em-

---

* Perip. Mar. Erythr. 34.
† Lib. ii. 124. B.

peror Justinian, we have no new information concerning the intercourse with the East by sea, or the progress which was made in the discovery of its remote regions. Under Justinian, Cosmas, an Egyptian merchant, in the course of his traffic, made some voyages to India, whence he acquired the sirname of Indicopleustes; but afterwards, by a transition not uncommon in that superstitious age, he renounced all the concerns of this life, and assumed the monastic character. In the solitude and leisure of a cell he composed several works, one of which, dignified by him with the name of *Christian Topography*, has reached us. The main design of it is, to combat the opinion of those philosophers who assert the earth to be of a spherical figure, and to prove that it is an oblong plane, of twelve thousand miles in length from east to west, and of six thousand miles in breadth from north to south, surrounded by high walls, covered by the firmament as with a canopy or vault; that the vicissitude of day and night was occasioned by a mountain of prodigious height, situated in the extremities of the north, round which the sun moved; that when it appeared on one side of this mountain, the earth was illuminated; when concealed on the other side, the earth was left involved in darkness.* But amidst those wild reveries, more suited to the credulity of his new profession than to the sound sense characteristic of that in which

---

* Cosmas, ap. Montfaucon Collect. Patrum, ii. 113, &c. 138.

he was formerly engaged, Cosmas seems to relate what he himself had observed in his travels, or what he had learned from others, with great simplicity and regard for truth.

He appears to have been well acquainted with the west coast of the Indian peninsula, and names several places situated upon it; he describes it as the chief seat of the pepper trade, and mentions Male, in particular, as one of the most frequented ports on that account.* From Male, it is probable that this side of the continent has derived its modern name of Malabar; and the cluster of islands contiguous to it, that of the Maldives. From him too we learn, that the island of Taprobane, which he supposes to lie at an equal distance from the Persian Gulf on the west, and the country of the Sinæ on the east, had become, in consequence of this commodious situation, a great staple of trade; that into it were imported the silk of the Sinæ, and the precious spices of the eastern countries, which were conveyed thence to all parts of India, to Persia, and to the Arabian Gulf. To this island he gives the name of Sielediba,† nearly the same with that of Selendib, or Serendib, by which it is still known all over the East.

To Cosmas we are also indebted for the first information of a new rival to the Romans in trade having appeared in the Indian seas. The Per-

---

* Cosm. lib. ii. p. 138. lib. xi. 337.   † Lib. xi. 336.

sians, after having overturned the empire of the Parthians, and re-established the line of their ancient monarchs, seem to have surmounted entirely the aversion of their ancestors to maritime exertion, and made early and vigorous efforts in order to acquire a share in the lucrative commerce with India. All its considerable ports were frequented by traders from Persia, who, in return for some productions of their own country in request among the Indians, received the precious commodities, which they conveyed up the Persian Gulf, and by means of the great rivers Euphrates and Tigris, distributed them through every province of their empire. As the voyage from Persia to India was much shorter than that from Egypt, and attended with less expense and danger, the intercourse between the two countries increased rapidly. A circumstance is mentioned by Cosmas which is a striking proof of this. In most of the cities of any note in India he found Christian churches established, in which the functions of religion were performed by priests ordained by the Archbishop of Seleucia, the capital of the Persian empire, and who continued subject to his jurisdiction.* India appears to have been more thoroughly explored at this period than it was in the age of Ptolemy, and a greater number of strangers seem to have been settled there. It is remarkable, however, that according to the account of Cosmas, none of these strangers were accustomed to visit the eastern regions

---

* Cosm. lib. iii. 178.

of Asia, but rested satisfied with receiving their silk, their spices, and other valuable productions, as they were imported into Ceylon, and conveyed thence to the various marts of India.*

The frequency of open hostilities between the emperors of Constantinople and the monarchs of Persia, together with the increasing rivalship of their subjects in the trade with India, gave rise to an event which produced a considerable change in the nature of that commerce. As the use of silk, both in dress and furniture, became gradually more general in the court of the Greek emperors, who imitated and surpassed the sovereigns of Asia in splendour and magnificence; and as China, in which, according to the concurring testimony of Oriental writers, the culture of silk was originally known,† still continued to be the only country which produced that valuable commodity; the Persians, improving the advantages which their situation gave them over the merchants from the Arabian Gulf, supplanted them in all the marts of India to which silk was brought by sea from the East. Having it likewise in their power to molest or to cut off the caravans which, in order to procure a supply for the Greek empire, travelled by land to China, through the northern provinces of their kingdom, they entirely engrossed that branch of commerce. Constantinople was obliged to depend on the rival power for an article which lux-

---

* Lib. xi. 337.   † Herbelot, Biblioth. Orient. art. *Harir*.

ury viewed and desired as essential to elegance. The Persians, with the usual rapacity of monopolists, raised the price of silk to such an exorbitant height,* that Justinian, eager not only to obtain a full and certain supply of a commodity which was become of indispensable use, but solicitous to deliver the commerce of his subjects from the exactions of his enemies, endeavoured, by means of his ally, the Christian monarch of Abyssinia, to wrest some portion of the silk trade from the Persians. In this attempt he failed; but when he least expected it, he, by an unforeseen event, attained, in some measure, the object which he had in view. Two Persian monks having been employed as missionaries in some of the Christian churches, which were established (as we are informed by Cosmas) in different parts of India, had penetrated into the country of the Seres, or China. There they observed the labours of the silk-worm, and became acquainted with all the arts of man in working up its productions into such a variety of elegant fabrics. The prospect of gain, or perhaps an indignant zeal, excited by seeing this lucrative branch of commerce engrossed by unbelieving nations, prompted them to repair to Constantinople. There they explained to the emperor the origin of silk, as well as the various modes of preparing and manufacturing it, mysteries hitherto unknown, or very imperfectly understood in Europe; and encouraged by

marginalia: SECT. II. — A. D. 55.

---

* Procop. Hist. Arcan. c. 25.

his liberal promises, they undertook to bring to the capital a sufficient number of those wonderful insects, to whose labours man is so much indebted. This they accomplished by conveying the eggs of the silk-worm in a hollow cane. They were hatched by the heat of a dunghill, fed with the leaves of a wild mulberry-tree, and they multiplied and worked in the same manner as in those climates where they first became objects of human attention and care.[*] Vast numbers of these insects were soon reared in different parts of Greece, particularly in the Peloponnesus. Sicily afterwards undertook to breed silk-worms with equal success, and was imitated from time to time in several towns of Italy. In all these places, extensive manufactures were established and carried on with silk of domestic production. The demand for silk from the East diminished of course, the subjects of the Greek emperors were no longer obliged to have recourse to the Persians for a supply of it, and a considerable change took place in the nature of the commercial intercourse between Europe and India.[†]

---

[*] Procop. de Bello Gothic. lib. iv. c. 17.
[†] See NOTE XXXVI. Page 330.

AN HISTORICAL DISQUISITION CONCERNING ANCIENT INDIA.

SECTION III.

Intercourse with India, from the Conquest of Egypt by the Mahomedans, to the Discovery of the Passage by the Cape of Good Hope, and the Establishment of the Portuguese Dominion in the East.

ABOUT fourscore years after the death of Justinian, an event happened, which occasioned a revolution still more considerable in the intercourse of Europe with the East. Mahomet, by publishing a new religion, seems to have animated his countrymen with a new spirit, and to have called forth latent passions and talents into exertion. The greatest part of the Arabians, satisfied from the earliest times with national independence and personal liberty, tended their camels, or reared their palm-trees within the precincts of their own peninsula, and had little intercourse with the rest of mankind, unless when they sallied out to plunder a caravan, or to rob a traveller. In some districts, however, they had begun to add the labours of agriculture, and the business of commerce, to the occupations of pastoral life.* These different orders of men, when prompted by the enthusiastic ardour with which the exhortations and example of Mahomet inspired them, displayed at once all the zeal of missionaries, and the ambition of conquerors. They spread the doctrine of their prophet, and extended the dominion of his successors, from the shores of the Atlantic to the frontier of China, with a rapidity of success to which there is nothing similar in the history of mankind. Egypt was one of their earliest conquests; and as they settled in that inviting country, and kept possession of it, the Greeks were excluded from all intercourse with Alexandria, to which they had long resorted as the chief mart of Indian goods. Nor was this the only effect which the progress of the Mahomedan arms had upon the commerce of Europe with India. Prior to their invasion of Egypt, the Arabians had subdued the great kingdom of Persia, and added it to the empire of their Caliphs. They found their new subjects engaged in prosecuting that extensive trade with India, and the country to the east of it, the commencement and progress of which in Persia I have already mentioned; and they were so sensible of the great advantages derived from it, that they became desirous to partake of them. As the active powers of the human mind, when roused to vigorous exertions in one line, are most capable of operating with force in other directions; the

---

* Sale's Koran, Prelim. Disc. p. 32, 33.

Arabians, from impetuous warriors, soon became enterprising merchants. They continued to carry on the trade with India in its former channel from the Persian Gulf, but it was with that ardour which characterizes all the early efforts of Mahomet's followers. In a short time they advanced far beyond the boundaries of ancient navigation, and brought many of the most precious commodities of the East directly from the countries which produced them. In order to engross all the profit arising from the sale of them, the Caliph Omar,* a few years after the conquest of Persia, founded the city of Bassora, on the western banks of the great stream formed by the junction of the Euphrates and Tigris, with a view of securing the command of these two rivers, by which goods imported from India were conveyed into all parts of Asia. With such discernment was the situation chosen, that Bassora soon became a place of trade hardly inferior to Alexandria.

This general information with respect to the trade of the Arabians with India, which is all that can be derived from the historians of that period, is confirmed and illustrated by the Relation of a Voyage from the Persian Gulf towards the East, written by an Arabian merchant in the year of the Christian era eight hundred and fifty-one, about two centuries after Persia was subjected to the Caliphs, and explained by the Commentary

---

* Herbel. Biblioth. Orient. artic. *Basrah.* Abul. Pharas. Hist. Dynast. p. 113.

of another Arabian, who had likewise visited the eastern parts of Asia.* This curious Relation, which enables us to fill up a chasm in the history of mercantile communication with India, furnishes materials for describing more in detail the extent of the Arabian discoveries in the East, and the manner in which they made them.

Though some have imagined that the wonderful property of the magnet, by which it communicates such virtue to a needle or slender rod of iron, as to make it point towards the poles of the earth, was known in the East long before it was observed in Europe, it is manifest, both from the Relation of the Mahomedan merchant, and from much concurring evidence, that not only the Arabians, but the Chinese, were destitute of this faithful guide, and that their mode of navigation was not more adventurous than that of the Greeks and Romans.† They steered servilely along the coast, seldom stretching out to sea so far as to lose sight of land; and as they shaped their course in this timid manner, their mode of reckoning was defective, and liable to the same errors which I observed in that of the Greeks and Romans.‡

Notwithstanding these disadvantages, the progress of the Arabians towards the East extended far beyond the Gulf of Siam, the boun-

---

* See Note XXXVII. Page 331. † Relation, p. 2, 3, &c.
‡ Renaudot. Inquiry into the Time when the Mahomedans first entered China, p. 143.

dary of European navigation. They became acquainted with Sumatra, and the other islands of the great Indian Archipelago, and advanced as far as the city of Canton in China. Nor are these discoveries to be considered as the effect of the enterprising curiosity of individuals; they were owing to a regular commerce carried on from the Persian Gulf with China, and all the intermediate countries. Many Mahomedans, imitating the example of the Persians described by Cosmas Indicopleustes, settled in India and the countries beyond it. They were so numerous in the city of Canton, that the Emperor (as the Arabian authors relate) permitted them to have a Cadi or Judge of their own sect, who decided controversies among his countrymen by their own laws, and presided in all the functions of religion.* In other places proselytes were gained to the Mahomedan faith, and the Arabian language was understood and spoken in almost every sea-port of any note. Ships from China and different places of India traded in the Persian Gulf,† and by the frequency of mutual intercourse, all the nations of the East became better acquainted with each other.‡

A STRIKING proof of this is the new information concerning China and India we receive from the two authors I have mentioned. They point out the situation of Canton, now so well known to Europeans, with a considerable degree of exact-

---

* Relation, 7. Remarks, p. 19. Inquiry, p. 171, &c.
† See NOTE XXXVIII. Page 333. ‡ Relation, p. 8.

SECT. III. ness. They take notice of the general use of silk among the Chinese. They are the first who mention their celebrated manufacture of porcelain, which, on account of its delicacy and transparency, they compare to glass.* They describe the tea-tree, and the mode of using its leaves; and from the great revenue which was levied (as they inform us) from the consumption of it, tea seems to have been as universally the favourite beverage of the Chinese in the ninth century, as it is at present.†

EVEN with respect to those parts of India which the Greeks and Romans were accustomed to visit, the Arabians had acquired more perfect information. They mention a great empire established on the Malabar Coast, governed by monarchs whose authority was paramount to that of every power in India. These monarchs were distinguished by the appellation of *Balchara*, a name yet known in India;‡ and it is probable that the Samorin, or Emperor of Calicut, so frequently mentioned in the accounts of the first voyages of the Portuguese to India, possessed some portion of their dominions. They celebrate the extraordinary progress which the Indians had made in astronomical knowledge; a circumstance which seems to have been little known to the Greeks and Romans; and assert, that in this branch of science they were far superior to the most en-

---

* See NOTE XXXIX. Page 335. † Relation, p. 21. 25.
‡ Herbelot, artic. *Hend. & Belhar*.

lightened nations of the East, on which account their sovereign was denominated the King of Wisdom.* Other peculiarities in the political institutions, the mode of judicial proceedings, the pastimes and the superstitions of the Indians, particularly the excruciating mortifications and penances of the Faquirs, might be produced as proofs of the superior knowledge which the Arabians had acquired of the manners of that people.

The same commercial spirit, or religious zeal, which prompted the Mahomedans of Persia to visit the remotest regions of the East, animated the Christians of that kingdom. The Nestorian churches planted in Persia, under the protection first of its native sovereigns, and afterwards of its conquerors the Caliphs, were numerous, and governed by respectable ecclesiastics. They had early sent missionaries into India, and established churches in different parts of it, particularly, as I have formerly related, in the island of Ceylon. When the Arabians extended their navigation as far as China, a more ample field, both for their commerce and their zeal, opened to their view. If we may rely on the concurring evidence of Christian authors, in the East as well as in the West, confirmed by the testimony of the two Mahomedan travellers, their pious labours were attended with such success, that in the ninth and tenth centuries the number of Christians in

---

* Relation, p. 37. 58.

India and China was very considerable.* As the churches in both these countries received all their ecclesiastics from Persia, where they were ordained by the *Catholicos*, or Nestorian Primate, whose supremacy they acknowledged, this became a regular channel of intercourse and intelligence; and to the combined effect of all these circumstances, we are indebted for the information we receive from the two Arabian writers,† concerning those regions of Asia which the Greeks and Romans never visited.

But while both the Mahomedan and Christian subjects of the Caliphs continued to extend their knowledge of the East, the people of Europe found themselves excluded almost entirely from any intercourse with it. To them the great port of Alexandria was now shut, and the new lords of the Persian Gulf, satisfied with supplying the demand for Indian commodities in their own extensive dominions, neglected to convey them, by any of the usual channels, to the trading towns on the Mediterranean. The opulent inhabitants of Constantinople and other great cities of Europe, bore this deprivation of luxuries, to which they had been long accustomed, with such impatience, that all the activity of commerce was exerted, in order to find a remedy for an evil which they deemed intolerable. The difficulties which were to be surmounted in order to accomplish this, afford the most striking proof of the high estima-

---

* See Note XL. Page 335.   † Relation, p. 39.

tion in which the commodities of the East were held at that time. The silk of China was purchased in Chensi, the westernmost province of that empire, and conveyed thence by a caravan, in a march of eighty or a hundred days, to the banks of the Oxus, where it was embarked, and carried down the stream of that river to the Caspian. After a dangerous voyage across that sea, and ascending the river Cyrus as far as it is navigable, it was conducted by a short land carriage of five days to the river Phasis,* which falls into the Euxine or Black Sea. Thence, by an easy and well known course, it was transported to Constantinople. The conveyance of commodities from that region of the East now known by the name of Indostan, was somewhat less tedious and operose. They were carried from the banks of the Indus by a route early frequented, and which I have already described, either to the river Oxus, or directly to the Caspian, from which they held the same course to Constantinople.

It is obvious, that only commodities of small bulk, and of considerable value, could bear the expense of such a mode of conveyance; and in regulating the price of those commodities, not only the expense, but the risk and danger of conveying them, were to be taken into account. In their journey across the vast plain extending from Samarcand to the frontier of China, caravans were exposed to the assaults and depredations of

---
* Plin. Nat. Hist. lib. vi. c. 17.

the Tartars, the Huns, the Turks, and other roving tribes which infest the north-east of Asia, and which have always considered the merchant and traveller as their lawful prey; nor were they exempt from insult and pillage in their journey from the Cyrus to the Phasis, through the kingdom of Colchis, a country noted, both in ancient and in modern times, for the thievish disposition of its inhabitants. Even under all these disadvantages, the trade with the East was carried on with ardour. Constantinople became a considerable mart of Indian and Chinese commodities, and the wealth which flowed into it in consequence of this, not only added to the splendour of that great city, but seems to have retarded, for some time, the decline of the empire of which it was the capital.

As far as we may venture to conjecture, from the imperfect information of contemporary historians, it was chiefly by the mode of conveyance which I have described, perilous and operose as it was, that Europe was supplied with the commodities of the East, during more than two centuries. Throughout that period the Christians and Mahomedans were engaged in almost uninterrupted hostilities, prosecuted with all the animosity which rivalship for power, heightened by religious zeal, naturally excites. Under circumstances which occasioned such alienation, commercial intercourse could hardly subsist, and the merchants of Christendom either did not resort at all to Alexandria and the ports of Syria, the ancient staples for the commodities of the East, after they were in possession of the Mahomedans; or if the love of gain, surmounting their abhorrence of the Infidels, prompted them to visit the marts which they had long frequented, it was with much caution and distrust.

WHILE the difficulties of procuring the productions of the East were thus augmented, the people of Europe became more desirous of obtaining them. About this time some cities of Italy, particularly Amalphi and Venice, having acquired a greater degree of security or independence than they formerly possessed, began to cultivate the arts of domestic industry, with an ardour and ingenuity uncommon in the middle ages. The effect of these exertions was such an increase of wealth as created new wants and desires, and formed a taste for elegance and luxury, which induced them to visit foreign countries in order to gratify it. Among men in this stage of their advancement, the productions of India have always been held in high estimation, and from this period they were imported into Italy in larger quantities, and came into more general use. Several circumstances which indicate this revival of a commercial spirit, are collected by the industrious Muratori, and from the close of the seventh century, an attentive observer may discern faint traces of its progress.*

---

* Antiquit. Ital. medij Ævi, ii. 400. 408. 410. 883. 885. 894. Rer. Ital. Script. ii. 487. Histoire du Commerce de la Russie, par M. Scherer, tom. i. p. 11, &c.

SECT. III.

Even in enlightened ages, when the transactions of nations are observed and recorded with the greatest care, and the store of historical materials seems to be abundantly ample, so little attention has been paid to the operations of commerce, that every attempt towards a regular deduction of them has been found an undertaking of the utmost difficulty. The era, however, to which I have conducted this Disquisition, is one of the periods in the annals of mankind concerning which history furnishes most scanty information. As it was chiefly in the Greek empire, and in some cities of Italy, that any efforts were made to procure the commodities of India, and the other regions of the East, it is only from the historians of those countries we can expect to find any account of that trade. But from the age of Mahomet, until the time when the Comneni ascended the throne of Constantinople, a period of more than four centuries and a half, the Byzantine history is contained in meagre chronicles, the compilers of which seldom extended their views beyond the intrigues in the palace, the factions in the theatre, or the disputes of theologians. To them the monkish annalists of the different states and cities of Italy, during the same period, are, if possible, far inferior in merit; and in the early accounts of those cities which have been most celebrated for their commercial spirit, we search with little success for the origin or nature of that trade* by which they

---

* See Note XLI. Page 335.

first rose to eminence. It is manifest, however, from the slightest attention to the events which happened in the seventh and eighth centuries, that the Italian states, while their coasts were continually infested by the Mahomedans, who had made some settlements there, and had subjected Sicily almost entirely to their dominion, could not trade with much confidence and security in Egypt and Syria. With what implacable hatred Christians viewed Mahomedans, as the disciples of an impostor, is well known; and as all the nations which professed the Christian faith, both in the East and West, had mingled the worship of angels and saints with that of the Supreme Being, and had adorned their churches with pictures and statues, the true Moslems considered themselves as the only assertors of the unity of God, and beheld Christians of every denomination with abhorrence, as idolaters. Much time was requisite to soften this mutual animosity, so far as to render intercourse in any degree cordial.

MEANWHILE a taste for the luxuries of the East continued not only to spread in Italy, but, from imitation of the Italians, or from some improvement in their own situation, the people of Marseilles and other towns of France on the Mediterranean, became equally fond of them. But the profits exacted by the merchants of Amalphi or Venice, from whom they received those precious commodities, were so exorbitant as prompted them to make some effort to supply their own demands. With this view, they not only opened a trade with Constantinople, but ventured at times to visit the ports of Egypt and Syria.* This eagerness of the Europeans, on the one hand, to obtain the productions of India, and on the other hand, considerable advantages which both the Caliphs and their subjects derived from the sale of them, induced both so far to conceal their reciprocal antipathy, as to carry on a traffic manifestly for their common benefit. How far this traffic extended, and in what mode it was conducted by these new adventurers, the scanty information which can be gathered from contemporary writers does not enable me to trace with accuracy. It is probable, however, that this communication would have produced insensibly its usual effect, of familiarizing and reconciling men of hostile principles and discordant manners to one another, and a regular commerce might have been established gradually between Christians and Mahomedans upon such equal terms, that the nations of Europe might have received all the luxuries of the East by the same channels in which they were formerly conveyed to them, first by the Tyrians, then by the Greeks of Alexandria, next by the Romans, and at last by the subjects of the Constantinopolitan empire.

But whatever might have been the influence of this growing correspondence, it was prevented from operating with full effect by the Crusades, or expeditions for the recovery of the Holy Land,

---

* Mem. de Litterat. tom. xxxvii. p. 467, &c. 483.

which, during two centuries, occupied the professors of the two rival religions, and contributed to alienate them more than ever from each other. I have, in another work,* contemplated mankind while under the dominion of this phrensy, the most singular, perhaps, and the longest continued, of any that occurs in the history of our species; and I pointed out such effects of it upon government, upon property, upon manners and taste, as were suited to what were then the objects of my inquiry. At present my attention is confined to observe the commercial consequences of the Crusades, and how far they contributed to retard or to promote the conveyance of Indian commodities into Europe.

To fix an idea of peculiar sanctity to that country which the Author of our religion selected as the place of his residence while on earth, and in which he accomplished the redemption of mankind, is a sentiment so natural to the human mind, that, from the first establishment of Christianity, the visiting of the holy places in Judea was considered as an exercise of piety, tending powerfully to awaken and to cherish a spirit of devotion. Through succeeding ages, the practice continued and increased in every part of Christendom. When Jerusalem was subjected to the Mahomedan empire, and danger was added to the fatigue and expense of a distant pilgrimage,

---

* Hist. of Charles V. vol. i. p. 26. edit. 1787.

the undertaking was viewed as still more meritorious. It was sometimes enjoined as a penance to be performed by heinous transgressors: It was more frequently a duty undertaken with voluntary zeal; and in both cases it was deemed an expiation for all past offences. From various causes, which I have elsewhere enumerated,[*] these pious visits to the Holy Land multiplied amazingly during the tenth and eleventh centuries. Not only individuals in the lower and middle ranks of life, but persons of superior condition, attended by large retinues, and numerous caravans of opulent pilgrims, resorted to Jerusalem.

In all their operations, however, men have a wonderful dexterity in mingling some attention to interest with those functions which seem to be most purely spiritual. The Mahomedan caravans, which, in obedience to the injunctions of their religion, visit the holy temple of Mecca, are not composed, as I shall hereafter explain more fully, of devout pilgrims only, but of merchants, who, both in going and returning, are provided with such an assortment of goods, that they carry on a considerable traffic.[†] Even the Faquirs of India, whose wild enthusiasm seems to elevate them above all solicitude about the concerns of this world, have rendered their frequent pilgrimages subservient to their interest, by trading in

---

[*] Hist. of Charles V. vol. i. p. 27. 285.
[†] Viagi di Ramusio, vol. i. p. 151, 152,

every country through which they travel.* In like manner, it was not by devotion alone that such numerous bands of Christian pilgrims were induced to visit Jerusalem. To many of them commerce was the chief motive of undertaking that distant voyage; and, by exchanging the productions of Europe for the more valuable commodities of Asia, particularly those of India, which at that time were diffused through every part of the Caliph's dominions, they enriched themselves, and furnished their countrymen with such an additional supply of eastern luxuries as augmented their relish for them.†

But, how faint soever the lines may be, which, prior to the Crusades, mark the influence of the frequent pilgrimages to the East upon commerce, they became so conspicuous after the commencement of these expeditions, as to meet the eye of every observer. Various circumstances concurred towards this, from an enumeration of which it will appear, that, by attending to the progress and effects of the Crusades, considerable light is thrown upon the subject of my inquiries. Great armies, conducted by the most illustrious princes and nobles of Europe, and composed of men of the most enterprising spirit in all the kingdoms of it, marched towards Palestine, through countries far advanced beyond those which they left

---

* See Note XLII. Page 338.
† Gul. Tyr. lib. xvii. c. 4. p. 933. ap. Gesta Dei per Francos.

in every species of improvement. They beheld the dawn of prosperity in the republics of Italy, which had begun to vie with each other in the arts of industry, and in their efforts to engross the lucrative commerce with the East. They next admired the more advanced state of opulence and splendour in Constantinople, raised to a pre-eminence above all the cities then known by its extensive trade, particularly that which it carried on with India and the countries beyond it. They afterwards served in those provinces of Asia through which the commodities of the East were usually conveyed, and became masters of several cities which had been staples of that trade. They established the kingdom of Jerusalem, which subsisted near two hundred years. They took possession of the throne of the Greek empire, and governed it above half a century. Amidst such a variety of events and operations, the ideas of the fierce warriors of Europe gradually opened and improved; they became acquainted with the policy and arts of the people whom they subdued; they observed the sources of their wealth, and availed themselves of all this knowledge. Antioch and Tyre, when conquered by the Crusaders, were flourishing cities, inhabited by opulent merchants, who supplied all the nations trading in the Mediterranean with the productions of the East;[*] and, as far as can be gathered from incidental occurrences mentioned

---

[*] Gul. Tyr. lib. xiii. c. 5. Alb. Aquens. Hist. Hieros. ap. Gesta Dei, vol. i. p. 247.

by the historians of the Holy War, who, being mostly priests and monks, had their attention directed to objects very different from those relating to commerce, there is reason to believe, that both in Constantinople, while subject to the Franks, and in the ports of Syria, acquired by the Christians, the long established trade with the East continued to be protected and encouraged.

But though commerce may have been only a secondary object with the martial leaders of the Crusades, engaged in perpetual hostilities with the Turks on one hand, and with the Soldans of Egypt on the other, it was the primary object with the associates, in conjunction with whom they carried on their operations. Numerous as the armies were which assumed the cross, and enterprising as the fanatical zeal was with which they were animated, they could not have accomplished their purpose, or even have reached the seat of their warfare, without securing the assistance of the Italian states. None of the other European powers could either furnish a sufficient number of transports to convey the armies of the Crusaders to the coast of Dalmatia, whence they marched to Constantinople, the place of general rendezvous; or were able to supply them with military stores and provisions in such abundance as to enable them to invade a distant country. In all the successive expeditions, the fleets of the Genoese, of the Pisans, or of the Venetians, kept on the coast as the armies advanced by land, and supplying them from time to time with whatever was wanting, engrossed all the profits of a branch of commerce, which, in every age, has been extremely lucrative. It was with all the interested attention of merchants, that the Italians afforded their aid. On the reduction of any place in which they found it for their interest to settle, they obtained from the Crusaders valuable immunities of different kinds; freedom of trade; an abatement of the usual duties paid for what was imported and exported, or a total exemption from them; the property of entire suburbs in some cities, and of extensive streets in others; and a privilege granted to every person who resided within their precincts, or who traded under their protection, of being tried by their own laws, and by Judges of their own appointment.* In consequence of so many advantages, we can trace, during the progress of the Crusades, a rapid increase of wealth and of power in all the commercial states of Italy. Every port open to trade was frequented by their merchants, who, having now engrossed entirely the commerce of the East, strove with such active emulation to find new markets for the commodities which it furnished, that they extended a taste for them to many parts of Europe, in which they had hitherto been little known.

Two events happened prior to the termination of the Holy War, which, by acquiring to the Venetians and Genoese the possession of several

---

* Hist. of Charles V. vol. i. p. 34.

provinces in the Greek empire, enabled them to supply Europe more abundantly with all the productions of the East. The first was the conquest of Constantinople in the year one thousand two hundred and four, by the Venetians, and the leaders of the fourth Crusade. An account of the political interests and intrigues which formed this alliance, and turned the hallowed arms destined to deliver the Holy City from the dominion of Infidels, against a Christian monarch, is foreign from the design of this Disquisition. Constantinople was taken by storm, and plundered by the confederates. An Earl of Flanders was placed on the imperial throne. The dominions which still remained subject to the successors of Constantine were divided into four parts, one of which being allotted to the new emperor, for supporting the dignity and expense of government, an equal partition of the other three was made between the Venetians and the chiefs of the Crusade. The former, who, both in concerting and in conducting this enterprise, kept their eyes steadily fixed on what might be most for the emolument of their commerce, secured the territories of greatest value to a trading people. They obtained some part of the Peloponnesus, at that time the seat of flourishing manufactures, particularly of silk. They became masters of several of the largest and best cultivated islands in the Archipelago,* and established a chain of settle-

---

* Danduli Chronic. ap. Murat. Script. Rer. Ital. vol. xii. p. 328. Mar. Sanuto Vite de Duchi di Venez. Murat. vol. xxii. p. 532.

ments, partly military and partly commercial, extending from the Adriatic to the Bosphorus. Many Venetians settled in Constantinople, and without obstruction from their warlike associates, little attentive to the arts of industry, they engrossed the various branches of trade which had so long enriched that capital. Two of these particularly attracted their attention; the silk trade, and that with India. From the reign of Justinian, it was mostly in Greece, and some of the adjacent islands, that silk-worms, which he first introduced into Europe, were reared. The product of their labours was manufactured into stuffs of various kinds, in many cities of the empire. But it was in Constantinople, the seat of opulence and luxury, that the demand for a commodity of such high price was greatest, and there, of consequence, the commerce of silk naturally centered. In assorting cargoes for the several ports in which they traded, the Venetians had for some time found silk to be an essential article, as it continued to grow more and more into request in every part of Europe. By the residence of so many of their citizens in Constantinople, and by the immunities granted to them, they not only procured silk in such abundance, and on such terms, as enabled them to carry on trade more extensively, and with greater profit than formerly, but they became so thoroughly acquainted with every branch of the silk manufacture, as induced them to attempt the establishment of it in their own dominions. The measures taken for this purpose by individuals, as well as the regulations framed by the state, were concerted with so much prudence, and executed with such success, that in a short time the silk fabrics of Venice vied with those of Greece and Sicily, and contributed both to enrich the republic, and to enlarge the sphere of its commerce. At the same time the Venetians availed themselves of the influence which they had acquired in Constantinople, in order to improve their Indian trade. The capital of the Greek empire, besides the means of being supplied with the productions of the East, which it enjoyed in common with the other commercial cities of Europe, received a considerable portion of them by a channel peculiar to itself. Some of the most valuable commodities of India and China were conveyed over land, by routes which I have described, to the Black Sea, and thence by a short navigation to Constantinople. To this market, the best stored of any except Alexandria, the Venetians had now easy access, and the goods which they purchased there made an addition of great consequence to what they were accustomed to acquire in the ports of Egypt and Syria. Thus, while the Latin empire in Constantinople subsisted, the Venetians possessed such advantages over all their rivals, that their commerce extended greatly, and it was chiefly from them every part of Europe received the commodities of the East.

THE other event which I had in view, was the subversion of the dominion of the Latins in Constantinople, and the re-establishment of the Imperial family on the throne. This was effected after a period of fifty-seven years, partly by a transient effort of vigour, with which indignation at a foreign yoke animated the Greeks, and partly by the powerful assistance which they received from the republic of Genoa. The Genoese were so sensible of the advantages which the Venetians, their rivals in trade, derived from their union with the Latin emperors of Constantinople, that, in order to deprive them of these, they surmounted the most deep-rooted prejudices of their age, and combined with the schismatic Greeks to dethrone a monarch protected by the papal power, setting at defiance the thunders of the Vatican, which at that time made the greatest princes tremble. This undertaking, bold and impious as it was then deemed, proved successful. In recompense for their signal services, the gratitude or weakness of the Greek emperor, among other donations, bestowed upon the Genoese Pera, the chief suburb of Constantinople, to be held as a fief of the empire, together with such exemption from the accustomed duties on goods imported and exported, as gave them a decided superiority over every competitor in trade. With the vigilant attention of merchants, the Genoese availed themselves of this favourable situation. They surrounded their new settlement in Pera with fortifications. They rendered their factories on the adjacent coast places of strength.[*] They were masters of the harbour of Constan-

---

[*] Niceph. Gregor. lib. xi. c. 1. § 6. lib. xvii. c. 1. § 2.

tinople more than the Greeks themselves. The whole trade of the Black Sea came into their hands; and not satisfied with this, they took possession of part of the Chersonesus Taurica, the modern Crimea, and rendered Caffa, its principal town, the chief seat of their trade with the East, and the port in which all its productions, conveyed to the Black Sea by the different routes I have formerly described, were landed.*

In consequence of this revolution, Genoa became the greatest commercial power in Europe; and if the enterprising industry and intrepid courage of its citizens had been under the direction of wise domestic policy, it might have long held that rank. But never was there a contrast more striking, than between the internal administration of the two rival republics of Venice and Genoa. In the former, government was conducted with steady systematic prudence; in the latter, it was consistent in nothing but a fondness for novelty, and a propensity to change. The one enjoyed a perpetual calm, the other was agitated with all the storms and vicissitudes of faction. The increase of wealth which flowed into Genoa from the exertions of its merchants, did not counterbalance the defects in its political constitution; and, even in its most prosperous

---

* Folieta Hist. Genuens. ap. Græv. Thes. Antiq. Ital. i. 387. De Marinis de Genuens. Dignit. ib. 1486. Niceph. Greg. lib. xiii. c. 12. Murat. Annal. d'Ital. lib. vii. c. 351. See Note XLIII. Page 339.

SECT. III.

state, we may discern the appearance of symptoms which foreboded a diminution of its opulence and power.

As long, however, as the Genoese retained the ascendant which they had acquired in the Greek empire, the Venetians felt their commercial transactions with it to be carried on upon such unequal terms, that their merchants visited Constantinople seldom, and with reluctance; and in order to procure the commodities of the East in such quantities as were demanded in the various parts of Europe which they were accustomed to supply, they were obliged to resort to the ancient staples of that trade. Of these Alexandria was the chief, and the most abundantly supplied, as the conveyance of Indian goods by land through Asia, to any of the ports of the Mediterranean, was often rendered impracticable by the incursions of Turks, Tartars, and other hordes, which successively desolated that fertile country, or contended for the dominion of it. But under the military and vigorous government of the Soldans of the Mamelukes, security and order were steadily maintained in Egypt, and trade, though loaded with heavy duties, was open to all. In proportion to the progress of the Genoese in engrossing the commerce of Constantinople and the Black Sea,[*] the Venetians found it more and more necessary to enlarge their transactions with Alexandria.

---

[*] See Note XLIV. Page 339.

But such an avowed intercourse with Infidels being considered, in that age, as unbecoming the character of Christians, the senate of Venice, in order to silence its own scruples, or those of its subjects, had recourse to the infallible authority of the Pope, who was supposed to be possessed of power to dispense with the rigorous observation of the most sacred laws, and obtained permission from him to fit out annually a specified number of ships for the ports of Egypt and of Syria.* Under this sanction the republic concluded a treaty of commerce with the Soldans of Egypt, on equitable terms; in consequence of which the senate appointed one consul to reside in Alexandria, and another in Damascus, in a public character, and to exercise a mercantile jurisdiction, authorized by the Soldans. Under their protection, Venetian merchants and artisans settled in each of these cities. Ancient prejudices and antipathies were forgotten, and their mutual interest established, for the first time, a fair and open trade between Christians and Mahomedans.†

While the Venetians and Genoese were alternately making those extraordinary efforts, in order to engross all the advantages of supplying Europe with the productions of the East, the republic of Florence, originally a commercial democracy, applied with such persevering vigour to

---

* See Note XLV. Page 340.
† Sandi Storia Civile Veneziana, lib. v. c. 15. p. 248, &c.

SECT. III. trade, and the genius of the people, as well as the nature of their institutions, were so favourable to its progress, that the state advanced rapidly in power, and the people in opulence. But as the Florentines did not possess any commodious sea-port, their active exertions were directed chiefly towards the improvement of their manufactures and domestic industry. About the beginning of the fourteenth century, the Florentine manufactures of various kinds, particularly those of silk and woollen cloth, appear, from the enumeration of a well-informed historian, to have been very considerable.* The connexion which they formed in different parts of Europe, by furnishing them with the productions of their own industry, led them to engage in another branch of trade, that of banking. In this they soon became so eminent, that the money transactions of almost every kingdom in Europe passed through their hands, and in many of them they were intrusted with the collection and administration of the public revenues. In consequence of the activity and success with which they conducted their manufactures and money transactions; the former always attended with certain though moderate profit, the latter lucrative in an high degree, at a period when neither the interest of money, nor the premium on bills of exchange, were settled with accuracy, Florence became

---

* Giov. Villani Hist. Florent. ap. Murat. Script. Rer. Ital. vol. xiii. p. 823. Dell' Istorie Florentine, di Scip. Ammirato, lib. iv. p. 151. lib. viii. p. 299.

one of the first cities in Christendom, and many of its citizens extremely opulent. Cosmo di Medici, the head of a family which rose from obscurity by its success in trade, was reckoned the most wealthy merchant ever known in Europe;* and in acts of public munificence, as well as of private generosity, in the patronage of learning, and in the encouragement of useful and elegant arts, no monarch of the age could vie with him. Whether the Medici, in their first mercantile transactions, carried on any commerce with the East, I have not been able to discover.† It is more probable, I should think, that their trade was confined to the same articles with that of their countrymen. But as soon as the commonwealth, by the conquest of Pisa, had acquired a communication with the ocean, Cosmo di Medici, who had the chief direction of its affairs, endeavoured to procure for his country a share in that lucrative commerce which had raised Venice and Genoa so far above all the other Italian states. With this view ambassadors were sent to Alexandria, in order to prevail with the Soldan to open that and the other ports of his dominions to the subjects of the republic, and to admit them to a participation in all the commercial privileges which were enjoyed by the Venetians. The negociation terminated with such success, that the Florentines seem to have obtained some share in

A.C. 1406.

A.C. 1425.

---

* Fr. Mich. Brutus Hist. Flor. p. 37. 62. Chron. Eugubinum ap. Murat. Script. Rer. Ital. vol. xiv. p. 1007. Denina Revol. d'Italie, tom. vi. p. 263, &c.

† See NOTE XLVI. Page 340.

the Indian trade;* and soon after this period, we find spices enumerated among the commodities imported by the Florentines into England.†

In some parts of this Disquisition concerning the nature and course of trade with the East, I have been obliged to grope my way, and often under the guidance of very feeble lights. But as we are now approaching to the period, when the modern ideas with respect to the importance of commerce began to unfold, and attention to its progress and effects became a more considerable object of policy, we may hope to carry on what researches yet remain to be made, with greater certainty and precision. To this growing attention we are indebted for the account which Marino Sanudo, a Venetian nobleman, gives of the Indian trade, as carried on by his countrymen about the beginning of the fourteenth century. They were supplied, as he informs us, with the productions of the East in two different ways. Those of small bulk and high value, such as cloves, nutmegs, mace, gems, pearls, &c. were conveyed from the Persian Gulf up the Tigris to Bassora, and thence to Bagdat, from which they were carried to some port on the Mediterranean. All more bulky goods, such as pepper, ginger, cinnamon, &c. together with some portion of the more valuable articles, were conveyed by the ancient route to the Red Sea, and thence across the desert, and down the Nile, to Alexandria. The

---

* See Note XLVII. Page 341. † Hakluyt, vol. i. p. 193.

goods received by the former route were, as Sanudo observes, of superior quality, but from the tediousness and expense of a distant land carriage the supply was often scanty; nor can he conceal (though contrary to a favourite project which he had in view when he wrote the treatise to which I refer) that, from the state of the countries through which the caravans passed, this mode of conveyance was frequently precarious and attended with danger.*

It was in Alexandria only that the Venetians found always a certain and full supply of Indian goods; and as these were conveyed thither chiefly by water carriage, they might have purchased them at a moderate price, if the Soldans had not imposed upon them duties which amounted to a third part of their full value. Under this and every other disadvantage, however, it was necessary to procure them, as from many concurring circumstances, particularly a more extensive intercourse established among the different nations of Europe, the demand for them continued to increase greatly during the fourteenth century. By the irruptions of the various hostile tribes of Barbarians who took possession of the greater part of Europe, that powerful bond by which the Romans had united together all the people of their vast empire was entirely dissolved, and such

---

* Mar. Sanuti Secreta Fidelium Crucis, p. 22, &c. ap. Bongarsium.

discouragement was given to the communication of one nation with another, as would appear altogether incredible, if the evidence of it rested wholly upon the testimony of historians, and were not confirmed by what is still more authentic, the express enactment of laws. Several statutes of this kind, which disgrace the jurisprudence of almost every European nation, I have enumerated and explained in another work.* But when the wants and desires of men multiplied, and they found that other countries could furnish the means of supplying and gratifying them, the hostile sentiments which kept nations at a distance from each other abated, and mutual correspondence gradually took place. From the time of the Crusades, which first brought people, hardly known to one another, to associate and to act in concert, during two centuries, in pursuit of one common end, several circumstances had co-operated towards accelerating this general intercourse. The people around the Baltic, hitherto dreaded and abhorred by the rest of Europe as pirates and invaders, assumed more pacific manners, and began now to visit their neighbours as merchants. Occurrences foreign from the subject of the present inquiry, united them together in the powerful commercial confederacy so famous in the middle ages, under the name of the Hanseatic League, and led them to establish the staple of their trade with the southern parts of Europe in Bruges. Thither the merchants of Italy, particularly those

---

* Hist. of Charles V. vol. i. p. 92. 291, &c.

of Venice, resorted; and in return for the productions of the East, and the manufactures of their own country, they received not only the naval stores and other commodities of the north, but a considerable supply of gold and silver from the mines in various provinces of Germany, the most valuable and productive of any known at that time in Europe.* Bruges continued to be the great mart or storehouse of European trade during the period to which my inquiries extend. A regular communication, formerly unknown, was kept up there among all the kingdoms into which our continent is divided, and we are enabled to account for the rapid progress of the Italian states in wealth and power, by observing how much their trade, the source from which both were derived, must have augmented upon the vast increase in the consumption of Asiatic goods, when all the extensive countries towards the north-east of Europe were opened for their reception.

During this prosperous and improving state of Indian commerce, Venice received from one of its citizens such new information concerning the countries which produced the precious commodities that formed the most valuable article of its trade, as gave an idea of their opulence, their population, and their extent, which rose far above all the former conceptions of Europeans. From the time that the Mahomedans became masters

---

* Zimmerman's Polit. Survey of Europe, p. 102.

of Egypt, as no Christian was permitted to pass through their dominions to the East,* the direct intercourse of Europeans with India ceased entirely. The account of India by Cosmas Indicopleustes in the sixth century, is, as far as I know, the last which the nations of the West received from any person who had visited that country. But about the middle of the thirteenth century, the spirit of commerce, now become more enterprising, and more eager to discover new routes which led to wealth, induced Marco Polo, a Venetian of a noble family, after trading for some time in many of the opulent cities of the Lesser Asia, to penetrate into the more eastern parts of that continent, as far as to the court of the Great Khan on the frontier of China. During the course of twenty-six years, partly employed in mercantile transactions, and partly in conducting negociations with which the Great Khan intrusted him, he explored many regions of the East which no European had ever visited.

He describes the great kingdom of Cathay, the name by which China is still known in many parts of the East,† and travelled through it from Chambalu, or Peking, on its northern frontier, to some of its most southern provinces. He visited different parts of Indostan, and is the first

---

* Sanuto, p. 23.
† Herbelot Bib. Orient. artic. *Khathai*. Stewart, Account of Thibet, Phil. Trans. lxvii. 474. Voyage of A. Jinkinson, Hakluyt, i. 333.

who mentions Bengal and Guzzerat, by their present names, as great and opulent kingdoms. Besides what he discovered on his journies by land, he made more than one voyage in the Indian Ocean, and acquired some information concerning an island which he calls Zipangri, or Cipango, probably Japan. He visited in person Java, Sumatra, and several islands contiguous to them, the island of Ceylon, and the coast of Malabar, as far as the Gulf of Cambay, to all which he gives the names that they now bear. This was the most extensive survey hitherto made of the East, and the most complete description of it ever given by any European; and, in an age which had hardly any knowledge of those regions but what was derived from the geography of Ptolemy, not only the Venetians, but all the people of Europe, were astonished at the discovery of immense countries open to their view, beyond what had hitherto been reputed the utmost boundary of the earth in that quarter.*

But while men of leisure and speculation occupied themselves with examining the discoveries of Marco Polo, which gave rise to conjectures and theories productive of most important consequences, an event happened that drew the attention of all Europe, and had a most conspicuous effect upon the course of that trade, the progress of which I am endeavouring to trace.

---

* See Note XLVIII. Page 342.

SECT. III.
A.D. 1453.

A.D. 1474.

The event to which I allude is, the final conquest of the Greek empire by Mahomet II. and the establishing the seat of the Turkish government in Constantinople. The immediate effect of this great revolution was, that the Genoese residing in Pera, involved in the general calamity, were obliged not only to abandon that settlement, but all those which they had made on the adjacent sea-coast, after they had been in their possession near two centuries. Not long after, the victorious arms of the Sultan expelled them from Caffa, and every other place which they held in the Crimea.* Constantinople was no longer a mart open to the nations of the West for Indian commodities, and no supply of them could now be obtained but in Egypt and the ports of Syria, subject to the Soldans of the Mamelukes. The Venetians, in consequence of the protection and privileges which they had secured by their commercial treaty with those powerful Princes, carried on trade in every part of their dominions with such advantage, as gave them a superiority over every competitor. Genoa, which had long been their most formidable rival, humbled by the loss of its possessions in the East, and weakened by domestic dissensions, declined so fast, that it was obliged to court foreign protection, and submitted alternately to the dominion of the Dukes of Milan and the Kings of France. In consequence of this diminution of their political power,

---

* Folieta Hist. Genu. 602. 626. Murat. Annali d'Ital. ix. 451.

the commercial exertions of the Genoese became less vigorous. A feeble attempt which they made to recover that share of the Indian trade which they had formerly enjoyed, by offering to enter into treaty with the Soldans of Egypt upon terms similar to those which had been granted to the Venetians, proved unsuccessful; and during the remainder of the fifteenth century, Venice supplied the greater part of Europe with the productions of the East, and carried on trade to an extent far beyond what had been known in those times.

THE state of the other European nations was extremely favourable to the commercial progress of the Venetians. England, desolated by the civil wars which the unhappy contest between the houses of York and Lancaster excited, had hardly begun to turn its attention towards those objects and pursuits to which it is indebted for its present opulence and power. In France, the fatal effects of the English arms and conquests were still felt, and the King had neither acquired power, nor the people inclination, to direct the national genius and activity to the arts of peace. The union of the different kingdoms of Spain was not yet completed; some of its most fertile provinces were still under the dominion of the Moors, with whom the Spanish monarchs waged perpetual war; and, except by the Catalans, little attention was paid to foreign trade. Portugal, though it had already entered upon that career of discovery which terminated with most splendid success, had not yet made such progress in it as to be entitled to any high rank among the commercial states of Europe. Thus the Venetians, almost without rival or competitor, except from some of the inferior Italian states, were left at liberty to concert and to execute their mercantile plans; and their trade with the cities of the Hanseatic League, which united the north and south of Europe, and which hitherto had been common to all the Italians, was now engrossed, in a great measure, by them alone.

WHILE the increasing demand for the productions of Asia induced all the people of Europe to court intercourse with the Venetians so eagerly, as to allure them, by various immunities, to frequent their sea-ports, we may observe a peculiarity in their mode of carrying on trade with the East, which distinguishes it from what has taken place in other countries in any period of history. In the ancient world, the Tyrians, the Greeks who were masters of Egypt, and the Romans, sailed to India in quest of those commodities with which they supplied the people of the West. In modern times, the same has been the practice of the Portuguese, the Dutch, the English, and, after their example, of other European nations. In both periods loud complaints have been made, that in carrying on this trade every state must be drained of the precious metals, which, in the course of it, flow incessantly from the West to the East, never to return. From whatever loss might have been occasioned by this gradual but unavoidable diminution of their gold and silver, (whether a real or only an imaginary loss, it is not incumbent upon me in this place to inquire or to determine), the Venetians were, in a great measure, exempted. They had no direct intercourse with India. They found in Egypt, or in Syria, warehouses filled with all the commodities of the East, imported by the Mahomedans; and from the best accounts we have with respect to the nature of their trade, they purchased them more frequently by barter than with ready money. Egypt, the chief mart for Indian goods, though a most fertile country, is destitute of many things requisite in an improved state of society, either for accommodation or for ornament. Too limited in extent, and too highly cultivated to afford space for forests; too level to have mines of the useful metals; it must be supplied with timber for building, with iron, lead, tin and brass, by importation from other countries. The Egyptians, while under the dominion of the Mamelukes, seem not themselves to have traded in the ports of any Christian state, and it was principally from the Venetians that they received all the articles which I have enumerated. Besides these, the ingenuity of the Venetian artists furnished a variety of manufactures of woollen cloths, silk stuffs of various fabric, camblets, mirrors, arms, ornaments of gold and silver, glass, and many other articles, for all which they found a ready market in Egypt and Syria. In return, they received from the merchants of Alexandria, spices of every kind, drugs, gems, pearls, ivory, cotton and silk, unwrought as well as manufactured in many different forms, and other productions of the East, together with several valuable articles of Egyptian growth or fabric. In Aleppo, Baruth, and other cities, besides the proper commodities of India brought thither by land, they added to their cargoes the carpets of Persia, the rich wrought silks of Damascus, still known by the name taken from that city, and various productions of art and nature peculiar to Syria, Palestine, and Arabia. If at any time their demand for the productions of the East went beyond what they could procure in exchange for their own manufactures, that trade with the cities of the Hanseatic League which I have mentioned, furnished them, from the mines of Germany, with a regular supply of gold and silver, which they could carry with advantage to the markets of Egypt and Syria.

From a propensity, remarkable in all commercial states, to subject the operations of trade to political regulation and restraint, the authority of the Venetian government seems to have been interposed, both in directing the importation of Asiatic goods, and in the mode of circulating them among the different nations of Europe. To every considerable staple in the Mediterranean, a certain number of large vessels, known by the name of *Galeons* or *Caracks*, was fitted out on the public account,[*] and returned loaded with the

---

[*] Sabellicus, Hist. Rer. Venet. Dec. iv. lib. iii. p. 868. Denina, Revol. d'Italie, tom. vi. 340.

richest merchandise, the profit arising from the sale of which must have been no slender addition to the revenue of the republic. Citizens, however, of every class, particularly persons of noble families, were encouraged to engage in foreign trade, and whoever employed a vessel of a certain burden for this purpose, received a considerable bounty from the state.* It was in the same manner, partly in ships belonging to the public, and partly in those of private traders, that the Venetians circulated through Europe the goods imported from the East, as well as the produce of their own dominions and manufactures.

THERE are two different ways by which we may come at some knowledge of the magnitude of those branches of commerce carried on by the Venetians. The one, by attending to the great variety and high value of the commodities which they imported into Bruges, the storehouse from which the more northern nations of Europe were supplied. A full enumeration of these is given by a well-informed author, in which is contained almost every article deemed in that age essential to accommodation or to elegance.† The other, by considering the effects of the Venetian trade upon the cities admitted to a participation of its advantages. Never did wealth appear more conspicuously in the train of commerce. The citizens of Bruges, enriched by it, displayed in their

---

* Sandi Stor. Civ. Venez. lib. viii. 891.
† Lud. Guicciardini Descript. de Paesi Bassi, p. 173.

dress, their buildings, and mode of living, such magnificence, as even to mortify the pride and excite the envy of royalty.* Antwerp, when the staple was removed thither, soon rivalled Bruges in opulence and splendour. In some cities of Germany, particularly in Augsburg, the great mart for Indian commodities in the interior parts of that extensive country, we meet with early examples of such large fortunes accumulated by mercantile industry, as raised the proprietors of them to high rank and consideration in the empire.

From observing this remarkable increase of opulence in all the places where the Venetians had an established trade, we are led to conclude, that the profit accruing to themselves from the different branches of it, especially that with the East, must have been still more considerable. It is impossible, however, without information much more minute than that to which we have access, to form an estimate of this with accuracy; but various circumstances may be produced to establish, in general, the justness of this conclusion. From the first revival of a commercial spirit in Europe, the Venetians possessed a large share of the trade with the East. It continued gradually to increase, and during a great part of the fifteenth century, they had nearly a monopoly of it. This was productive of consequences attending all monopolies. Wherever there is no competition, and the merchant has it in his power to re-

---

* See Note XLIX. Page 344.

gulate the market, and to fix the price of the commodities which he vends, his gains will be exorbitant. Some idea of their magnitude, during several centuries, may be formed by attending to the rate of the premium or interest then paid for the use of money. This is undoubtedly the most exact standard by which to measure the profit arising from the capital stock employed in commerce; for, according as the interest of money is high or low, the gain acquired by the use of it must vary, and become excessive or moderate. From the close of the eleventh century to the commencement of the sixteenth, the period during which the Italians made their chief commercial exertions, the rate of interest was extremely high. It was usually twenty per cent, sometimes above that; and so late as the year one thousand five hundred, it had not sunk below ten or twelve per cent in any part of Europe.* If the profits of a trade so extensive as that of the Venetians corresponded to this high value of money, it could not fail of proving a source of great wealth, both public and private.† The condition of Venice, accordingly, during the period under review, is described, by writers of that age, in terms which are not applicable to that of any other country in Europe. The revenues of the republic, as well as the wealth amassed by individuals, exceeded whatever was elsewhere known. In the magnificence of their houses, in richness of furniture,

---

* Hist. of Charles V. vol. i. p. 401, &c.
† See NOTE L. Page 345.

in profusion of plate, and in every thing which contributed either towards elegance or parade in their mode of living, the nobles of Venice surpassed the state of the greatest monarchs beyond the Alps. Nor was all this display the effect of an ostentatious and inconsiderate dissipation; it was the natural consequence of successful industry, which having accumulated wealth with ease, is entitled to enjoy it in splendour.*

NEVER did the Venetians believe the power of their country to be more firmly established, or rely with greater confidence on the continuance and increase of its opulence, than towards the close of the fifteenth century, when two events (which they could neither foresee nor prevent) happened, that proved fatal to both. The one was the discovery of America: The other was the opening a direct course of navigation to the East-Indies by the Cape of Good Hope. Of all occurrences in the history of the human race, these are undoubtedly among the most interesting; and as they occasioned a remarkable change of intercourse among the different quarters of the globe, and finally established those commercial ideas and arrangements which constitute the chief distinction between the manners and policy of ancient and of modern times, an account of them is intimately connected with the subject of this Disquisition, and will bring it to that period which I have fixed upon for its boundary. But as I have

---

* See NOTE LI. Page 345.

elated the rise and progress of these discoveries at great length in another work,* a rapid view of them is all that is requisite in this place.

The admiration or envy with which the other nations of Europe beheld the power and wealth of Venice, led them naturally to inquire into the causes of this pre-eminence; and among these, its lucrative commerce with the East appeared to be by far the most considerable. Mortified with being excluded from a source of opulence, which to the Venetians had proved so abundant, different countries had attempted to acquire a share of the Indian trade. Some of the Italian states endeavoured to obtain admission into the ports of Egypt and Syria, upon the same terms with the Venetians; but either by the superior interest of the Venetians in the court of the Soldans, their negociations for that purpose were rendered unsuccessful; or from the manifold advantages which merchants, long in possession of any branch of trade, have in a competition with new adventurers, all their exertions did not produce effects of any consequence.† In other countries, various schemes were formed with the same view. As early as the year one thousand four hundred and eighty, the inventive and enterprising genius of Columbus conceived the idea of opening a shorter and more certain communication with India, by holding a direct westerly course towards those re-

---

* Hist. of America, Books I. and II.
† See Note LII. Page 347.

gions, which, according to Marco Polo and other travellers, extended eastward far beyond the utmost limits of Asia known to the Greeks or Romans. This scheme, supported by arguments deduced from a scientific acquaintance with cosmography, from his own practical knowledge of navigation, from the reports of skilful pilots, and from the theories and conjectures of the ancients, he proposed first to the Genoese his countrymen, and next to the King of Portugal, into whose service he had entered. It was rejected by the former from ignorance, and by the latter with circumstances most humiliating to a generous mind. By perseverance, however, and address, he at length induced the most wary and least adventurous court in Europe, to undertake the execution of his plan; and Spain, as the reward of this deviation from its usual cautious maxims, had the glory of discovering a new world, hardly inferior in magnitude to a third part of the habitable globe. Astonishing as the success of Columbus was, it did not fully accomplish his own wishes, or conduct him to those regions of the East, the expectation of reaching which was the *original* object of his voyage. The effects, however, of his discoveries were great and extensive. By giving Spain the possession of immense territories, abounding in rich mines, and many valuable productions of nature, several of which had hitherto been deemed peculiar to India, wealth began to flow so copiously into that kingdom, and thence was so diffused over Europe, as gradually awakened a general spirit of industry, and called forth exertions, which alone must have soon turned the course of commerce into new channels.

But this was accomplished more speedily, as well as more completely, by the other great event which I mentioned, the discovery of a new route of navigation to the East by the Cape of Good Hope. When the Portuguese, to whom mankind are indebted for opening this communication between the most remote parts of the habitable globe, undertook their first voyage of discovery, it is probable that they had nothing farther in view than to explore those parts of the coast of Africa which lay nearest to their own country. But a spirit of enterprise, when roused and put in motion, is always progressive; and that of the Portuguese, though slow and timid in its first operations, gradually acquired vigour, and prompted them to advance along the western shore of the African continent, far beyond the utmost boundary of ancient navigation in that direction. Encouraged by success, this spirit became more adventurous, despised dangers which formerly appalled it, and surmounted difficulties which it once deemed insuperable. When the Portuguese found in the torrid zone, which the ancients had pronounced to be uninhabitable, fertile countries occupied by numerous nations, and perceived that the continent of Africa, instead of extending in breadth towards the west, according to the opinion of Ptolemy, appeared to contract itself and to bend eastwards, more extensive prospects opened to their view, and inspired them with hopes of reaching India, by continuing to hold the same course which they had so long pursued.

After several unsuccessful attempts to accomplish what they had in view, a small squadron sailed from the Tagus, under the command of Vasco de Gama, an officer of rank, whose abilities and courage fitted him to conduct the most difficult and arduous enterprises. From unacquaintance, however, with the proper season and route of navigation in that vast ocean through which he had to steer his course, his voyage was long and dangerous. At length he doubled that promontory, which for several years had been the object of terror and of hope to his countrymen. From that, after a prosperous navigation along the south-east of Africa, he arrived at the city of Melinda, and had the satisfaction of discovering there, as well as at other places where he touched, people of a race very different from the rude inhabitants of the western shore of that continent, which alone the Portuguese had hitherto visited. These he found to be so far advanced in civilization, and acquaintance with the various arts of life, that they carried on an active commerce, not only with the nations on their own coast, but with remote countries of Asia. Conducted by their pilots, (who held a course with which experience had rendered them well acquainted), he sailed across the Indian Ocean, and landed at Calecut, on the coast of Malabar, on the twenty-second of May, one thousand four hundred and ninety-eight, ten months and two days after his departure from the port of Lisbon.

The Samorin, or monarch of the country, astonished at this unexpected visit of an unknown people, whose aspect, and arms, and manners, bore no resemblance to any of the nations accustomed to frequent his harbours, and who arrived in his dominions by a route hitherto deemed impracticable, received them, at first, with that fond admiration which is often excited by novelty. But in a short time, as if he had been inspired with foresight of all the calamities now approaching India by this fatal communication opened with the inhabitants of Europe, he formed various schemes to cut off Gama and his followers. But from every danger to which he was exposed, either by the open attacks or secret machinations of the Indians, the Portuguese admiral extricated himself with singular prudence and intrepidity, and at last sailed from Calecut with his ships loaded, not only with the commodities peculiar to that coast, but with many of the rich productions of the eastern parts of India.

On his return to Lisbon, he was received with the admiration and gratitude due to a man, who, by his superior abilities and resolution, had conducted to such an happy issue an undertaking of the greatest importance, which had long occupied the thoughts of his sovereign, and excited

SECT. III.

the hopes of his fellow-subjects.* Nor did this event interest the Portuguese alone. No nation in Europe beheld it with unconcern. For although the discovery of a new world, whether we view it as a display of genius in the person who first conceived an idea of that undertaking which led mankind to the knowledge of it, whether we contemplate its influence upon science by giving a more complete knowledge of the globe which we inhabit, or whether we consider its effects upon the commercial intercourse of mankind, be an event far more splendid than the voyage of Gama, yet the latter seems originally to have excited more general attention. The former, indeed, filled the minds of men with astonishment; it was some time, however, before they attained such a sufficient knowledge of that portion of the earth now laid open to their view, as to form any just idea, or even probable conjecture, with respect to what might be the consequences of communication with it. But the immense value of the Indian trade, which both in ancient and in modern times had enriched every nation by which it was carried on, was a subject familiar to the thoughts of all intelligent men, and they at once perceived that the discovery of this new route of navigation to the East must occasion great revolutions, not only in the course of commerce, but in the political state of Europe.

---

* Asia de João de Barros, dec. i. lib. iv. c. 11. Castagaeda, Hist. de l'Inde, trad. en François, lib. i. c. 2—28.

WHAT these revolutions were most likely to be, and how they would operate, were points examined with particular attention in the cities of Lisbon and of Venice, but with feelings very different. The Portuguese, founding upon the rights which, in that age, priority of discovery, confirmed by a papal grant, were supposed to confer, deemed themselves entitled to an exclusive commerce with the countries which they had first visited, began to enjoy, by anticipation, all the benefits of it, and to fancy that their capital would soon be what Venice then was, the great storehouse of eastern commodities to all Europe, and the seat of opulence and power. On the first intelligence of Gama's successful voyage, the Venetians, with the quick-sighted discernment of merchants, foresaw the immediate consequence of it to be the ruin of that lucrative branch of commerce which had contributed so greatly to enrich and aggrandize their country; and they observed this with more poignant concern, as they were apprehensive that they did not possess any effectual means of preventing, or even retarding, its operation.

THE hopes and fears of both were well founded. The Portuguese entered upon the new career opened to them with activity and ardour, and made exertions, both commercial and military, far beyond what could have been expected from a kingdom of such inconsiderable extent. All these were directed by an intelligent monarch, capable of forming plans of the greatest magnitude with calm systematic wisdom, and of prosecuting them with unremitting perseverance. The prudence and vigour of his measures, however, would have availed little without proper instruments to carry them into execution. Happily for Portugal, the discerning eye of Emanuel selected a succession of officers to take the supreme command in India, who, by their enterprising valour, military skill, and political sagacity, accompanied with disinterested integrity, public spirit, and love of their country, have a title to be ranked with the persons most eminent for virtue and abilities in any age or nation. Greater things perhaps were achieved by them than were ever accomplished in so short a time. Before the close of Emanuel's reign, twenty-four years only after the voyage of Gama, the Portuguese had rendered themselves masters of the city of Malacca, in which the great staple of trade carried on among the inhabitants of all those regions in Asia which Europeans have distinguished by the general name of the East Indies, was then established. To this port, situated nearly at an equal distance from the eastern and western extremities of these countries, and possessing the command of that strait by which they keep communication with each other,* the merchants of China, of Japan, of every kingdom on the continent, of the Moluccas, and all the islands in the Archipelago, resorted from the East; and those

---

* Decad. de Carros, dec. i. lib. viii. c. 1. Osor. de reb. Eman. lib. vii. 213, &c.

of Malabar, of Ceylon, of Coromandel, and of Bengal, from the West. This conquest secured to the Portuguese great influence over the interior commerce of India, while, at the same time, by their settlements at Goa and Diu, they were enabled to engross the trade of the Malabar Coast, and to obstruct greatly the long established intercourse of Egypt with India by the Red Sea. Their ships frequented every port in the East where valuable commodities were to be found, from the Cape of Good Hope to the river of Canton; and along this immense stretch of coast, extending upwards of four thousand leagues,* they had established, for the conveniency or protection of trade, a chain of forts or factories. They had likewise taken possession of stations most favourable to commerce along the southern coast of Africa, and in many of the islands which lie between Madagascar and the Moluccas. In every part of the East they were received with respect; in many they had acquired the absolute command. They carried on trade there without rival or controul; they prescribed to the natives the terms of their mutual intercourse; they often set what price they pleased on goods which they purchased; and were thus enabled to import from Indostan and the regions beyond it, whatever is useful, rare, or agreeable, in greater abundance, and of more various kinds, than had been known formerly in Europe.

---

* Hist. Gener. des Voyages, tom. i. p. 140.

SECT. III.

Not satisfied with this ascendant which they had acquired in India, the Portuguese early formed a scheme, no less bold than interested, of excluding all other nations from participating of the advantages of commerce with the East. In order to effect this, it was necessary to obtain possession of such stations in the Arabian and Persian Gulfs, as might render them masters of the navigation of these two inland seas, and enable them both to obstruct the ancient commercial intercourse between Egypt and India, and to command the entrance of the great rivers, which facilitated the conveyance of Indian goods, not only through the interior provinces of Asia, but as far as Constantinople. The conduct of the measures for this purpose was committed to Alphonso Albuquerque, the most eminent of all the Portuguese generals who distinguished themselves in India. After the utmost efforts of genius and valour, he was able to accomplish one-half only of what the ambition of his countrymen had planned. By wresting the island of Ormuz, which commanded the mouth of the Persian Gulf, from the petty princes who, as *tribu*taries to the monarchs of Persia, had established their dominion there, he secured to Portugal that extensive trade with the East which the Persians had carried on for several centuries. In the hands of the Portuguese, Ormuz soon became the great mart from which the Persian empire, and all the provinces of Asia to the west of it, were supplied with the productions of India; and a city which they built on that barren island, destitute of water, was rendered one of the chief seats of opulence, splendour, and luxury in the Eastern World.*

The operations of Albuquerque in the Red Sea were far from being attended with equal success. Partly by the vigorous resistance of the Arabian princes, whose ports he attacked, and partly by the damage his fleet sustained in a sea of which the navigation is remarkably difficult and dangerous, he was constrained to retire without effecting any settlement of importance.† The ancient channel of intercourse with India by the Red Sea still continued open to the Egyptians; but their commercial transactions in that country were greatly circumscribed and obstructed, by the influence which the Portuguese had acquired in every port to which they were accustomed to resort.

In consequence of this, the Venetians soon began to feel that decrease of their own Indian trade which they had foreseen and dreaded. In order to prevent the farther progress of this evil, they persuaded the Soldan of the Mamelukes, equally alarmed with themselves at the rapid success of the Portuguese in the East, and no less interested to hinder them from engrossing that

---

* Osorius de reb. gestis Eman. lib. x. p. 274, &c. Tavernier's Travels, book v. c. 29. Kœmpfer Amœnit. Exot. p. 756, &c.

† Osorius, lib. ix. p. 248, &c.

commerce, which had so long been the chief source of opulence both to the monarchs and to the people of Egypt, to enter into a negociation with the Pope and the King of Portugal. The tone which the Soldan assumed in this negociation was such as became the fierce chief of a military government. After stating his exclusive right to the trade with India, he forewarned Julius II. and Emanuel, that if the Portuguese did not relinquish that new course of navigation by which they had penetrated into the Indian Ocean, and cease from encroaching on that commerce which from time immemorial had been carried on between the east of Asia and his dominions, he would put to death all the Christians in Egypt, Syria, and Palestine, burn their churches, and demolish the holy sepulchre itself.* This formidable threat, which, during several centuries, would have made all Christendom tremble, seems to have made so little impression, that the Venetians, as the last expedient, had recourse to a measure which, in that age, was deemed not only reprehensible but impious. They incited the Soldan to fit out a fleet in the Red Sea, and to attack those unexpected invaders of a gainful monopoly, of which he and his predecessors had long enjoyed undisturbed possession. As Egypt did not produce timber proper for building ships of force, the Venetians permitted the Soldan to cut it in their forests of Dalmatia, whence it was

---

* Osorius de rebus Eman. lib. iv. p. 110. edit. 1580. Asia de Barros, decad. i. lib. viii. c. 2.

conveyed to Alexandria, and then carried partly by water and partly by land to Suez. There twelve ships of war were built, on board of which a body of Mamelukes was ordered to serve, under the command of an officer of merit. These new enemies, far more formidable than the natives of India with whom the Portuguese had hitherto contended, they encountered with undaunted courage, and, after some conflicts, they entirely ruined the squadron, and remained masters of the Indian Ocean.*

Soon after this disaster, the dominion of the Mamelukes was overturned, and Egypt, Syria, and Palestine were subjected to the Turkish empire by the victorious arms of Selim I. Their mutual interest quickly induced the Turks and Venetians to forget ancient animosities, and to co-operate towards the ruin of the Portuguese trade in India. With this view Selim confirmed to the Venetians the extensive commercial privileges which they had enjoyed under the government of the Mamelukes, and published an edict permitting the free entry of all the productions of the East, imported directly from Alexandria, into every part of his dominions, and imposing heavy duties upon such as were brought from Lisbon.†

---

* Asia de Barros, dec. ii. lib. ii. c. 6. Lafitau, Hist. de Decouvertes des Portugais, i. 292, &c. Osor. lib. iv. p. 120.
† Sandi Stor. Civ. Venez. part ii. 901. part iii. 432.

SECT. III.

But all these were unavailing efforts against the superior advantages which the Portuguese possessed in supplying Europe with the commodities of the East, in consequence of having opened a new mode of communication with it. At the same time, the Venetians, brought to the brink of ruin by the fatal league of Cambray, which broke the power and humbled the pride of the republic, were incapable of such efforts for the preservation of their commerce, as they might have made in the more vigorous age of their government, and were reduced to the feeble expedients of a declining state. Of this there is a remarkable instance in an offer made by them to the King of Portugal, in the year one thousand five hundred and twenty-one, to purchase at a stipulated price all the spices imported into Lisbon, over and above what might be requisite for the consumption of his own subjects. If Emanuel had been so inconsiderate as to close with this proposal, Venice would have recovered all the benefit of the gainful monopoly which she had lost. But the offer met with the reception that it merited, and was rejected without hesitation.*

The Portuguese, almost without obstruction, continued their progress in the East, until they established there a commercial empire; to which, whether we consider its extent, its opulence, the slender power by which it was formed, or the

---

* Osor. de reb. Eman. lib. xii. 265.

splendour with which the government of it was conducted, there had hitherto been nothing comparable in the history of nations. Emanuel, who laid the foundation of this stupendous fabric, had the satisfaction to see it almost completed. Every part of Europe was supplied by the Portuguese with the productions of the East; and if we except some inconsiderable quantity of them, which the Venetians still continued to receive by the ancient channels of conveyance, our quarter of the globe had no longer any commercial intercourse with India, and the regions of Asia beyond it, but by the Cape of Good Hope.

Though from this period the people of Europe have continued to carry on their trade with India by sea, yet a considerable portion of the valuable productions of the East is still conveyed to other regions of the earth by land carriage. In tracing the progress of trade with India, this branch of it is an object of considerable magnitude, which has not been examined with sufficient attention. That the ancients should have had recourse frequently to the tedious and expensive mode of transporting goods by land, will not appear surprising, when we recollect the imperfect state of navigation among them: The reason of this mode of conveyance being not only continued, but increased, in modern times, demands some explanation.

If we inspect a map of Asia, we cannot fail to observe, that the communication throughout all the countries of that great continent, to the west of Indostan and China, though opened in some degree towards the south by the navigable rivers Euphrates and Tigris, and towards the north by two inland seas, the Euxine and Caspian, must be carried on in many extensive provinces wholly by land. This, as I have observed, was the first mode of intercourse between different countries, and, during the infancy of navigation, it was the only one. Even after that art had attained some degree of improvement, the conveyance of goods by the two rivers formerly mentioned, extended so little way into the interior country, and the trade of the Euxine and Caspian Seas was so often obstructed by the barbarous nations scattered along their shores, that partly on that account, and partly from the adherence of mankind to ancient habits, the commerce of the various provinces of Asia, particularly that with India and the regions beyond it, continued to be conducted by land.

The same circumstances which induced the inhabitants of Asia to carry on such a considerable part of their commerce with each other in this manner, operated with still more powerful effect in Africa. That vast continent, which little resembles the other divisions of the earth, is not penetrated with inland seas, like Europe and Asia, or by a chain of lakes like North America, or opened by rivers (the Nile alone excepted) of extended navigation. It forms one uniform, continuous surface, between the various parts of which there could be no intercourse from the earliest times but by land. Rude as all the people of Africa are, and slender as the progress is which they have made in the arts of life, such a communication appears to have been early opened and always kept up. How far it extended in the more early periods to which my researches have been directed, and by what different routes it was carried on, I have not sufficient information to determine with accuracy. It is highly probable, that, from time immemorial, the gold, the ivory, the perfumes, both of the southern parts of Africa and of its more northern districts, were conveyed either to the Arabian Gulf or to Egypt, and exchanged for the spices and other productions of the East.

The Mahomedan religion, which spread with amazing rapidity over all Asia, and a considerable part of Africa, contributed greatly towards the increase of commercial intercourse by land in both these quarters of the globe, and has given it additional vigour, by mingling with it a new principle of activity, and by directing it to a common centre. Mahomet enjoined all his followers to visit once in their lifetime the Caaba, or square building in the temple of Mecca, the immemorial object of veneration among his countrymen, not only on account of its having been chosen (according to their tradition) to be the residence of man at his creation,* but because it was the first

---
* Abul-Ghazi Bayadur Khan, Hist. Gen. des Tartars, p. 15.

SECT. III.

spot on this earth which was consecrated to the worship of God:* In order to preserve continually upon their minds a sense of obligation to perform this duty, he directed, that in all the multiplied acts of devotion which his religion prescribes, true believers should always turn their faces towards that holy place.† In obedience to a precept solemnly enjoined and sedulously inculcated, large caravans of pilgrims assemble annually in every country where the Mahomedan faith is established. From the shores of the Atlantic on one hand, and from the most remote regions of the East on the other, the votaries of the Prophet advance to Mecca. Commercial ideas and objects mingle with those of devotion; the numerous camels‡ of each caravan are loaded with those commodities of every country which are of easiest carriage and most ready sale. The holy city is crowded, not only with zealous devotees, but with opulent merchants. During the few days they remain there, the fair of Mecca is the greatest, perhaps, on the face of the earth. Mercantile transactions are carried on in it to an immense value, of which the despatch, the silence, the mutual confidence and good faith in conducting them, are the most unequivocal proof. The productions and manufactures of India form a capital article in this great traffic, and the cara-

---

* Ohsson Tableau General de l'Empire Othoman, tom. iii. p. 150, &c. 289. edit. 8vo.
† Herbelot Biblioth. Orient. artic. *Caaba* & *Keblah*.
‡ See NOTE LIII. Page 347.

vans on their return disseminate them through every part of Asia and Africa. Some of these are deemed necessary, not only to the comfort, but to the preservation of life, and others contribute to its elegance and pleasure. They are so various as to suit the taste of mankind in every climate, and in different stages of improvement; and are in high request among the rude natives of Africa, as well as the more luxurious inhabitants of Asia. In order to supply their several demands, the caravans return loaded with the muslins and chintzes of Bengal and the Deccan, the shawls of Cachemire, the pepper of Malabar, the diamonds of Golconda, the pearls of Kilcare, the cinnamon of Ceylon, the nutmeg, cloves, and mace of the Moluccas, and an immense number of other Indian commodities.

BESIDES these great caravans, formed partly by respect for a religious precept, and partly with a view to extend a lucrative branch of commerce, there are other caravans, and these not inconsiderable, composed entirely of merchants, who have no object but trade. These, at stated seasons, set out from different parts of the Turkish and Persian dominions, and proceeding to Indostan, and even to China, by routes which were anciently known, they convey by land carriage the most valuable commodities of these countries to the remote provinces of both empires. It is only by considering the distance to which large quantities of these commodities are carried, and frequently across extensive deserts, which, without the aid of camels, would have been impassable, that we can form any idea of the magnitude of the trade with India by land, and are led to perceive, that in a Disquisition concerning the various modes of conducting this commerce, it is well entitled to the attention which I have bestowed in endeavouring to trace it.*

---

* See Note LIV. Page 349.

AN HISTORICAL DISQUISITION CONCERNING ANCIENT INDIA.

SECTION IV.

General Observations.

THUS I have endeavoured to describe the progress of trade with India, both by sea and by land, from the earliest times in which history affords any authentic information concerning it, until an entire revolution was made in its nature, and the mode of carrying it on, by that great discovery which I originally fixed as the utmost boundary of my inquiries. Here, then, this Disquisition might have been terminated. But as I have conducted my readers to that period when a new order of ideas, and new arrangements of policy began to be introduced into Europe, in consequence of the value and importance of commerce being so thoroughly understood, that in almost every country the encouragement of it became a chief object of public attention; as we have now reached that point whence a line may

SECT. IV.

be drawn which marks the chief distinction between the manners and political institutions of ancient and modern times, it will render the work more instructive and useful, to conclude it with some general observations, which naturally arise from a survey of both, and a comparison of the one with the other. These observations, I trust, will be found not only to have an intimate connexion with the subject of my researches, and to throw additional light upon it; but will serve to illustrate many particulars in the general history of commerce, and to point out effects or consequences of various events, which have not been generally observed, or considered with that attention which they merited.

I. AFTER viewing the great and extensive effects of finding a new course of navigation to India by the Cape of Good Hope, it may appear surprising to a modern observer, that a discovery of such importance was not made, or even attempted, by any of the commercial states of the ancient world. But in judging with respect to the conduct of nations in remote times, we never err more widely, than when we decide with regard to it, not according to the ideas and views of their age, but of our own. This is not, perhaps, more conspicuous in any instance, than in that under consideration. It was by the Tyrians, and by the Greeks, who were masters of Egypt, that the different people of Europe were first supplied with the productions of the East. From the account that has been given of the manner in which they procured these, it is manifest that they had neither the same inducements with modern nations to wish for any new communication with India, nor the same means of accomplishing it. All the commercial transactions of the ancients with the East were confined to the ports on the Malabar Coast, or extended, at farthest, to the island of Ceylon. To these staples the natives of all the different regions in the eastern parts of Asia brought the commodities which were the growth of their several countries, or the product of their ingenuity, in their own vessels, and with them the ships from Tyre and from Egypt completed their investments. While the operations of their Indian trade were carried on within a sphere so circumscribed, the conveyance of a cargo by the Arabian Gulf, notwithstanding the expense of land carriage, either from Elath to Rhinocolura, or across the desert to the Nile, was so safe and commodious, that the merchants of Tyre and Alexandria had little reason to be solicitous for the discovery of any other. The situation of both these cities, as well as that of the other considerable commercial states of antiquity, was very different from that of the countries to which, in later times, mankind have been indebted for keeping up intercourse with the remote parts of the globe. Portugal, Spain, England, Holland, which have been most active and successful in this line of enterprise, all lie on the Atlantic Ocean, (in which every European voyage of discovery must commence), or have immediate access to it. But Tyre was situated at the eastern extremity of the Mediterranean, Alexandria not far from it; Rhodes, Athens, Corinth, which came afterwards to be ranked among the most active trading cities of antiquity, lay considerably advanced towards the same quarter in that sea. The commerce of all these states was long confined within the precincts of the Mediterranean; and in some of them, never extended beyond it. The Pillars of Hercules, or the Straits of Gibraltar, were long considered as the utmost boundary of navigation. To reach this was deemed a signal proof of naval skill; and before any of these states could give a beginning to an attempt towards exploring the vast unknown ocean which lay beyond it, they had to accomplish a voyage (according to their ideas) of great extent and much danger. This was sufficient to deter them from engaging in an arduous undertaking, from which, even if attended with success, their situation prevented their entertaining hopes of deriving great advantage.*

But could we suppose the discovery of a new passage to India to have become an object of desire or pursuit to any of these states, their science as well as practice of navigation was so defective, that it would have been hardly possible for them to attain it. The vessels which the ancients employed in trade were so small, as not to afford stowage for provisions sufficient to subsist a crew

---

* See Note LV. Page 355.

during a long voyage. Their construction was such, that they could seldom venture to depart far from land, and their mode of steering along the coast (which I have been obliged to mention often) so circuitous and slow, that from these, as well as from other circumstances which I might have specified,* we may pronounce a voyage from the Mediterranean to India, by the Cape of Good Hope, to have been an undertaking beyond their power to accomplish, in such a manner as to render it, in any degree, subservient to commerce. To this decision, the account preserved by Herodotus, of a voyage performed by some Phœnician ships employed by a king of Egypt, which, taking their departure from the Arabian Gulf, doubled the southern promontory of Africa, and arrived, at the end of three years, by the Straits of Gades, or Gibraltar, at the mouth of the Nile,† can hardly be considered as repugnant; for several writers of the greatest eminence among the ancients, and most distinguished for their proficiency in the knowledge of geography, regarded this account rather as an amusing tale than the history of a real transaction; and either entertained doubts concerning the possibility of sailing round Africa, or absolutely denied it.‡ But if what Herodotus relates concerning the course held by these Phœnician ships had ever

---

* Goguet, Orig. des Loix des Arts, &c. ii. 303. 329.
† Lib. iv. c. 42.
‡ Polyb. lib. iii. p. 193. edit. Casaub. Plin. Nat. Hist. lib. ii. c. 6. Ptol. Geogr. lib. iv. c. 9. See Note LVI. Page 355.

been received by the ancients with general assent, we can hardly suppose that any state could have been so wildly adventurous as to imagine, that a voyage which it required three years to complete, could be undertaken with a prospect of commercial benefit.

II. The rapid progress of the moderns in exploring India, as well as the extensive power and valuable settlements which they early acquired there, mark such a distinction between their mode of conducting naval operations, and that of the ancients, as merits to be considered and explained with attention. From the reign of the first Ptolemy to the conquest of Egypt by the Mahomedans, Europe had been supplied with the productions of the East by the Greeks of Alexandria, by the Romans while they were masters of Egypt, and by the subjects of the Emperors of Constantinople, when that kingdom became a province of their dominions. During this long period, extending almost to a thousand years, none of those people, the most enlightened, undoubtedly, in the ancient world, ever advanced by sea farther towards the east than the Gulf of Siam, and had no regular established trade but with the ports on the coast of Malabar, or those in the island of Ceylon. They attempted no conquests in any part of India, they made no settlements, they erected no forts. Satisfied with an intercourse merely commercial, they did not aim at acquiring any degree of power or dominion in the countries where they traded, though it seems to be probable that they might have established it without much opposition from the natives, a gentle effeminate people, with whom, at that time, no foreign and more warlike race was mingled. But the enterprising activity of the Portuguese was not long confined within the same limits; a few years after their arrival at Calcout, they advanced towards the east, into regions unknown to the ancients. The kingdoms of Cambodia, Cochin-China, Tonquin, the vast empire of China, and all the fertile islands in the great Indian Archipelago, from Sumatra to the Philippines, were discovered, and the Portuguese, though opposed in every quarter by the Mahomedans of Tartar or Arabian origin settled in many parts of India, enemies much more formidable than the natives, established there that extensive influence and dominion which I have formerly described.

Of this remarkable difference between the progress and operations of the ancients and moderns in India, the imperfect knowledge of the former, with respect both to the theory and practice of navigation, seems to have been the principal cause. From the coast of Malabar to the Philippines, was a voyage of an extent far beyond any that the ancients were accustomed to undertake, and, according to their manner of sailing, must have required a great length of time to perform it. The nature of their trade with India was such, that they had not (as has been formerly observed) the same inducements with the moderns to prosecute discovery with ardour; and, according to the description given of the vessels in which the merchants of Alexandria carried on their trade from the Arabian Gulf, they appear to have been very unfit for that purpose. On all these accounts, the ancients remained satisfied with a slender knowledge of India; and influenced by reasons proceeding from the same cause, they attempted neither conquest nor settlement there. In order to accomplish either of these, they must have transported a considerable number of men into India. But, from the defective structure of their ships, as well as from the imperfection of their art in navigating them, the ancients seldom ventured to convey a body of troops to any distance by sea. From Berenice to Musiris was to them, even after Hippalus had discovered the method of steering a direct course, and when their naval skill had attained to its highest state of improvement, a voyage of no less than seventy days. By the ancient route along the coast of Persia, a voyage from the Arabian Gulf to any part of India must have been of greater length, and accomplished more slowly. As no hostile attack was ever made upon India by sea, either by the Greek monarchs of Egypt, though the two first of them were able and ambitious princes, or by the most enterprising of the Roman Emperors, it is evident that they must have deemed it an attempt beyond their power to execute. Alexander the Great, and, in imitation of him, his successors, the monarchs of Syria, were the only persons in the ancient world who formed an idea of establishing their dominion in any part of India; but it was with armies led thither by land that they hoped to achieve this.

III. The sudden effect of opening a direct communication with the East, in lowering the price of Indian commodities, is a circumstance that merits observation. How compendious soever the ancient intercourse with India may appear to have been, it was attended with considerable expense. The productions of the remote parts of Asia, brought to Ceylon, or to the ports on the Malabar Coast, by the natives, were put on board the ships which arrived from the Arabian Gulf. At Berenice they were landed, and carried by camels two hundred and fifty-eight miles to the banks of the Nile. There they were again embarked, and conveyed down the river to Alexandria, whence they were despatched to different markets. The addition to the price of goods by such a multiplicity of operations must have been considerable, especially when the rate chargeable on each operation was fixed by monopolists, subject to no controul. But, after the passage to India by the Cape of Good Hope was discovered, its various commodities were purchased at first hand in the countries of which they were the growth or manufacture. In all these, particularly in Indostan and in China, the subsistence of man is more abundant than in any other part of the earth. The people live chiefly upon rice, the most prolific of all grains; population, of consequence, is so great, and labour so extremely cheap, that every production of nature or of art is sold at a very low price. When these were shipped in different parts of India, they were conveyed directly to Lisbon, by a navigation, long indeed, but uninterrupted and safe, and thence circulated through Europe. The carriage of mercantile goods by water is so much less expensive than by any other mode of conveyance, that as soon as the Portuguese could import the productions of India in sufficient quantities to supply the demands of Europe, they were able to afford them at such a reduced price, that the competition of the Venetians ceased almost entirely, and the full stream of commerce flowed in its natural direction towards the cheapest market. In what proportion the Portuguese lowered the price of Indian commodities, I cannot ascertain with precision, as I have not found in contemporary writers sufficient information with respect to that point. Some idea, however, of this, approaching perhaps near to accuracy, may be formed from the computations of Mr Munn, an intelligent English merchant. He has published a table of the prices paid for various articles of goods in India, compared with the prices for which they were sold in Aleppo, from which the difference appears to be nearly as three to one; and he calculates, that, after a reasonable allowance for the expense of the voyage from India, the same goods may be sold in England at half the price which they bear in Aleppo. The expense of conveying the productions of India up the Persian Gulf to Bassora, and thence either through the Great or Little Desert to Aleppo, could not, I should imagine, differ considerably from that by the Red Sea to Alexandria. We may therefore suppose, that the Venetians might purchase them from the merchants of that city, at nearly the same rate for which they were sold in Aleppo; and when we add to this, what they must have charged as their own profit in all the markets which they frequented, it is evident that the Portuguese might afford to reduce the commodities of the East to a price below that which has been mentioned, and might supply every part of Europe with them more than one-half cheaper than formerly. The enterprising schemes of the Portuguese monarchs were accomplished sooner, as well as more completely, than in the hour of most sanguine hope they could have presumed to expect; and, early in the sixteenth century, their subjects became possessed of a monopoly of the trade with India, founded upon the only equitable title, that of furnishing its productions in greater abundance, and at a more moderate price.

IV. We may observe, that in consequence of a more plentiful supply of Indian goods, and at a cheaper rate, the demand for them increased rapidly in every part of Europe. To trace the progress of this in detail, would lead me far beyond the period which I have fixed as the limit of this Disquisition, but some general remarks concerning it will be found intimately connected with the subject of my inquiries. The chief articles of importation from India, while the Romans had the direction of the trade with that country, have been formerly specified. But upon the subversion of their empire, and the settlement of the fierce warriors of Scythia and Germany in the various countries of Europe, the state of society, as well as the condition of individuals, became so extremely different, that the wants and desires of men were no longer the same. Barbarians, many of them not far advanced in their progress beyond the rudest state of social life, had little relish for those accommodations, and that elegance, which are so alluring to polished nations. The curious manufactures of silk, the precious stones and pearls of the East, which had been the ornament and pride of the wealthy and luxurious citizens of Rome, were not objects of desire to men, who, for a considerable time after they took possession of their new conquests, retained the original simplicity of their pastoral manners. They advanced, however, from rudeness to refinement in the usual course of progression which nations are destined to hold, and an increase of wants and desires requiring new objects to gratify them, they began to acquire a relish for some of the luxuries of India. Among these they had a singular predilection for the spiceries and aromatics which that country yields in such variety and abundance. Whence their peculiar fondness for these arose, it is not of importance to inquire. Whoever consults the writers of the middle ages, will find many particulars which confirm this observation. In every enumeration of Indian commodities which they give, spices are always mentioned as the most considerable and precious article.* In their cookery, all dishes were highly seasoned with them. In every entertainment of parade, a profusion of them was deemed essential to magnificence. In every medical prescription they were principal ingredients.† But, considerable as the demand for spices had become, the mode in which the nations of Europe had hitherto been supplied with them was extremely disadvantageous. The ships employed by the merchants of Alexandria never ventured to visit those remote regions which produce the most valuable spices, and before they could be circulated through Europe, they were loaded with the accumulated profits received by four or five different hands through which they had passed. But the Portuguese, with a bolder spirit of navigation, having penetrated into every part of Asia, took in their cargo of spices in the places where they grew, and could afford to dispose of them at such a price, that, from being an expensive luxury, they became an article of such general use as greatly augmented the demand for them. An effect similar to this may be observed with respect to the demand for other commodities imported

---

* Jac. de Vitriac. Hist. Hieros. ap. Bongars, i. p. 1099. Wilh. Tyr. lib. xii. c. 23.
† Du Cange, Glossar. Verb. *Aromata, Species.* Henry's Hist. of Great Brit. vol. iv. p. 597, 598.

from India, upon the reduction of their price by the Portuguese. From that period a growing taste for Asiatic luxuries may be traced in every country of Europe, and the number of ships fitted out for that trade at Lisbon continued to increase every year.*

V. Lucrative as the trade with India was, and had long been deemed, it is remarkable that the Portuguese were suffered to remain in the undisturbed and exclusive possession of it, during the course of almost a century. In the ancient world, though Alexandria, from the peculiar felicity of its situation, could carry on an intercourse with the East by sea, and circulate its productions through Europe with such advantage as gave it a decided superiority over every rival; yet various attempts (which have been described in their proper places) were made, from time to time, to obtain some share in a commerce so apparently beneficial. From the growing activity of the commercial spirit in the sixteenth century, as well as from the example of the eager solicitude with which the Venetians and Genoese exerted themselves alternately to shut out each other from any share in the Indian trade, it might have been expected that some competitor would have arisen to call in question the claim of the Portuguese to an exclusive right of traffic with the East, and to wrest from them some portion of it. There were, however, at that time, some

---

* See Note LVII. Page 356.

peculiar circumstances in the political state of all those nations in Europe, whose intrusion, as rivals, the Portuguese had any reason to dread, which secured to them the quiet enjoyment of their monopoly of Indian commerce, during such a long period. From the accession of Charles V. to the throne, Spain was either so much occupied in a multiplicity of operations in which it was engaged by the ambition of that monarch and of his son Philip II. or so intent on prosecuting its own discoveries and conquests in the New World, that although, by the successful enterprise of Magellan, its fleets were unexpectedly conducted by a new course to that remote region of Asia which was the seat of the most gainful and alluring branch of trade carried on by the Portuguese, it could make no considerable effort to avail itself of the commercial advantages which it might have derived from that event. By the acquisition of the crown of Portugal, in the year one thousand five hundred and eighty, the Kings of Spain, instead of the rivals, became the protectors of the Portuguese trade, and the guardians of all its exclusive rights. Throughout the sixteenth century, the strength and resources of France were so much wasted by the fruitless expeditions of their monarchs into Italy, by their unequal contest with the power and policy of Charles V. and by the calamities of the civil wars which desolated the kingdom upwards of forty years, that it could neither bestow much attention upon objects of commerce, nor engage in any scheme of dis-

A. D. 1521.

tant enterprise. The Venetians, how sensibly soever they might feel the mortifying reverse of being excluded, almost entirely, from the Indian trade, of which their capital had been formerly the chief seat, were so debilitated and humbled by the League of Cambray, that they were no longer capable of engaging in any undertaking of magnitude. England, weakened (as was formerly observed) by the long contest between the houses of York and Lancaster, and just beginning to recover its proper vigour, was restrained from active exertion, during one part of the sixteenth century, by the cautious maxims of Henry VII.; and wasted its strength, during another part of it, by engaging inconsiderately in the wars between the princes on the continent. The nation, though destined to acquire territories in India more extensive and valuable than were ever possessed by any European power, had no such presentiment of its future eminence there, as to take an early part in the commerce or transactions of that country, and a great part of the century elapsed before it began to turn its attention towards the East.

WHILE the most considerable nations in Europe found it necessary, from the circumstances which I have mentioned, to remain inactive spectators of what passed in the East, the Seven United Provinces of the Low-Countries, recently formed into a small state, still struggling for political existence, and yet in the infancy of its power, ventured to appear in the Indian Ocean as the rivals of the Portuguese; and, despising their pretensions to an exclusive right of commerce with the extensive countries to the eastward of the Cape of Good Hope, invaded that monopoly which they had hitherto guarded with such jealous attention. The English soon followed the example of the Dutch; and both nations, at first by the enterprising industry of private adventurers, and afterwards by the more powerful efforts of trading companies, under the protection of public authority, advanced with astonishing ardour and success in this new career opened to them. The vast fabric of power which the Portuguese had erected in the East (a superstructure much too large for the basis on which it had to rest), was almost entirely overturned, in as short time, and with as much facility, as it had been raised. England and Holland, by driving them from their most valuable settlements, and seizing the most lucrative branches of their trade, have attained to that pre-eminence in naval power and commercial opulence, by which they are distinguished among the nations of Europe.

VI. The coincidence, in point of time, of the discoveries made by Columbus in the West, and those of Gama in the East, is a singular circumstance, which merits observation, on account of the remarkable influence of those events in forming or strengthening the commercial connexion of the different quarters of the globe with each other. In all ages, gold and silver, particularly the latter, have been the commodities exported with the greatest profit to India. In no part of the earth do the natives depend so little upon foreign countries, either for the necessaries or luxuries of life. The blessings of a favourable climate and fertile soil, augmented by their own ingenuity, afford them whatever they desire. In consequence of this, trade with them has always been carried on in one uniform manner, and the precious metals have been given in exchange for their peculiar productions, whether of nature or art. But when the communication with India was rendered so much more easy, that the demand for its commodities began to increase far beyond what had been formerly known, if Europe had not been supplied with the gold and silver which it was necessary to carry to the markets of the East from sources richer and more abundant than her own barren and impoverished mines, she must either have abandoned the trade with India altogether, or have continued it with manifest disadvantage. By such a continual drain of gold and silver, as well as by the unavoidable waste of both in circulation and in manufactures, the quantity of those metals must have gone on diminishing, and their value would have been so much enhanced, that they could not have continued long to be of the same utility in the commercial transactions between the two countries. But before the effects of this diminution could be very sensibly felt, America opened her mines, and poured in treasures upon Europe in the most copious stream to which mankind ever had access. This treasure, in spite of innumerable anxious precautions to prevent it, flowed to the markets where the commodities necessary for supplying the wants, or gratifying the luxury of the Spaniards, were to be found; and from that time to the present, the English and Dutch have purchased the productions of China and Indostan, with silver brought from the mines of Mexico and Peru. The immense exportation of silver to the East, during the course of two centuries, has not only been replaced by the continual influx from America, but the quantity of it has been considerably augmented, and at the same time the proportional rate of its value in Europe and in India has varied so little, that it is chiefly with silver that many of the capital articles imported from the East are still purchased.

While America contributed in this manner to facilitate and extend the intercourse of Europe with Asia, it gave rise to a traffic with Africa, which, from slender beginnings, has become so considerable, as to form the chief bond of commercial connexion with that continent. Soon after the Portuguese had extended their discoveries on the coast of Africa beyond the river Senegal, they endeavoured to derive some benefit from their new settlements there, by the sale of slaves. Various circumstances combined in favouring the revival of this odious traffic. In every part of America of which the Spaniards took possession, they found that the natives, from the feebleness of their frame, from their indolence, or from the injudicious manner of treating them, were incapable of the exertions requisite either for working mines, or for cultivating the earth.

SECT. IV.

Eager to find hands more industrious and efficient, the Spaniards had recourse to their neighbours the Portuguese, and purchased from them negro slaves. Experience soon discovered that they were men of a more hardy race, and so much better fitted for enduring fatigue, that the labour of one negro was computed to be equal to that of four Americans;* and from that time the number employed in the New World has gone on increasing with rapid progress. In this practice, no less repugnant to the feelings of humanity than to the principles of religion, the Spaniards have unhappily been imitated by all the nations of Europe who have acquired territories in the warmer climates of the New World. At present the number of negro slaves in the settlements of Great Britain and France in the West Indies, exceeds a million; and as the establishment of servitude has been found, both in ancient and in modern times, extremely unfavourable to population, it requires an annual importation from Africa of at least fifty-eight thousand to keep up the stock.† If it were possible to ascertain, with equal exactness, the number of slaves in the Spanish dominions, and in North America, the total number of negro slaves might be well reckoned at as many more.

Thus the commercial genius of Europe, which has given it a visible ascendant over the three

---

* Hist. of America, vol. i. p. 311.
† Report of Lords of the Privy-Council, A. D. 1788.

other divisions of the earth, by discerning their respective wants and resources, and by rendering them reciprocally subservient to one another, has established an union among them, from which it has derived an immense increase of opulence, of power, and of enjoyments.

VII. Though the discovery of a New World in the West, and the opening of a more easy and direct communication with the remote regions of the East, co-operated towards extending the commerce, and adding to the enjoyments of Europe, a remarkable difference may be observed, with respect both to the time and the manner in which they produced these effects. When the Portuguese first visited the different countries of Asia, stretching from the coast of Malabar to China, they found them possessed by nations highly civilized, which had made considerable progress in elegant as well as useful arts, which were accustomed to intercourse with strangers, and well acquainted with all the advantages of commerce. But when the Spaniards began to explore the New World which they discovered, the aspect which it presented to them was very different. The islands were inhabited by naked savages, so unacquainted with the simplest and most necessary arts of life, that they subsisted chiefly on the spontaneous productions of a fertile soil and genial climate. The continent appeared to be a forest of immense extent, along the coast of which were scattered some feeble tribes, not greatly superior to the islanders

SECT. IV.

in industry or improvement. Even its two large monarchies, which have been dignified with the appellation of civilized states, had not advanced so far beyond their countrymen as to be entitled to that name. The inhabitants both of Mexico and Peru, unacquainted with the useful metals, and destitute of the address requisite for acquiring such command of the inferior animals as to derive any considerable aid from their labour, had made so little progress in agriculture, the first of all arts, that one of the greatest difficulties with which the small number of Spaniards who overturned those highly extolled empires had to struggle, was how to procure in them what was sufficient for their subsistence.

It was, of consequence, with a very different spirit that the intercourse with two countries, resembling each other so little in their degree of improvement, was begun and carried on. The Portuguese, certain of finding in the East, not only the productions with which the bountiful hand of nature has enriched that part of the globe, but various manufactures which had long been known and admired in Europe, engaged in this alluring trade with the greatest eagerness. The encouragement of it their monarchs considered as a chief object of government, towards which they directed all the power of the kingdom, and roused their subjects to such vigorous exertions in the prosecution of it, as occasioned that astonishing rapidity of progress which I have described. The sanguine hopes with which the Spaniards entered upon their career of discovery, met not with the same speedy gratification. From the industry of the rude inhabitants of the New World, they did not receive a single article of commerce. Even the natural productions of the soil and climate, when not cherished and multiplied by the fostering and active hand of man, were of little account. Hope, rather than success, incited them to persist in extending their researches and conquests; and as government derived little immediate benefit from these, it left the prosecution of them chiefly to private adventurers, by whose enterprising activity, more than by any effort of the state, the most valuable possessions of Spain in America were acquired. Instead of the instantaneous and great advantages which the Portuguese derived from their discoveries, above half a century elapsed before the Spaniards reaped any benefit of consequence from their conquests, except the small quantities of gold which the islanders were compelled to collect, and the plunder of the gold and silver employed by the Mexicans and Peruvians, as ornaments of their persons and temples, or as utensils of sacred or domestic use. It was not until the discovery of the mines of Potosi in Peru, in the year one thousand five hundred and forty-five, and of those of Sacotecas in Mexico, soon after, that the Spanish territories in the New World brought a permanent and valuable addition of wealth and revenue to the mother country.

SECT. IV.

Nor did the trade with India differ more from that with America, in respect of the particular circumstances which I have explained, than in respect to the manner of carrying it on, after it grew to be a considerable object of political attention. Trade with the East was a simple mercantile transaction, confined to the purchase either of the natural productions of the country, such as spices, precious stones, pearls, &c. or of the manufactures which abounded among an industrious race of men, such as silk and cotton stuffs, porcelain, &c. Nothing more was requisite in conducting this trade, than to settle a few skilful agents in proper places, to prepare a proper assortment of goods for completing the cargoes of ships as soon as they arrived from Europe, or at the utmost to acquire the command of a few fortified stations, which might secure them admission into ports where they might careen in safety, and find protection from the insults of any hostile power. There was no necessity of making any attempt to establish colonies, either for the cultivation of the soil or the conduct of manufactures. Both these remained, as formerly, in the hands of the natives.

But as soon as that wild spirit of enterprise, which animated the Spaniards who first explored and subdued the New World, began to subside; and when, instead of roving as adventurers from province to province in quest of gold and silver, they seriously turned their thoughts towards rendering their conquests beneficial by cultivation and industry, they found it necessary to establish colonies in every country which they wished to improve. Other nations imitated their example in the settlements which they afterwards made in some of the islands, and on the continent of North America. Europe, after having desolated the New World, began to repeople it, and under a system of colonization (the spirit and regulations of which it is not the object of this Disquisition to explain) the European race has multiplied there amazingly. Every article of commerce imported from the New World, if we except the furs and skins purchased from the independent tribes of hunters in North America, and from a few tribes in a similar state on the southern continent, is the produce of the industry of Europeans settled there. To their exertions, or to those of hands which they have taught or compelled to labour, we are indebted for sugar, rum, cotton, tobacco, indigo, rice, and even the gold and silver extracted from the bowels of the earth. Intent on those lucrative branches of industry, the inhabitants of the New World pay little attention to those kinds of labour which occupy a considerable part of the members of other societies, and depend, in some measure, for their subsistence, and entirely for every article of elegance and luxury, upon the ancient continent. Thus the Europeans have become manufacturers for America, and their industry has been greatly augmented by the vast demands for supplying the wants of extensive countries, the population of which is continually increasing.

SECT. IV.

Nor is the influence of this demand confined solely to the nations which have a more immediate connexion with the American colonies; it is felt in every part of Europe that furnishes any article exported to them, and gives activity and vigour to the hand of the artisan in the inland provinces of Germany, as well as to those in Great Britain and other countries, which carry on a direct trade with the New World.

But while the discovery and conquest of America is allowed to be one principal cause of that rapid increase of industry and wealth, which is conspicuous in Europe during the two last centuries, some timid theorists have maintained, that throughout the same period Europe has been gradually impoverished, by being drained of its treasure in order to carry on its trade with India. But this apprehension has arisen from inattention to the nature and use of the precious metals. They are to be considered in two different lights; either as the signs which all civilized nations have agreed to employ, in order to estimate or represent the value both of labour and of all commodities, and thus to facilitate the purchase of the former and the conveyance of the latter from one proprietor to another; or gold and silver may be viewed as being themselves commodities, or articles of commerce, for which some equivalent must be given by such as wish to acquire them. In this light the exportation of the precious metals to the East should be regarded; for, as the nation by which they are exported must purchase them with the produce of its own labour and ingenuity, this trade must contribute, though not in the same obvious and direct manner as that with America, towards augmenting the general industry and opulence of Europe. If England, as the price of Mexican and Peruvian dollars which are necessary for carrying on its trade with India, must give a certain quantity of its woollen or cotton cloth, or hard-ware, then the hands of an additional number of manufacturers are rendered active, and work to a certain amount must be executed, for which, without this trade, there would not have been any demand. The nation reaps all the benefit arising from a new creation of industry. With the gold and silver which her manufacturers have purchased in the West, she is enabled to trade in the markets of the East, and the exportation of treasure to India, which has been so much dreaded, instead of impoverishing, enriches the kingdom.

VIII. It is to the discovery of the passage to India by the Cape of Good Hope, and to the vigour and success with which the Portuguese prosecuted their conquests and established their dominion there, that Europe has been indebted for its preservation from the most illiberal and humiliating servitude that ever oppressed polished nations. For this observation I am indebted to an author, whose ingenuity has illustrated, and whose eloquence has adorned, the History of the Settlements and Commerce of Modern Nations in the East and West Indies;* and it appears to me so well founded as to merit more ample investigation. A few years after the first appearance of the Portuguese in India, the dominion of the Mamelukes was overturned by the irresistible power of the Turkish arms, and Egypt and Syria were annexed as provinces to the Ottoman empire. If after this event the commercial intercourse with India had continued to be carried on in its ancient channels, the Turkish Sultans, by being masters of Egypt and Syria, must have possessed the absolute command of it, whether the productions of the East were conveyed by the Red Sea to Alexandria, or were transported by land carriage from the Persian Gulf to Constantinople and the ports of the Mediterranean. The monarchs who were then at the head of this great empire, were neither destitute of abilities to perceive the pre-eminence to which this would have elevated them, nor of ambition to aspire to it. Selim, the conqueror of the Mamelukes, by confirming the ancient privileges of the Venetians in Egypt and Syria, and by his regulations concerning the duties on Indian goods, which I have already mentioned, early discovered his solicitude to secure all the advantages of commerce with the East to his own dominions. The attention of Solyman the Magnificent, his successor, seems to have been equally directed towards the same object. More enlightened than any monarch of the Ottoman race, he attended to all the transactions of

---

* M. L'Àbbé Raynal.

the European states, and had observed the power as well as opulence to which the republic of Venice had attained by engrossing the commerce with the East. He now beheld Portugal rising towards the same elevation by the same means. Eager to imitate and to supplant them, he formed a scheme suitable to his character for political wisdom, and the appellation of *Institutor of Rules,* by which the Turkish historians have distinguished him, and established, early in his reign, a system of commercial laws in his dominions, by which he hoped to render Constantinople the great staple of Indian trade, as it had been in the prosperous ages of the Greek empire.* For accomplishing this scheme, however, he did not rely on the operation of laws alone; he fitted out about the same time a formidable fleet in the Red Sea, under the conduct of a confidential officer, with such a body of janizaries on board of it, as he deemed sufficient not only to drive the Portuguese out of all their new settlements in India, but to take possession of some commodious station in that country, and to erect his standard there. The Portuguese, by efforts of valour and constancy entitled to the splendid success with which they were crowned, repulsed this powerful armament in every enterprise it undertook, and compelled the shattered remains of the Turkish fleet and army to return with ignominy to the harbours from which they had taken their departure,

A.D.1539

---

* Paruta, Hist. Venet. lib. vii. p. 589. Sandi Stor. Civil. Venez. part ii. p. 901.

SECT. IV. with the most sanguine hopes of terminating the expedition in a very different manner.* Solyman, though he never relinquished the design of expelling the Portuguese from India, and of acquiring some establishment there, was so occupied, during the remainder of his reign, by the multiplicity of arduous operations in which an insatiable ambition involved him, that he never had leisure to resume the prosecution of it with vigour.

If either the measures of Selim had produced the effect which he expected, or if the more adventurous and extensive plan of Solyman had been carried into execution, the command of the wealth of India, together with such a marine as the monopoly of trade with that country has, in every age, enabled the power which possessed it to create and maintain, must have brought an accession of force to an empire already formidable to mankind, that would have rendered it altogether irresistible. Europe, at that period, was not in a condition to have defended itself against the combined exertions of such naval and military power, supported by commercial wealth, and under the direction of a monarch whose comprehensive genius was able to derive from each its peculiar advantages, and to employ all with the greatest effect. Happily for the human race, the despotic system of Turkish government, founded on such illiberal fanaticism as has ex-

---

* Asia de Barros, dec. iv. lib. x. c. 1, &c.

tinguished science in Egypt, in Assyria, and in Greece, its three favourite mansions in ancient times, was prevented from extending its dominion over Europe, and from suppressing liberty, learning, and taste, when beginning to make successful efforts to revive there, and again to bless, to enlighten, and to polish mankind.

APPENDIX.

I SHALL now endeavour to fulfil an engagement which I came under,* to make some observations upon the genius, the manners, and institutions of the people of India, as far as they can be traced from the earliest ages to which our knowledge of them extends. Were I to enter upon this wide field with an intention of surveying its whole extent; were I to view each object which it presents to a philosophical inquirer, under all its different aspects, it would lead me into researches and speculations, not only of immense length, but altogether foreign from the subject of this disquisition. My inquiries and reflections shall therefore be confined to what is intimately connected with the design of this work. I shall collect the facts which the ancients have transmitted to us concerning the institutions peculiar to the natives of India, and by comparing them with what we

---

* See Page 23.

now know of that country, endeavour to deduce such conclusions as tend to point out the circumstances which have induced the rest of mankind, in every age, to carry on commercial intercourse to so great an extent with that country.

Of this intercourse there are conspicuous proofs in the earliest periods concerning which history affords information. Not only the people contiguous to India, but remote nations, seem to have been acquainted, from time immemorial, with its commodities, and to have valued them so highly, that in order to procure them they undertook fatiguing, expensive, and dangerous journeys. Whenever men give a decided preference to the commodities of any particular country, this must be owing either to its possessing some valuable natural productions peculiar to its soil and climate, or to some superior progress which its inhabitants have made in industry, arts, and elegance. It is not to any peculiar excellence in the natural productions of India, that we must ascribe entirely the predilection of ancient nations for its commodities; for, pepper excepted, an article, it must be allowed, of great importance, they are little different from those of other tropical countries; and Ethiopia or Arabia might have fully supplied the Phœnicians, and other trading people of antiquity, with the spices, the perfumes, the precious stones, the gold and silver, which formed the principal articles of their commerce.

WHOEVER, then, wishes to trace the commerce with India to its source, must search for it, not so much in any peculiarity of the natural productions of that country, as in the superior improvement of its inhabitants. Many facts have been transmitted to us, which, if they are examined with proper attention, clearly demonstrate, that the natives of India were not only more early civilized, but had made greater progress in civilization than any other people. These I shall endeavour to enumerate, and to place them in such a point of view, as may serve both to throw light upon the institutions, manners, and arts of the Indians, and to account for the eagerness of all nations to obtain the productions of their ingenious industry.

By the ancient Heathen writers, the Indians were reckoned among those races of men which they denominated *Autochthones* or *Aborigines*, whom they considered as natives of the soil, whose origin could not be traced.* By the inspired writers, the wisdom of the East (an expression which is to be understood as a description of their extraordinary progress in science and arts) was early celebrated.† In order to illustrate and confirm these explicit testimonies concerning the ancient and high civilization of the inhabitants of India, I shall take a view of

---

* Diod. Sic. lib. ii. p. 151. † 1 Kings, iv. 31.

their rank and condition as individuals; of their civil policy; of their laws and judicial proceedings; of their useful and elegant arts; of their sciences; and of their religious institutions; as far as information can be gathered from the accounts of the Greek and Roman writers, compared with what still remains of their ancient acquirements and institutions.

I. From the most ancient accounts of India we learn, that the distinction of ranks and separation of professions were completely established there. This is one of the most undoubted proofs of a society considerably advanced in its progress. Arts in the early stages of social life are so few, and so simple, that each man is sufficiently master of them all, to gratify every demand of his own limited desires. A savage can form his bow, point his arrows, rear his hut, and hollow his canoe, without calling in the aid of any hand more skilful than his own.* But when time has augmented the wants of men, the productions of art become so complicated in their structure, or so curious in their fabric, that a particular course of education is requisite towards forming the artist to ingenuity in contrivance and expertness in execution. In proportion as refinement spreads, the distinction of professions increases, and they branch out into more numerous and minute subdivisions. Prior to the records of authentic his-

---

* Hist. of Amer. vol. ii. p. 177, &c.

tory, and even before the most remote era to which their own traditions pretend to reach, this separation of professions had not only taken place among the natives of India, but the perpetuity of it was secured by an institution, which must be considered as the fundamental article in the system of their policy. The whole body of the people was divided into four orders or casts. The members of the first, deemed the most sacred, had it for their province to study the principles of religion; to perform its functions; and to cultivate the sciences. They were the priests, the instructors, and philosophers of the nation. The members of the second order were intrusted with the government and defence of the state. In peace, they were its rulers and magistrates; in war, they were the generals who commanded its armies, and the soldiers who fought its battles. The third was composed of husbandmen and merchants; and the fourth of artisans, labourers, and servants. None of these can ever quit his own cast, or be admitted into another.* The station of every individual is unalterably fixed; his destiny is irrevocable; and the walk of life is marked out, from which he must never deviate. This line of separation is not only established by civil authority, but confirmed and sanctioned by religion; and each order or cast is said to have proceeded from the Divinity in such a different manner, that to

---

* Ayeen Akbery, iii. 81, &c. Sketches relating to the History, &c. of the Hindoos, p. 107, &c.

mingle and confound them would be deemed an act of most daring impiety.* Nor is it between the four different tribes alone that such insuperable barriers are fixed: the members of each cast adhere invariably to the professions of their forefathers. From generation to generation, the same families have followed, and will always continue to follow, one uniform line of life.

Such arbitrary arrangements of the various members which compose a community, seem, at first view, to be adverse to improvement either in science or in arts; and by forming around the different orders of men artificial barriers, which it would be impious to pass, tend to circumscribe the operations of the human mind within a narrower sphere than nature has allotted to them. When every man is at full liberty to direct his efforts towards those objects and that end which the impulse of his own mind prompts him to prefer, he may be expected to attain that high degree of eminence to which the uncontrolled exertions of genius and industry naturally conduct. The regulations of Indian policy with respect to the different orders of men, must necessarily, at some times, check genius in its career, and confine to the functions of an inferior cast, talents fitted to shine in an higher sphere. But the arrangements of civil government are made, not for what is extraordinary, but for what is common;

---

* See Note LVIII. Page 357.

not for the few, but for the many. The object of the first Indian legislators was to employ the most effectual means of providing for the subsistence, the security, and happiness of all the members of the community over which they presided. With this view they set apart certain races of men for each of the various professions and arts necessary in a well ordered society, and appointed the exercise of them to be transmitted from father to son in succession. This system, though extremely repugnant to the ideas which we, by being placed in a very different state of society, have formed, will be found, upon attentive inspection, better adapted to attain the end in view, than a careless observer, at first sight, is apt to imagine. The human mind bends to the law of necessity, and is accustomed not only to accommodate itself to the restraints which the condition of its nature, or the institutions of its country, impose, but to acquiesce in them. From his entrance into life, an Indian knows the station allotted to him, and the functions to which he is destined by his birth. The objects which relate to these are the first that present themselves to his view. They occupy his thoughts, or employ his hands; and, from his earliest years, he is trained to the habit of doing with ease and pleasure that which he must continue through life to do. To this may be ascribed that high degree of perfection conspicuous in many of the Indian manufactures; and though veneration for the practices of their ancestors may check the spirit of invention, yet, by adhering to these, they acquire such an expertness and delicacy of hand, that Europeans, with all the advantages of superior science, and the aid of more complete instruments, have never been able to equal the exquisite execution of their workmanship. While this high improvement of their more curious manufactures excited the admiration, and attracted the commerce of other nations, the separation of professions in India, and the early distribution of the people into classes, attached to particular kinds of labour, secured such abundance of the more common and useful commodities, as not only supplied their own wants, but ministered to those of the countries around them.

To this early division of the people into casts, we must likewise ascribe a striking peculiarity in the state of India; the permanence of its institutions, and the immutability in the manners of its inhabitants. What now is in India, always was there, and is likely still to continue: neither the ferocious violence and illiberal fanaticism of its Mahomedan conquerors, nor the power of its European masters, have effected any considerable alteration.* The same distinctions of condition take place, the same arrangements in civil and domestic society remain, the same maxims of religion are held in veneration, and the same sciences and arts are cultivated. Hence, in all ages, the

---

* See Note LIX. Page 361.

trade with India has been the same: Gold and silver have uniformly been carried thither, in order to purchase the same commodities with which it now supplies all nations; and from the age of Pliny to the present times, it has been always considered and execrated as a gulf which swallows up the wealth of every other country, that flows incessantly towards it, and from which it never returns.* According to the accounts which I have given of the cargoes anciently imported from India, they appear to have consisted of nearly the same articles with those of the investments in our own times; and whatever difference we may observe in them seems to have arisen, not so much from any diversity in the nature of the commodities which the Indians prepared for sale, as from a variety in the tastes, or in the wants of the nations which demanded them.

II. ANOTHER proof of the early and high civilization of the people of India, may be deduced from considering their political constitution and form of government. The Indians trace back the history of their own country through an immense succession of ages, and assert, that all Asia, from the mouth of the Indus on the west, to the confines of China on the east, and from the mountains of Thibet on the north, to Cape Comorin on the south, formed a vast empire, subject to one mighty sovereign, under whom

---

* See NOTE LX. Page 363.

ruled several hereditary Princes and Rajahs. But their chronology, which measures the life of man in ancient times by thousands of years, and computes the length of the several periods during which it supposes the world to have existed, by millions, is so wildly extravagant as not to merit any serious discussion. We must rest satisfied, then, until some more certain information is obtained with respect to the ancient history of India, with taking the first accounts of that country, which can be deemed authentic, from the Greeks who served under Alexander the Great. They found kingdoms of considerable magnitude established in that country. The territories of Porus and of Taxiles comprehended a great part of the Panjab, one of the most fertile and best cultivated countries in India. The kingdom of the Prasij, or Gandaridæ, stretched to a great extent on both sides of the Ganges. All the three, as appears from the ancient Greek writers, were powerful and populous.

This description of the partition of India into states of such magnitude, is alone a convincing proof of its having advanced far in civilization. In whatever region of the earth there has been an opportunity of observing the progress of men in social life, they appear at first in small independent tribes or communities. Their common wants prompt them to unite; and their mutual jealousies, as well as the necessity of securing subsistence, compel them to drive to a distance every rival who might encroach on those domains which they consider as their own. Many ages elapse before they coalesce, or acquire sufficient foresight to provide for the wants, or sufficient wisdom to conduct the affairs of a numerous society, even under the genial climate, and in the rich soil of India, more favourable perhaps to the union and increase of the human species than any other part of the globe: The formation of such extensive states as were established in that country when first visited by Europeans, must have been a work of long time; and the members of them must have been long accustomed to exertions of useful industry.

Though monarchical government was established in all the countries of India to which the knowledge of the ancients extended, the sovereigns were far from possessing uncontrolled or despotic power. No trace, indeed, is discovered there of any assembly, or public body, the members of which, either in their own right or as representatives of their fellow-citizens, could interpose in enacting laws, or in superintending the execution of them. Institutions destined to assert and guard the rights belonging to men in social state, how familiar soever the idea may be to the people of Europe, never formed a part of the political constitution in any great Asiatic kingdom. It was to different principles that the natives of India were indebted for restrictions which limited the exercise of regal power. The rank of individuals was unalterably fixed, and the privileges of the different casts were deemed inviolable. The monarchs of India, who were all taken from the second of the four classes formerly described, which is intrusted with the functions of government and exercise of war, behold among their subjects an order of men far superior to themselves in dignity, and so conscious of their own pre-eminence, both in rank and in sanctity, that they would deem it degradation and pollution if they were to eat of the same food with their sovereign.* Their persons are sacred, and even for the most heinous crimes they cannot be capitally punished; their blood must never be shed.† To men in this exalted station, monarchs must look up with respect, and reverence them as the ministers of religion and the teachers of wisdom. On important occasions, it is the duty of sovereigns to consult them, and to be directed by their advice. Their admonitions, and even their censures, must be received with submissive respect. This right of the Brahmins to offer their opinion with respect to the administration of public affairs, was not unknown to the ancients;‡ and in some accounts preserved in India of the events which happened in their own country, princes are mentioned, who, having violated the privileges of the casts,

---

* Orme's Dissert. vol. i. p. 4. Sketches, &c. p. 113.
† Code of Gentoo Laws, c. xxi. § 10. p. 275. 283, &c.
‡ Strabo, lib. xv. p. 1029. C.

and disregarded the remonstrances of the Brahmins, were deposed by their authority, and put to death.*

WHILE the sacred rights of the Brahmins opposed a barrier against the encroachments of regal power on the one hand, it was circumscribed on the other by the ideas which those who occupied the highest stations in society entertained of their own dignity and privileges. As none but the members of the cast next in rank to that which religion has rendered sacred, could be employed in any function of the state, the sovereigns of the extensive kingdoms anciently established in India, found it necessary to intrust them with the superintendence of the cities and provinces too remote to be under their own immediate inspection. In these stations they often acquired such wealth and influence, that offices conferred during pleasure, continued hereditarily in their families, and they came gradually to form an intermediate order between the sovereign and his subjects; and, by the vigilant jealousy with which they maintained their own dignity and privileges, they constrained their rulers to respect them, and to govern with moderation and equity.

---

* Account of the Qualities requisite in a Magistrate, prefixed by the Pundits to the Code of Gentoo Laws, p. cii. and cxvi.

Nor were the benefits of these restraints upon the power of the sovereign confined wholly to the two superior orders in the state; they extended, in some degree, to the third class, employed in agriculture. The labours of that numerous and useful body of men are so essential to the preservation and happiness of society, that the greatest attention was paid to render their condition secure and comfortable. According to the ideas which prevailed among the natives of India (as we are informed by the first Europeans who visited their country), the sovereign is considered as the sole universal proprietor of all the land in his dominions, and from him is derived every species of tenure by which his subjects can hold it. These lands were let out to the farmers who cultivated them at a stipulated rent, amounting usually to a fourth part of their annual produce, paid in kind.* In a country where the price of work is extremely low, and where the labour of cultivation is very inconsiderable, the earth yielding its productions almost spontaneously, where subsistence is amazingly cheap, where few clothes are needed, and houses are built and furnished at little expense, this rate cannot be deemed exorbitant or oppressive. As long as the husbandman continued to pay the established rent, he retained possession of the farm, which descended, like property, from father to son.

---

* Strabo, lib. xv. p. 1030. A. Diod. Sic. lib. ii. p. 53.

THESE accounts, given by ancient authors, of the condition and tenure of the renters of land in India, agree so perfectly with what now takes place, that it may be considered almost as a description of the present state of its cultivation. In every part of India where the native Hindoo Princes retain dominion, the *Ryots*, the modern name by which the renters of land are distinguished, hold their possessions by a lease, which may be considered as perpetual, and at a rate fixed by ancient surveys and valuations. This arrangement has been so long established, and accords so well with the ideas of the natives, concerning the distinctions of casts, and the functions allotted to each, that it has been inviolably maintained in all the provinces subject either to Mahomedans or Europeans; and, to both, it serves as the basis on which their whole system of finance is founded.* In a more remote period, before the original institutions of India were subverted by foreign invaders, the industry of the husbandmen, on which every member of the community depended for subsistence, was as secure as the tenure by which he held his lands was equitable. Even war did not interrupt his labours, or endanger his property. It was not uncommon, we are informed, that while two hostile armies were fighting a battle in one field, the peasants were ploughing or reaping in the next field in perfect tranquillity.* These

---

* See NOTE LXI. Page 363. † Strabo, lib. xv. p. 1030. A.

maxims and regulations of the ancient legislators of India have a near resemblance to the system of those ingenious speculators on political economy in modern times, who represent the produce of land as the sole source of wealth in every country; and who consider the discovery of this principle, according to which they contend that the government of nations should be conducted, as one of the greatest efforts of human wisdom. Under a form of government which paid such attention to all the different orders of which the society is composed, particularly the cultivators of the earth, it is not wonderful that the ancients should describe the Indians as a most happy race of men; and that the most intelligent modern observers should celebrate the equity, the humanity, and mildness of Indian policy. A Hindoo Rajah, as I have been informed by persons well acquainted with the state of India, resembles more a father presiding in a numerous family of his own children, than a sovereign ruling over inferiors, subject to his dominion. He endeavours to secure their happiness with vigilant solicitude; they are attached to him with the most tender affection and inviolable fidelity. We can hardly conceive men to be placed in any state more favourable to their acquiring all the advantages derived from social union. It is only when the mind is perfectly at ease, and neither feels nor dreads oppression, that it employs its active powers in forming numerous arrangements of police, for securing its enjoyments, and increasing them. Many arrangements of this nature, the Greeks, though accustomed to their own institutions, the most perfect at that time in Europe, observed, and admired among the Indians, and mention them as instances of high civilization and improvement. There were established among the Indians three distinct classes of officers, one of which had it in charge to inspect agriculture, and every kind of country work. They measured the portions of land allotted to each renter. They had the custody of the *Tanks*, or public reservoirs of water, without a regular distribution of which, the fields in a torrid climate cannot be rendered fertile. They marked out the course of the high-ways, along which, at certain distances, they erected stones, to measure the road and direct travellers.* To officers of a second class was committed the inspection of the police in cities: their functions, of course, were many and various; some of which only I shall specify. They appropriated houses for the reception of strangers; they protected them from injury, provided for their subsistence, and when seized with any disease, they appointed physicians to attend them; and, on the event of their death, they not only buried them with decency, but took charge of their effects, and restored them to their relations. They kept exact registers of births and of deaths. They visited the public markets, and examined weights and measures. The third class of officers

---

* See Note LXII. Page 367.

superintended the military department; but, as the objects to which their attention was directed are foreign from the subject of my inquiries, it is unnecessary to enter into any detail with respect to them.*

As manners and customs in India descend almost without variation from age to age, many of the peculiar institutions which I have enumerated still subsist there. There is still the same attention to the construction and preservation of tanks, and the distribution of their waters. The *direction of roads,* and placing stones along *them,* is still an object of police. *Choultries,* or houses built for the accommodation of travellers, are frequent in every part of the country, and are useful as well as noble monuments of Indian munificence and humanity. It is only among men in the most improved state of society, and under the best forms of government, that we discover institutions similar to those which I have described; and many nations have advanced far in their progress, without establishing arrangements of police equally perfect.

III. In estimating the progress which any nation has made in civilization, the object that merits the greatest degree of attention, next to its political constitution, is the spirit of the laws and nature of the forms by which its judicial

---

* Strabo, lib. xv. p. 1034. A. &c. Diod. Sicul. lib. ii. p. 154.

proceedings are regulated. In the early and rude ages of society, the few disputes with respect to property which arise, are terminated by the interposition of the old men, or by the authority of the chiefs in every small tribe or community; their decisions are dictated by their own discretion, or founded on plain and obvious maxims of equity. But as the controversies multiply, cases similar to such as have been formerly determined must recur, and the awards upon these grow gradually into precedents, which serve to regulate future judgments. Thus, long before the nature of property is defined by positive statutes, or any rules prescribed concerning the mode of acquiring or conveying it, there is gradually formed, in every state, a body of customary or common law, by which judicial proceedings are directed, and every decision conformable to it is submitted to with reverence, as the result of the accumulated wisdom and experience of ages.

In this state the administration of justice seems to have been in India when first visited by Europeans. Though the Indians, according to their account, had no written laws, but determined every controverted point by recollecting what had been formerly decided,[*] they assert that justice was dispensed among them with great accuracy, and that crimes were most severely punished.[†] But in this general observation is con-

---

[*] Strabo, lib. xv. 1035. D.   [†] Diod. Sicul. lib. ii. p. 154.

tained all the intelligence which the ancients furnish concerning the nature and forms of judicial proceedings in India. From the time of Megasthenes, no Greek or Roman of any note appears to have resided long enough in the country, or to have been so much acquainted with the customs of the natives, as to be capable of entering into any detail with respect to a point of so great importance in their policy. Fortunately, the defects of their information have been amply supplied by the more accurate and extensive researches of the moderns. During the course of almost three centuries, the number of persons who have resorted from Europe to India has been great. Many of them, who have remained long in the country, and were persons of liberal education and enlarged minds, have lived in such familiar intercourse with the natives, and acquired so competent a knowledge of their languages, as enabled them to observe their institutions with attention, and to describe them with fidelity. Respectable as their authority may be, I shall not, in what I offer for illustrating the judicial proceedings of the Hindoos, rest upon it alone, but shall derive my information from sources higher and more pure.

Towards the middle of the sixteenth century, Akber, the sixth in descent from Tamerlane, mounted the throne of Indostan. He is one of the few sovereigns entitled to the appellation both of Great and Good, and the only one of

Mahomedan race whose mind appears to have risen so far above all the illiberal prejudices of that fanatical religion in which he was educated, as to be capable of forming a plan worthy of a monarch who loved his people, and was solicitous to render them happy. As, in every province of his extensive dominions, the Hindoos formed the great body of his subjects, he laboured to acquire a perfect knowledge of their religion, their sciences, their laws, and institutions; in order that he might conduct every part of his government, particularly the administration of justice, in a manner as much accommodated as possible to their own ideas.* In this generous undertaking he was seconded with zeal by his vizier Abul Fazel, a minister whose understanding was not less enlightened than that of his master. By their assiduous researches, and consultation of learned men,† such information was obtained as enabled Abul Fazel to publish a brief compendium of Hindoo jurisprudence in the Ayeen Akbery,‡ which may be considered as the first genuine communication of its principles to persons of a different religion. About two centuries afterwards, the illustrious example of Akber was imitated and surpassed by Mr Hastings, the Governor-General of the British Settlements in India. By his authority, and under his inspection, the most eminent Pundits, or Brahmins learned

A.D. 1773.

---

* See NOTE LXIII. Page 367.
† Ayeen Akbery, A. vol. iii. p. 95.
‡ Ibid. vol. iii. p. 197, &c.

in the laws of the provinces over which he presided, were assembled at Calcutta; and, in the course of two years, compiled, from their most ancient and approved authors, sentence by sentence, without addition or diminution, a full code of Hindoo laws;* which is, undoubtedly, the most valuable and authentic elucidation of Indian policy and manners that has been hitherto communicated to Europe.

According to the Pundits, some of the writers upon whose authority they found the decrees which they have inserted in the Code, lived several millions of years before their time;† and they boast of having a succession of expounders of their laws from that period to the present. Without entering into any examination of what is so extravagant, we may conclude, that the Hindoos have in their possession treatises concerning the laws and jurisprudence of their country, of more remote antiquity than are to be found in any other nation. The truth of this depends not upon their own testimony alone, but it is put beyond doubt by one circumstance, that all these treatises are written in the Sanskreet language, which has not been spoken for many ages in any part of Indostan, and is now understood by none but the most learned Brahmins. That the Hindoos were a people highly civilized, at the time when their laws were composed, is most clearly

---

* Preface to the Code, p. x. † Ibid. p. xxxviii.

established by internal evidence contained in the Code itself. Among nations beginning to emerge from barbarism, the regulations of law are extremely simple, and applicable only to a few obvious cases of daily occurrence. Men must have been long united in a social state, their transactions must have been numerous and complex, and judges must have determined an immense variety of controversies to which these give rise, before the system of law becomes so voluminous and comprehensive as to direct the judicial proceedings of a nation far advanced in improvement. In that early age of the Roman republic when the laws of the Twelve Tables were promulgated, nothing more was required than the laconic injunctions which they contain for regulating the decisions of courts of justice; but, in a later period, the body of civil law, ample as its contents are, was found hardly sufficient for that purpose. To the jejune brevity of the Twelve Tables, the Hindoo Code has no resemblance; but with respect to the number and variety of points it considers, it will bear a comparison with the celebrated Digest of Justinian, or with the systems of jurisprudence in nations most highly civilized. The articles of which the Hindoo Code is composed, are arranged in natural and luminous order. They are numerous and comprehensive, and investigated with that minute attention and discernment which are natural to a people distinguished for acuteness and subtilty of understanding, who have been long accustomed to the accuracy of judicial proceedings, and acquainted with all the refinements of legal practice. The decisions concerning every point (with a few exceptions occasioned by local prejudices and peculiar customs) are founded upon the great and immutable principles of justice, which the human mind acknowledges and respects, in every age, and in all parts of the earth. Whoever examines the whole work, cannot entertain a doubt of its containing the jurisprudence of an enlightened and commercial people. Whoever looks into any particular title, will be surprised with a minuteness of detail and nicety of distinction, which, in many instances, seem to go beyond the attention of European legislation; and it is remarkable, that some of the regulations which indicate the greatest degree of refinement, were established in periods of the most remote antiquity. " In the first of the sacred law tracts, (as is observed by a person to whom Oriental literature, in all its branches, has been greatly indebted), which the Hindoos suppose to have been revealed by Menu, some millions of years ago, there is a curious passage on the legal interest of money, and the limited rate of it in different cases; with an exception in regard to adventures at sea; an exception which the sense of mankind approves, and which commerce absolutely requires, though it was not before the reign of Charles I. that our English jurisprudence fully admitted it in respect of maritime contracts."* It is like-

* Sir W. Jones's Third Discourse, Asiat. Research. p. 428.

wise worthy of notice, that though the natives of India have been distinguished in every age for the humanity and mildness of their disposition, yet such is the solicitude of their lawgivers to preserve the order and tranquillity of society, that the punishments which they inflict on criminals are (agreeably to an observation of the ancients already mentioned) extremely rigorous. "Punishment (according to a striking personification in the Hindoo Code) is the magistrate; punishment is the inspirer of terror; punishment is the nourisher of the subjects; punishment is the defender from calamity; punishment is the guardian of those that sleep; punishment, with a black aspect and a red eye, terrifies the guilty."*

IV. As the condition of the ancient inhabitants of India, whether we consider them as individuals or as members of society, appears from the preceding investigation to have been extremely favourable to the cultivation of useful and elegant arts; we are naturally led to inquire, whether the progress which they actually made in them was such as might have been expected from a people in that situation. In attempting to trace this progress, we have not the benefit of guidance equal to that which conducted our researches concerning the former articles of inquiry. The ancients, from their slender acquaintance with the interior state of India, have been able to communicate

---

* Code, ch. xxi. § 8.

little information with respect to the arts cultivated there; and though the moderns, during their continued intercourse with India for three centuries, have had access to observe them with great attention, it is of late only, that by studying the languages now and formerly spoken in India, and by consulting and translating their most eminent authors, they have begun to enter into that path of inquiry which leads with certainty to a thorough knowledge of the state of arts cultivated in that country.

One of the first arts which human ingenuity aimed at improving, beyond what mere necessity requires, was that of building. In the brief remarks which the subject of my inquiries leads me to make on the progress of this art in India, I shall confine my attention wholly to those of highest antiquity. The most durable monuments of human industry are public buildings. The productions of art, formed for the common purposes of life, waste and perish in using them; but works destined for the benefit of posterity subsist through ages, and it is according to the manner in which these are executed, that we form a judgment with respect to the degree of power, skill, and improvement to which the people by whom they were erected had attained. In every part of India monuments of high antiquity are found. These are of two kinds, such as were consecrated to the offices of religion, or fortresses built for the security of the country. In the former of these, to which Europeans, whatever their structure may be, give the general name of *Pagodas*, we may observe a diversity of style, which both marks the gradual progress of architecture, and throws light on the general state of arts and manners in different periods. The most early Pagodas appear to have been nothing more than excavations in mountainous parts of the country, formed probably in imitation of the natural caverns to which the first inhabitants of the earth retired for safety during the night, and where they found shelter from the inclemency of the seasons. The most celebrated, and, as there is reason to believe, the most ancient of all these, is the Pagoda in the island Elephanta, at no great distance from Bombay. It has been hewn by the hands of man out of a solid rock, about half way up a high mountain, and formed into a spacious area, nearly 120 feet square. In order to support the roof, and the weight of the mountain that lies above it, a number of massy pillars, and of a form not inelegant, have been cut out of the same rock, at such regular distances, as on the first entrance presents to the eye of the spectator an appearance both of beauty and of strength. Great part of the inside is covered with human figures in high relief, of gigantic size as well as singular forms, and distinguished by a variety of symbols, representing, it is probable, the attributes of the deities whom they worshipped, or the actions of the heroes whom they admired. In the isle of Salsette, still nearer to Bombay, are excavations in a similar style, hardly inferior in magnificence, and destined for the same religious purposes.

These stupendous works are of such high antiquity, that as the natives cannot, either from history or tradition, give any information concerning the time in which they were executed, they universally ascribe the formation of them to the power of superior beings. From the extent and grandeur of these subterraneous mansions, which intelligent travellers compare to the most celebrated monuments of human power and art in any part of the earth, it is manifest that they could not have been formed in that stage of social life where men continue divided into small tribes, unaccustomed to the efforts of persevering industry. It is only in states of considerable extent, and among people long habituated to subordination, and to act with concert, that the idea of such magnificent works is conceived, or the power of accomplishing them can be found.

That some such powerful state was established in India at the time when the excavations in the islands of Elephanta and Salsette were formed, is not the only conclusion to be drawn from a survey of them; the style in which the sculptures with which they are adorned is executed, indicates a considerable improvement in art at that early period. Sculpture is the imitative art in which man seems to have made the first trial of his own talents. But even in those countries where it has attained to the highest degree of perfection, its progress has been extremely slow. Whoever has attended to the history of this art in Greece, knows how far removed the first rude essay to represent the human form was from any complete delineation of it.* But the different groupes of figures which still remain entire in the Pagoda of Elephanta, however low they must rank if they be compared with the more elegant works of Grecian or even Etruscan artists, are finished in a style considerably superior to the hard inexpressive manner of the Egyptians, or to the figures in the celebrated palace of Persepolis. In this light they have appeared to persons abundantly qualified to appreciate their merit, and from different drawings, particularly those of Niebuhr, a traveller equally accurate in observing and faithful in describing, we must form a favourable opinion of the state of arts in India at that period.

It is worthy of notice, that although several of the figures in the caverns at Elephanta be so different from those now exhibited in the Pagodas as objects of veneration, that some learned Europeans have imagined they represent the rites of a religion more ancient than that now established in Indostan, yet by the Hindoos themselves the caverns are considered as hallow-

---

* Winkelman's Hist. de l'Art, chez les Anciens, tom. i. p. 32, &c.

ed places of their own worship, and they still resort thither to perform their devotions, and honour the figures there, in the same manner with those in their own Pagodas. In confirmation of this, I have been informed by an intelligent observer, who visited this subterraneous sanctuary in the year 1782, that he was accompanied by a sagacious Brahmin, a native of Benares, who, though he had never been in it before that time, recognized at once all the figures, was well acquainted with the parentage, education, and life of every deity or human personage there represented, and explained with fluency the meaning of the various symbols by which the images were distinguished. This may be considered as a clear proof, that the system of mythology now prevalent in Benares, is not different from that delineated in the caverns of Elephanta. Mr Hunter, who visited Elephanta in the year 1784, seems to consider the figures there as representing deities who are still objects of worship among the Hindoos.* One circumstance serves to confirm the justness of this opinion. Several of the most conspicuous personages in the groupes at Elephanta are decorated with the *Zennar*, the sacred string or cord peculiar to the order of Brahmins; an authentic evidence of the distinction of casts having been established in India at the time when these works were finished.

* Archæologia, vol. vii. p. 286, &c.

2. INSTEAD of caverns, the original places of worship, which could be formed only in particular situations, the devotion of the people soon began to raise temples in honour of their deities in other parts of India. The structure of these, was at first extremely simple. They were pyramids of large dimension, and had no light within but what came from a small door. After having been long accustomed to perform all the rites of religion in the gloom of caverns, the Indians were naturally led to consider the solemn darkness of such a mansion as sacred. Some Pagodas in this first style of building still remain in Indostan. Drawings of two of these at Deogur, and of a third near Tanjore in the Carnatic, all fabrics of great antiquity, have been published by Mr Hodges;* and though they are rude structures, they are of such magnitude as must have required the power of some considerable State to rear them.

3. IN proportion to the progress of the different countries of India in opulence and refinement, the structure of their temples gradually improved. From plain buildings they became highly ornamented fabrics, and, both by their extent and magnificence, are monuments of the power and taste of the people by whom they were erected. In this highly finished style there are Pagodas of great antiquity in different parts of

---
* NO. VI.

Indostan, particularly in the southern provinces, which were not exposed to the destructive violence of Mahomedan zeal.* In order to assist my readers in forming such an idea of these buildings as may enable them to judge with respect to the early state of arts in India, I shall briefly describe two, of which we have the most accurate accounts. The entry to the Pagoda of Chillambrum, near Porto Novo, on the Coromandel coast, held in high veneration on account of its antiquity, is by a stately gate under a pyramid an hundred and twenty-two feet in height, built with large stones above forty feet long, and more than five feet square, and all covered with plates of copper, adorned with an immense variety of figures neatly executed. The whole structure extends one thousand three hundred and thirty-two feet in one direction, and nine hundred and thirty-six in another. Some of the ornamental parts are finished with an elegance entitled to the admiration of the most ingenious artists.† The Pagoda of Seringham, superior in sanctity to that of Chillambrum, surpasses it as much in grandeur; and fortunately I can convey a more perfect idea of it by adopting the words of an elegant and accurate historian.‡ This Pagoda is situated about a mile from the western extremity of the

---

* See Note LXIV. Page 369.
† Mem. de Litterat. tom. xxxii. p. 44, &c. Voy. de M. Somerat, tom. i. p. 217.
‡ Orme's Hist. of Milit. Transact. of Indostan, vol. i. p. 178.

island of Seringham, formed by the division of the great river Caveri into two channels. " It is composed of seven square enclosures, one within the other, the walls of which are twenty-five feet high, and four thick. These enclosures are three hundred and fifty feet distant from one another, and each has four large gates, with a high tower; which are placed, one in the middle of each side of the enclosure, and opposite to the four cardinal points. The outward wall is near four miles in circumference, and its gateway to the south is ornamented with pillars, several of which are single stones thirty-three feet long, and nearly five in diameter; and those which form the roof are still larger: in the inmost enclosures are the chapels. About half a mile to the east of Seringham, and nearer to the Caveri than the Coleroon, is another large Pagoda, called Jembikisma; but this has only one enclosure. The extreme veneration in which Seringham is held, arises from a belief that it contains that identical image of the god Wistchnu, which used to be worshipped by the god Brahma. Pilgrims from all parts of the Peninsula come here to obtain absolution, and none come without an offering of money; and a large part of the revenue of the island is allotted for the maintenance of the Brahmins who inhabit the Pagoda; and these, with their families, formerly composed a multitude not less than forty thousand souls, maintained, without labour, by the liberality of superstition. Here, as in all the other great Pagodas of India, the Brahmins live in a subordination which knows no resistance, and slumber in a voluptuousness which knows no wants."

The other species of public buildings which I mentioned, were those erected for the defence of the country. From the immense plains of Indostan there arise, in different parts, eminences and rocks, formed by nature to be places of strength. Of these the natives early took possession, and, fortifying them with works of various kinds, rendered them almost impregnable stations. There seems to have been, in some distant age, a period of general turbulence and danger in India, when such retreats were deemed essentially necessary to public safety; for among the duties of magistrates prescribed by the Pundits, one is, " that he shall erect a strong fort in the place where he chooses to reside; and shall build a wall *on* all the four sides of it, with towers and battlements, and shall make a full ditch around it."* Of these fortresses several remain, which, both from the appearance of the buildings, and from the tradition of the natives, must have been constructed in very remote times. Mr Hodges has published views of three of these, one of Chunar Gur, situated upon the river Ganges, about sixteen miles above the city of Benares;† the second, of Gwallior, about eighty miles to the south of Agra;‡

---

* Introd. to Code of Gentoo Laws, p. cxi.
† No. I. ‡ No. II.

the third, of Bidjegur, in the territory of Benares.*
They are all, particularly Gwallior, works of considerable magnitude and strength. The fortresses in Bengal, however, are not to be compared with several in the Deccan. Asseergur, Burhampour, and Dowlatabad, are deemed by the natives to be impregnable;† and I am assured by a good judge, that Asseergur is indeed a most stupendous work, and so advantageously situated, that it would be extremely difficult to reduce it by force. Adoni, of which Tippoo Sultaun lately rendered himself master, is not inferior to any of them, either in strength or importance.‡

Nor is it only from surveying their public works that we are justified in asserting the early proficiency of the Indians in elegant and useful arts: we are led to form the same conclusion by a view of those productions of their ingenuity, which were the chief articles of their trade with foreign nations. Of these, the labours of the Indian loom and needle have, in every age, been the most celebrated; and fine linen is conjectured, with some probability, to have been called by the ancients *Sindon*, from the name of the river Indus or Sindus, near which it was wrought in the highest perfection.§ The cotton manufactures of India seem anciently to have been as

---

* NO. III.   † Rennell, Mem. p. 133. 139.
‡ Historical and Political View of the Deccan, p. 13.
§ Sir William Jones's Third Discourse, p. 428.

much admired as they are at present, not only for their delicate texture, but for the elegance with which some of them are embroidered, and the beautiful colour of the flowers with which others are adorned. From the earliest period of European intercourse with India, that country has been distinguished for the number and excellence of the substances for dying various colours, with which it abounded.* The dye of the deep blue colour in highest estimation among the Romans, bore the name of *Indicum*.† From India, too, the substance used in dying a bright red colour, seems to have been imported;‡ and it is well known, that both in the cotton and silk stuffs which we now receive from India, the blue and the red are the colours of most conspicuous lustre and beauty. But however much the ancients may have admired these productions of Indian art, some circumstances, which I have already mentioned, rendered their demand for the cotton manufactures of India far inferior to that of modern times; and this has occasioned the information concerning them which we receive from the Greek and Roman writers to be very imperfect. We may conclude, however, from the wonderful resemblance of the ancient

---

* Strabo, lib. xv. p. 1018. A. 1024. B.
† Plin. Nat. Hist. lib. xxxv. c. 6. § 27.
‡ Salmasius Exercit. Plinianæ in Solin. 180, &c. 810. Salmasius de Homionymis Hyles Jatrica, c. 107. See NOTE LXV. Page 371.

state of India to the modern, that, in every period, the productions of their looms were as various as beautiful. The ingenuity of the Indians in other kinds of workmanship, particularly in metals and in ivory, is mentioned with praise by ancient authors, but without any particular description of their nature.* Of these early productions of Indian artists, there are now some specimens in Europe, from which it appears that they were acquainted with the method of engraving upon the hardest stones and gems; and, both in the elegance of their designs and in neatness of execution, had arrived at a considerable degree of excellence. An ingenious writer maintains, that the art of engraving on gems was probably an Indian invention, and certainly was early improved there; and he supports this opinion by several plausible arguments.† The Indian engraved gems of which he has published descriptions, appear to be the workmanship of a very remote period, as the legends on them are in the Sanskreet language.‡

But it is not alone from the improved state of mechanic arts in India, that we conclude its inhabitants to have been highly civilized: a

---

* Strabo, lib. xv. p. 1044. B. Dionys. Perieges, ver. 1016.

† Raspe's Introd. to Tassie's Descript. Catal. of engraved gems, &c. p. xii. &c.

‡ Raspe's Introd. to Tassie's Descript. Catal. of engraved gems, vol. i. p. 74. vol. ii. plate xiii.

proof of this, still more convincing, may be deduced from the early and extraordinary productions of their genius in the fine arts. This evidence is rendered more interesting, by being derived from a source of knowledge which the laudable curiosity of our countrymen has opened to the people of Europe within these few years. That all the science and literature possessed by the Brahmins, were contained in books written in a language understood by a few only of the most learned among them, is a fact which has long been known; and all the Europeans settled in India during three centuries, have complained that the Brahmins obstinately refused to instruct any person in this language. But at length, by address, mild treatment, and a persuasion that the earnestness with which instruction was solicited, proceeded not from any intention of turning their religion into derision, but from a desire of acquiring a perfect knowledge of their sciences and literature, the scruples of the Brahmins have been overcome. Several British gentlemen are now completely masters of the Sanskreet language. The mysterious veil, formerly deemed impenetrable, is removed; and in the course of five years, the curiosity of the public has been gratified by two publications as singular as they were unexpected. The one is a translation by Mr Wilkins, of an Episode from the *Mahabarat*, an epic poem in high estimation among the Hindoos, composed, according to their account, by Kreeshna Dwypayen Veias, the most eminent of all their Brahmins, above three thousand years before the Christian era. The other is *Sacontala*, a dramatic poem, written about a century before the birth of Christ, translated by Sir W. Jones. I shall endeavour to give my readers such a view of the subject and composition of each of these, as may enable them to estimate, in some measure, the degree of merit which they possess.

THE Mahabarat is a voluminous poem, consisting of upwards of four hundred thousand lines. Mr Wilkins has translated more than a third of it; but only a short episode, entitled Baghvat-Geeta, is hitherto published; and from this specimen we must form an opinion with respect to the whole. The subject of the poem is a famous civil war between two branches of the royal house of Bhaurat. When the forces on each side were formed in the field, and ready to decide the contest by the sword, Arjoon, the favourite and pupil of the god Kreeshna, who accompanied him in this hour of danger, requested of him to cause his chariot to advance between the two hostile armies. He looked at both armies, and beheld on either side, none but grandsires, uncles, cousins, tutors, sons, and brothers, near relations, or bosom friends; and when he had gazed for a while, and saw these prepared for the fight, he was seized with extreme pity and compunction, and uttered his sorrow in the following words:—
" Having beheld, O *Kreeshna!* my kindred thus

waiting anxious for the fight, my members fail me, my countenance withereth, the hair standeth on end upon my body, and all my frame trembleth with horror; even *Gandeev*, my bow, escapeth from my hand, and my skin is parched and dried up.—When I have destroyed my kindred, shall I longer look for happiness? *I wish not for victory, Kreeshna;* I want not dominion; I want not pleasure: for what is dominion and the enjoyments of life, or even life itself, when those for whom dominion, pleasure, and enjoyment were to be coveted, have abandoned life and fortune, and stand here in the field ready for the battle. Tutors, sons and fathers, grandsires and grandsons, uncles, nephews, cousins, kindred, and friends! Although they would kill me, I wish not to fight them; no, not even for the dominion of the three regions of the universe, much less for this little earth."* In order to remove his scruples, Kreeshna informs him what was the duty of a prince of the Chehteree or military cast, when called to act in such a situation, and incites him to perform it by a variety of moral and philosophical arguments, the nature of which I shall have occasion to consider particularly in another part of this Dissertation. In this dialogue between Kreeshna and his pupil, there are several passages which give an high idea of the genius of the poet. The speech of Arjoon I have quoted, in which he expresses the anguish

---

* Baghvat-Geeta, p. 30, 31.

of his soul, must have struck every reader as beautiful and pathetic; and I shall afterwards produce a description of the Supreme Being, and of the reverence wherewith he should be worshipped, which is sublime. But while these excite our admiration, and confirm us in the belief of a high degree of civilization in that country where such a work was produced, we are surprised at the defect of taste and of art in the manner of introducing this Episode. Two powerful armies are drawn up in battle-array, eager for the fight; a young hero and his instructor are described as standing in a chariot of war between them: that surely was not the moment for teaching him the principles of philosophy, and delivering eighteen lectures of metaphysics and theology.

With regard, however, both to the dramatic and epic poetry of the Hindoos, we labour under the disadvantage of being obliged to form an opinion from a single specimen of each, and that of the latter, too, (as it is only a part of a large work), an imperfect one. But if, from such scanty materials, we may venture upon any decision, it must be, that of the two the drama seems to have been conducted with the most correct taste. This will appear from the observations which I now proceed to make upon Sacontala.

It is only to nations considerably advanced in refinement, that the drama is a favourite entertainment. The Greeks had been for a good time a polished people: Alcæus and Sappho had composed their Odes, and Thales and Anaximander had opened their schools, before tragedy made its first rude essay in the cart of Thespis; and a good time elapsed before it attained to any considerable degree of excellence. From the drama of Sacontala, then, we must form an advantageous idea of the state of improvement in that society to whose taste it was suited. In estimating its merit, however, we must not apply to it rules of criticism drawn from the literature and taste of nations with which its author was altogether unacquainted; we must not expect the unities of the Greek theatre; we must not measure it by our own standard of propriety. Allowance must be made for local customs, and singular manners, arising from a state of domestic society, an order of civil policy, and a system of religious opinions, very different from those established in Europe. Sacontalá is not a regular drama, but, like some of the plays early exhibited on the Spanish and English theatres, is an history in dialogue, unfolding events which happened in different places, and during a series of years. When viewed in this light, the fable is in general well arranged, many of the incidents are happily chosen, and the vicissitudes in the situation of the principal personages are sudden and unexpected. The unravelling of the piece, however, though some of the circumstances preparatory to it be introduced with skill, is at last brought about by the intervention of superior beings, which has always a bad effect, and discovers some want of art. But as Sacontala was descended of a celestial nymph, and under the protection of a holy hermit, this heavenly interposition may appear less marvellous, and is extremely agreeable to the Oriental taste. In many places of this drama it is simple and tender, in some pathetic; in others there is a mixture of comic with what is more serious. Of each, examples might be given. I shall select a few of the first, both because simplicity and tenderness are the characteristic beauties of the piece, and because they so little resemble the extravagant imagery and turgid style conspicuous in almost all the specimens of Oriental poetry which have hitherto been published.

SACONTALA, the heroine of the drama, a princess of high birth, had been educated by an holy hermit in a hallowed grove, and had passed the early part of her life in rural occupations and pastoral innocence. When she was about to quit this beloved retreat, and repair to the court of a great monarch, to whom she had been married, Cana, her foster-father, and her youthful companions, thus bewail their own loss, and express their wishes for her happiness, in a strain of sentiment and language perfectly suited to their pastoral character.

"HEAR, O ye trees of this hallowed forest, hear and proclaim that Sacontala is going to the palace of her wedded Lord; she who drank not, though thirsty, before you were watered; she who cropped not, through affection for you, one of your fresh leaves, though she would have been pleased with such an ornament for her locks; she, whose chief delight was in the season when your branches are spangled with flowers!

"*Chorus of Wood Nymphs.*—May her way be attended with prosperity! May propitious breezes sprinkle, for her delight, the odoriferous dust of rich blossoms! May pools of clear water, green with the leaves of the lotus, refresh her as she walks! and may shady branches be her defence from the scorching sun-beams!"

SACONTALA, just as she was departing from the grove, turns to Cana: "Suffer me, venerable father, to address this Madhavi-creeper, whose red blossoms inflame the grove."—*Cana.* "My child, I know thy affection for it."——*Sacont.* "O most radiant of shining plants, receive my embraces, and return them with thy flexible arms! from this day, though removed at a fatal distance, I shall for ever be thine.—O beloved father, consider this creeper as myself!" As she advances, she again addresses Cana: "Father! when yon female antelope, who now moves slowly from the weight of the young ones with which she is pregnant, shall be delivered of them, send me, I beg, a kind message with tidings of her safety.—Do not forget."——*Cana.* "My beloved, I will not forget it."———*Sacontala* [*stopping.*] "Ah! what is it that clings to the skirts of my robe and detains me!"———*Cana.* " It is thy adopted child, the little fawn, whose mouth, when the sharp points of Cusa grass had wounded it, has been so often smeared by thee with the healing oil of Ingudi; who has been so often fed by thee with a handful of Synmaka grains, and now will not leave the footsteps of his protectress."———*Sacont.* " Why dost thou weep, tender fawn, for me, who must leave our common dwelling-place?—As thou wast reared by me when thou hadst lost thy mother, who died soon after thy birth, so will my foster-father attend thee, when we are separated, with anxious care.—Return, poor thing, return,———we must part." [*She bursts into tears.*]——— *Cana.* " Thy tears, my child, ill suit the occasion; we shall all meet again; be firm; see the direct road before thee, and follow it. When the big tear lurks beneath thy beautiful eye-lashes, let thy resolution check its first efforts to disengage itself.—In thy passage over this earth, where the paths are now high, now low, and the true path seldom distinguished, the traces of thy feet must needs be unequal; but virtue will press thee right onward."[*]

FROM this specimen of the Indian drama, every reader of good taste, I should imagine, will be satisfied, that it is only among a people of polished

---

[*] Act IV. p. 47, &c.

manners and delicate sentiments that a composition so simple and correct could be produced or relished. I observe one instance in this drama of that wild extravagance so frequent in Oriental poetry. The monarch, in replacing a bracelet which had dropped from the arm of Sacontala, thus addresses her: " Look, my darling, this is the new moon which left the firmament in honour of superior beauty, and having descended on your enchanting wrist, hath joined both its horns round it in the shape of a bracelet."* But this is the speech of an enraptured young man to his mistress, and in every age and nation exaggerated praise is expected from the mouth of lovers. Dramatic exhibitions seem to have been a favourite amusement of the Hindoos as well as of other civilized nations. " The tragedies, comedies, farces, and musical pieces of the Indian theatre, would fill as many volumes as that of any nation in ancient or modern Europe. They are all in verse where the dialogue is elevated, and in prose where it is familiar; the men of rank and learning are represented speaking pure Sanskreet, and the women Pracrit, which is little more than the language of the Brahmins, melted down by a delicate articulation to the softness of Italian; while the low persons of the drama speak the vulgar dialects of the several provinces which they are supposed to inhabit."†

---

* Act III. p. 36.
† Preface to Sacont. by Sir William Jones, p. ix. See Note LXVI. Page 373.

V. The attainments of the Indians in science furnish an additional proof of their early civilization. By every person who has visited India in ancient or modern times, its inhabitants, either in transactions of private business, or in the conduct of political affairs, have been deemed not inferior to the people of any nation in sagacity or in acuteness of understanding. From the application of such talents to the cultivation of science, an extraordinary degree of proficiency might have been expected. The Indians were, accordingly, early celebrated on that account, and some of the most eminent of the Greek philosophers travelled into India, that, by conversing with the sages of that country, they might acquire some portion of the knowledge for which they were distinguished.* The accounts, however, which we receive from the Greeks and Romans, of the sciences which attracted the attention of the Indian philosophers, or of the discoveries which they had made in them, are very imperfect. To the researches of a few intelligent persons, who have visited India during the course of the three last centuries, we are indebted for more ample and authentic information. But from the reluctance with which the Brahmins communicate their sciences to strangers, and the inability of Europeans to acquire much knowledge of them, while, like the mysteries of their religion, they were concealed from vulgar eyes in an unknown tongue, this information was acquired

---

* Brukeri, Hist. Philosoph. vol. I. p. 190.

slowly, and with great difficulty. The same observation, however, which I made concerning our knowledge of the state of the fine arts among the people of India, is applicable to that of their progress in science, and the present age is the first furnished with sufficient evidence upon which to found a decisive judgment with respect to either.

Science, when viewed as disjoined from religion, the consideration of which I reserve for another head, is employed in contemplating either the operations of the understanding, the exercise of our moral powers, or the nature and qualities of external objects. The first is denominated logic; the second ethics; the third physics, or the knowledge of nature. With respect to the early progress in cultivating each of these sciences in India, we are in possession of facts which merit attention.

But, prior to the consideration of them, it is proper to examine the ideas of the Brahmins with respect to mind itself; for if these were not just, all their theories concerning its operations must have been erroneous and fanciful. The distinction between matter and spirit appears to have been early known by the philosophers of India, and to the latter they ascribed many powers of which they deemed the former to be incapable; and when we recollect how inadequate our conceptions are of every object that does not fall under the cognizance of the senses, we may affirm (if allowance be made for a peculiar notion of the Hindoos, which shall be afterwards explained) that no description of the human soul is more suited to the dignity of its nature than that given by the author of the Mahabarat. "Some," says he, "regard the soul as a wonder, others hear of it with astonishment, but no one knoweth it. The weapon divideth it not; the fire burneth it not; the water corrupteth it not; the wind drieth it not away; for it is indivisible, inconsumable, incorruptible; it is eternal, universal, permanent, immoveable; it is invisible, inconceivable, and unalterable."* After this view of the sentiments of the Brahmins concerning mind itself, we may proceed to consider their ideas with respect to each of the sciences, in that tripartite arrangement which I mentioned.

1st, Logic and Metaphysics. On no subject has the human understanding been more exercised than in analyzing its own operations. The various powers of the mind have been examined and defined. The origin and progress of our ideas have been traced; and proper rules have been prescribed, of proceeding from the observation of facts to the establishment of principles, or from the knowledge of principles to form arrangements of science. The philosophers of ancient Greece were highly celebrated for their proficiency in these abstruse speculations; and in

---

* Baghvat-Geeta, p. 37.

their discussions and arrangements, discovered such depth of thought and acuteness of discernment, that their systems of logic, particularly that of the Peripatetic School, have been deemed most distinguished efforts of human reason.

But since we became acquainted, in some degree, with the literature and science of the Hindoos, we find that as soon as men arrive at that stage in social life when they can turn their attention to speculative inquiries, the human mind will, in every region of the earth, display nearly the same powers, and proceed in its investigations and discoveries by nearly similar steps. From Abul Fazel's compendium of the philosophy* of the Hindoos, the knowledge of which he acquired, as he informs us, by associating intimately with the most learned men of the nation; from the specimen of their logical discussions contained in that portion of the Shastra published by Colonel Dow,† and from many passages in the Baghvat-Geeta, it appears that the same speculations which occupied the philosophers of Greece had engaged the attention of the Indian Brahmins; and the theories of the former, either concerning the qualities of external objects, or the nature of our own ideas, were not more ingenious than those of the latter. To define with accuracy, to distinguish with acuteness, and to reason

---

* Ayeen Akbery, vol. iii. p. 95, &c.
† Dissertation, p. xxxix. &c.

with subtlety, are characteristics of both; and in both the same excess of refinement, in attempting to analyze those operations of mind which the faculties of man were not formed to comprehend, led sometimes to the most false and dangerous conclusions. That sceptical philosophy, which denies the existence of the material world, and asserts nothing to be real but our own ideas, seems to have been known in India, as well as in Europe;[*] and the sages of the East, as they were indebted to philosophy for the knowledge of many important truths, were not more exempt than those of the West from its delusions and errors.

2d, ETHICS. This science, which has for its object to ascertain what distinguishes virtue from vice, to investigate what motives should prompt men to act, and to prescribe rules for the conduct of life, as it is of all others the most interesting, seems to have deeply engaged the attention of the Brahmins. Their sentiments with respect to these points were various, and, like the philosophers of Greece, the Brahmins were divided into sects, distinguished by maxims and tenets often diametrically opposite. That sect with whose opinions we are, fortunately, best acquainted, had established a system of morals founded on principles the most generous and dignified which unassisted reason is capable of discovering. Man, they taught, was formed not for speculation

---

[*] Dow's Dissertation, p. lvii. Ayeen Akbery, vol. iii. p. 128.

or indolence, but for action. He is born, not for himself alone, but for his fellow men. The happiness of the society of which he is a member, the good of mankind, are his ultimate and highest objects. In choosing what to prefer or to reject, the justness and propriety of his own choice are the only considerations to which he should attend. The events which may follow his actions are not in his own power; and whether they be prosperous or adverse, as long as he is satisfied with the purity of the motives which induced him to act, he can enjoy that approbation of his own mind which constitutes genuine happiness, independent of the power of fortune or the opinions of other men. " Man (says the author of the Mahabarat) enjoyeth not freedom from action. Every man is involuntarily urged to act by those principles which are inherent in his nature. He who restraineth his active faculties, and sitteth down with his mind attentive to the objects of his senses, may be called one of an astrayed soul. The man is praised, who having subdued all his passions, performeth with his active faculties all the functions of life, unconcerned about the event.* Let the motive be in the deed, and not in the event. Be not one whose motive for action is the hope of reward. Let not thy life be spent in inaction. Depend upon application, perform thy duty, abandon all thought of the consequence, and make the event equal, whether it terminate in good or in

---

* Baghvat-Geeta, p. 44.

evil; for such an equality is called *Yog* [*i. e.* attention to what is spiritual]. Seek an asylum then in wisdom alone; for the miserable and unhappy are so on account of the event of things. Men who are endued with true wisdom are unmindful of good or evil in this world. Study then to obtain this application of thy understanding, for such application in business is a precious art. Wise men who have abandoned all thought of the fruit which is produced from their actions, are freed from the chains of birth, and go to the regions of eternal happiness." *

FROM these and other passages which I might have quoted, we learn that the distinguishing doctrines of the Stoical school were taught in India many ages before the birth of Zeno, and inculcated with a persuasive earnestness nearly resembling that of Epictetus: and it is not without astonishment that we find the tenets of this manly active philosophy, which seem to be formed only for men of the most vigorous spirit, prescribed as the rule of conduct to a race of people more eminent (as is generally supposed) for the gentleness of their disposition than for the elevation of their minds.

3*d*, PHYSICS. In all the sciences which contribute towards extending our knowledge of nature, in mathematics, mechanics, and astronomy,

---

* Baghvat-Geeta, p. 40.

arithmetic is of elementary use. In whatever country, then, we find that such attention has been paid to the improvement of arithmetic as to render its operations most easy and correct, we may presume that the sciences depending upon it have attained a superior degree of perfection. Such improvement of this science we find in India. While, among the Greeks and Romans, the only method used for the notation of numbers was by the letters of the alphabet, which necessarily rendered arithmetical calculation extremely tedious and operose, the Indians had, from time immemorial, employed for the same purpose the ten cyphers, or figures, now universally known, and by means of them performed every operation in arithmetic with the greatest facility and expedition. By the happy invention of giving a different value to each figure according to its change of place, no more than ten figures are needed in calculations the most complex, and of any given extent; and arithmetic is the most perfect of all the sciences. The Arabians, not long after their settlement in Spain, introduced this mode of notation into Europe, and were candid enough to acknowledge that they had derived the knowledge of it from the Indians. Though the advantages of this mode of notation are obvious and great, yet so slowly do mankind adopt new inventions, that the use of it was for some time confined to science: by degrees, however, men of business relinquished the former cumbersome method of computation by letters, and the Indian arithmetic came into general use throughout Europe.* It is now so familiar and simple, that the ingenuity of the people to whom we are indebted for the invention is less observed, and less celebrated, than it merits.

The astronomy of the Indians is a proof still more conspicuous of their extraordinary progress in science. The attention and success with which they studied the motions of the heavenly bodies were so little known to the Greeks and Romans, that it is hardly mentioned by them but in the most cursory manner.† But as soon as the Mahomedans established an intercourse with the natives of India, they observed and celebrated the superiority of their astronomical knowledge. Of the Europeans who visited India after the communication with it by the Cape of Good Hope was discovered, M. Bernier, an inquisitive and philosophical traveller, was one of the first who learned that the Indians had long applied to the study of astronomy, and had made considerable progress in that science.‡ His information, however, seems to have been very general and imperfect. We are indebted for the first scientific proof of the great proficiency of the Indians in astronomical knowledge, to M. de la Loubere, who, on his return from his embassy to Siam, brought with him an extract from a Siamese ma- A.D. 1687.

---

* Montucla, Hist. des Mathemat. tom. i. p. 360, &c.
† Strabo, lib. xv. p. 1047. A. Dion. Perieg. v. 1173.
‡ Voyages, tom. ii. p. 145, &c.

nuscript, which contained tables and rules for calculating the places of the sun and moon. The manner in which these tables were constructed rendered the principles on which they were founded extremely obscure, and it required a commentator as conversant in astronomical calculation as the celebrated Cassini, to explain the meaning of this curious fragment. The epoch of the Siamese tables corresponds to the 21st of March A. D. 638. Another set of tables was transmitted from Chrisnabouram, in the Carnatic, the epoch of which answers to the 10th of March A. D. 1491. A third set of tables came from Narsapour, and the epoch of them goes no farther back than A. D. 1569. The fourth and most curious set of tables was published by M. le Gentil, to whom they were communicated by a learned Brahmin of Tirvalore, a small town on the Coromandel Coast, about twelve miles west of Negapatam. The epoch of these tables is of high antiquity, and coincides with the beginning of the celebrated era of the Calyougham or Collee Jogue, which commenced, according to the Indian account, three thousand one hundred and two years before the birth of Christ.*

These four sets of tables have been examined and compared by M. Bailly, who, with singular felicity of genius, has conjoined an uncommon degree of eloquence with the patient researches

---

* See Note LXVII. Page 377.

of an astronomer, and the profound investigations of a geometrician. His calculations have been verified, and his reasonings have been illustrated and extended by Mr Playfair, in a very masterly Dissertation, published in the Transactions of the Royal Society of Edinburgh.*

INSTEAD of attempting to follow them in reasonings and calculations, which from their nature are often abstruse and intricate, I shall satisfy myself with giving such a general view of them as is suited to a popular work. This, I hope, may convey a proper idea of what has been published concerning the astronomy of India, a subject too curious and important to be omitted in any account of the state of science in that country; and, without interposing any judgment of my own, I shall leave each of my readers to form his own opinion.

IT may be considered as the general result of all the inquiries, reasonings, and calculations, with respect to Indian astronomy, which have hitherto been made public, " That the motion of the heavenly bodies, and more particularly their situation at the commencement of the different epochs to which the four sets of tables refer, are ascertained with great accuracy; and that many of the elements of their calculations, especially for very remote ages, are verified by an astonish-

---

* Vol. ii. p. 135.

ing coincidence with the tables of the modern astronomy of Europe, when improved by the latest and most nice deductions from the theory of gravitation." These conclusions are rendered peculiarly interesting, by the evidence which they afford of an advancement in science unexampled in the history of rude nations. The Indian Brahmins, who annually circulate a kind of almanac, containing astronomical predictions of some of the more remarkable phenomena in the heavens, such as the new and full moons, the eclipses of the sun and moon, are in possession of certain methods of calculation, which, upon examination, are found to involve in them a very extensive system of astronomical knowledge. M. le Gentil, a French astronomer, had an opportunity, while in India, of observing two eclipses of the moon which had been calculated by a Brahmin, and he found the error in either to be very inconsiderable.

THE accuracy of these results is less surprising than the justness and scientific nature of the principles on which the tables, by which they calculate, are constructed; for the method of predicting eclipses which is followed by the Brahmins, is of a kind altogether different from any that has been found in the possession of rude nations in the infancy of astronomy. In Chaldea, and even in Greece, in the early ages, the method of calculating eclipses was founded on the observation of a certain period or cycle, after which the eclipses of the sun and moon return nearly in the same order; but there was no attempt to analyze the different circumstances on which the eclipse depends, or to deduce its phenomena from a precise knowledge of the motions of the sun and moon. This last was reserved for a more advanced period, when geometry, as well as arithmetic, were called in to the assistance of astronomy; and, if it was attempted at all, seems not to have been attempted with success before the age of Hipparchus. It is a method of this superior kind, founded on principles and on an analysis of the motions of the sun and moon, which guides the calculations of the Brahmins, and they never employ any of the grosser estimations, which were the pride of the first astronomers in Egypt and Chaldea.

THE Brahmins of the present times are guided in their calculations by these principles, though they do not now understand them: they know only the use of the tables which are in their possession, but are unacquainted with the method of their construction. The Brahmin who visited M. le Gentil at Pondicherry, and instructed him in the use of the Indian tables, had no knowledge of the principles of his art, and discovered no curiosity concerning the nature of M. le Gentil's observations, or about the instruments which he employed. He was equally ignorant with respect to the authors of these tables: and whatever is to be learned concerning the time or place of their construction, must be deduced from the tables themselves. One set of these tables (as was formerly observed) profess to be as old as the beginning of the Calyougham, or to go back to the year 3102 before the Christian era; but as nothing (it may be supposed) is easier than for an astronomer to give to his tables what date he pleases, and by calculating backwards, to establish an epoch of any assigned antiquity, the pretensions of the Indian astronomy to so remote an origin are not to be admitted without examination.

That examination has accordingly been instituted by M. Bailly, and the result of his inquiries is asserted to be, that the astronomy of India is founded on observations which cannot be of a much later date than the period above mentioned. For the Indian tables represent the state of the heavens at that period with astonishing exactness; and there is between them and the calculations of our modern astronomy such a conformity with respect to those ages, as could result from nothing but from the authors of the former having accurately copied from nature, and having delineated truly the face of the heavens, in the age wherein they lived. In order to give some idea of the high degree of accuracy in the Indian tables, I shall select a few instances of it, out of many that might be produced. The place of the sun for the astronomical epoch at the beginning of the Calyougham, as stated in the tables of Tirvalore, is only forty-seven minutes greater than by the tables of M. de la Caille, when corrected by the calculations of M. de la Grange. The place of the moon, in the same tables, for the same epoch, is only thirty-seven minutes different from the tables of Mayer. The tables of Ptolemy, for that epoch, are erroneous no less than ten degrees with respect to the place of the sun, and eleven degrees with respect to that of the moon. The acceleration of the moon's motion, reckoning from the beginning of the Calyougham to the present time, agrees, in the Indian tables, with those of Mayer to a single minute. The inequality of the sun's motion, and the obliquity of the ecliptic, which were both greater in former ages than they are now, as represented in the tables of Tirvalore, are almost of the precise quantity that the theory of gravitation assigns to them three thousand years before the Christian era. It is accordingly for those very remote ages (about 5000 years distant from the present) that their astronomy is most accurate, and the nearer we come down to our own times, the conformity of its results with ours diminishes. It seems reasonable to suppose, that the time when its rules are most accurate, is the time when the observations were made on which these rules are founded.

In support of this conclusion M. Bailly maintains, that none of all the astronomical systems of Greece or Persia, or of Tartary, from some of which it might be suspected that the Indian tables were copied, can be made to agree with them, especially when we calculate for very remote ages.

The superior perfection of the Indian tables becomes always more conspicuous as we go farther back into antiquity. This shows, likewise, how difficult it is to construct any astronomical tables, which will agree with the state of the heavens for a period so remote from the time when the tables were constructed, as four or five thousand years. It is only from astronomy in its most advanced state, such as it has attained in modern Europe, that such accuracy is to be expected.

WHEN an estimate is endeavoured to be made of the geometrical skill necessary for the construction of the Indian tables and rules, it is found to be very considerable; and, beside the knowledge of elementary geometry, it must have required plain and spherical trigonometry, or something equivalent to them, together with certain methods of approximating to the values of geometrical magnitudes, which seem to rise very far above the elements of any of those sciences. Some of these last mark also very clearly, (although this has not been observed by M. Bailly), that the places to which these tables are adapted must be situated between the Tropics, because they are altogether inapplicable at a greater distance from the Equator.

FROM this long induction, the conclusion which seems obviously to result is, that the Indian astronomy is founded upon observations which were made at a very early period; and when we consider the exact agreement of the places which they assign to the sun and moon, and other heavenly bodies, at that epoch, with those deduced from the tables of De la Caille and Mayer, it strongly confirms the truth of the position which I have been endeavouring to establish, concerning the early and high state of civilization in India.

BEFORE I quit this subject, there is one circumstance which merits particular attention. All the knowledge which we have hitherto acquired of the principles and conclusions of Indian astronomy, is derived from the southern part of the Carnatic, and the tables are adapted to places situated between the meridian of Cape Comorin and that which passes through the eastern part of Ceylon.* The Brahmins in the Carnatic acknowledge that their science of astronomy was derived from the north, and that their method of calculation is denominated *Fakiam*, or New, to distinguish it from the *Siddantam*, or ancient method established at Benares, which they allow to be much more perfect; and we learn from Abul Fazel, that all the astronomers of Indostan rely entirely upon the precepts contained in a book called *Soorej Sudhant*, composed in a very remote period.† It is manifestly from this book that the method to which the Brahmins of the south gave the name of Siddantam is taken. Benares has been from time immemorial the Athens of India,

---

* Bailly, Dis. Prelim. p. xvii.   † Ayeen Akbery, iii. p. 8.

the residence of the most learned Brahmins, and the seat both of science and literature. There, it is highly probable, whatever remains of the ancient astronomical knowledge and discoveries of the Brahmins is still preserved.* In an enlightened age and nation, and during a reign distinguished by a succession of the most splendid and successful undertakings to extend the knowledge of nature, it is an object worthy of public attention, to take measures for obtaining possession of all that time has spared of the philosophy and inventions of the most early and most highly civilized people of the East. It is with peculiar advantages Great Britain may engage in this laudable undertaking. Benares is subject to its dominion; the confidence of the Brahmins has been so far gained as to render them communicative; some of our countrymen are acquainted with that sacred language in which the mysteries both of religion and of science are recorded; movement and activity has been given to a spirit of inquiry throughout all the British establishments in India; persons who visited that country with other views, though engaged in occupations of a very different kind, are now carrying on scientific and literary researches with ardour and success. Nothing seems now to be wanting, but that those intrusted with the administration of the British

---

* M. Bernier, in the year 1668, saw a large hall in Benares filled with the works of the Indian philosophers, physicians, and poets. Voy. ii. p. 148.

empire in India, should enable some person capable, by his talents and liberality of sentiment, of investigating and explaining the more abstruse parts of Indian philosophy, to devote his whole time to that important object. Thus Great Britain may have the glory of exploring fully that extensive field of unknown science, which the academicians of France had the merit of first opening to the people of Europe.*

VI. THE last evidence which I shall mention of the early and high civilization of the ancient Indians, is deduced from the consideration of their religious tenets and practices. The institutions of religion, publicly established in all the extensive countries stretching from the banks of the Indus to Cape Comorin, present to view an aspect nearly similar. They form a regular and complete system of superstition, strengthened and upheld by every thing which can excite the reverence and secure the attachment of the people. The temples consecrated to their deities are magnificent, and adorned not only with rich offerings, but with the most exquisite works in painting and sculpture, which the artists highest in estimation among them were capable of executing. The rites and ceremonies of their worship are pompous and splendid, and the performance of them not only mingles in all the more momentous transactions of common life, but constitutes an essen-

---

* See NOTE LXVIII. Page 380.

tial part of them. The Brahmins, who, as ministers of religion, preside in all its functions, are elevated above every other order of men, by an origin deemed not only more noble, but acknowledged to be sacred. They have established among themselves a regular hierarchy and gradation of ranks, which, by securing subordination in their own order, adds weight to their authority, and gives them a more absolute dominion over the minds of the people. This dominion they support by the command of the immense revenues with which the liberality of princes, and the zeal of pilgrims and devotees, have enriched their Pagodas.*

It is far from my intention to enter into any minute detail with respect to this vast and complicated system of superstition. An attempt to enumerate the multitude of deities which are the objects of adoration in India; to describe the splendour of worship in their Pagodas, and the immense variety of their rites and ceremonies; to recount the various attributes and functions which the craft of priests, or the credulity of the people, have ascribed to their divinities; especially if I were to accompany all this with the review of the numerous and often fanciful speculations and theories of learned men on this subject, would require a work of great magnitude. I shall, therefore, on this, as on some of the for-

---

* Roger, Porte Ouverte, p. 39. 209, &c.

mer heads, confine myself to the precise point which I have kept uniformly in view; and by considering the state of religion in India, I shall endeavour not only to throw additional light on the state of civilization in that country, but I flatter myself that, at the same time, I shall be able to give what may be considered as a sketch and outline of the history and progress of superstition and false religion in every region of the earth.

I. WE may observe, that, in every country, the received mythology, or system of superstitious belief, with all the rites and ceremonies which it prescribes, is formed in the infancy of society, in rude and barbarous times. True religion is as different from superstition in its origin, as in its nature. The former is the offspring of reason cherished by science, and attains to its highest perfection in ages of light and improvement. Ignorance and fear give birth to the latter, and it is always in the darkest periods that it acquires the greatest vigour. That numerous part of the human species whose lot is labour, whose principal and almost sole occupation is to secure subsistence, has neither leisure nor capacity for entering into that path of intricate and refined speculation, which conducts to the knowledge of the principles of rational religion. When the intellectual powers are just beginning to unfold, and their first feeble exertions are directed towards a few objects of primary necessity and use; when the faculties of the mind are so limited as not to have formed general and abstract ideas; when language is so barren as to be destitute of names to distinguish any thing not perceivable by some of the senses; it is preposterous to expect that men should be capable of tracing the relation between effects and their causes; or to suppose that they should rise from the contemplation of the former to the discovery of the latter, and form just conceptions of one Supreme Being, as the Creator and Governor of the universe. The idea of creation is so familiar, wherever the mind is enlarged by science, and illuminated by revelation, that we seldom reflect how profound and abstruse the idea is, or consider what progress man must have made in observation and research, before he could arrive at any distinct knowledge of this elementary principle in religion. But even in its rude state, the human mind, formed for religion, opens to the reception of ideas which are destined, when corrected and refined, to be the great source of consolation amidst the calamities of life. These apprehensions, however, are originally indistinct and perplexed, and seem to be suggested rather by the dread of impending evils, than to flow from gratitude for blessings received. While nature holds on her course with uniform and undisturbed regularity, men enjoy the benefits resulting from it, without much inquiry concerning its cause. But every deviation from this regular course rouses and astonishes them. When they behold events to which they are not accustomed, they search for the causes of them with eager curiosity. Their understanding is often unable to discover these, but imagination, a more forward and ardent faculty of the mind, decides without hesitation. It ascribes the extraordinary occurrences in nature to the influence of invisible beings, and supposes the thunder, the hurricane, and the earthquake, to be the immediate effect of their agency. Alarmed by these natural evils, and exposed, at the same time, to many dangers and disasters which are unavoidable in the early and uncivilized state of society, men have recourse for protection to power superior to what is human, and the first rites or practices which bear any resemblance to acts of religion, have it for their object to avert evils which they suffer or dread.*

II. As superstition and false religion take their rise, in every country, from nearly the same sentiments and apprehensions, the invisible beings who are the first objects of veneration, have everywhere a near resemblance. To conceive an idea of one superintending mind, capable of arranging and directing all the various operations of nature, seems to be an attainment far beyond the powers of man in the more early stages of his progress.

---

* In the second volume of the History of America, p. 183. of fifth edition, I gave nearly a similar account of the origin of false religion. Instead of labouring to convey the same ideas in different language, I have inserted here some paragraphs in the same words I then used.

His theories, more suited to the limited sphere of his own observation, are not so refined. He supposes that there is a distinct cause of every remarkable effect, and ascribes to a separate power every event which attracts his attention, or excites his terror. He fancies that it is the province of one deity to point the lightning, and, with an awful sound, to hurl the irresistible thunderbolt at the head of the guilty; that another rides in the whirlwind, and, at his pleasure, raises or stills the tempest; that a third rules over the ocean; that a fourth is the god of battles; that while malevolent powers scatter the seeds of animosity and discord, and kindle in the breast those angry passions which give rise to war, and terminate in destruction, others of a nature more benign, by inspiring the hearts of men with kindness and love, strengthen the bonds of social union, augment the happiness, and increase the number of the human race.

WITHOUT descending farther into detail, or attempting to enumerate that infinite multitude of deities to which the fancy or the fears of men have allotted the direction of the several departments in nature, we may recognize a striking uniformity of features in the systems of superstition established throughout every part of the earth. The less men have advanced beyond the state of savage life, and the more slender their acquaintance with the operations of nature, the fewer were their deities in number, and the more compendious was their theological creed; but as their mind gradually opened, and their knowledge continued to extend, the objects of their veneration multiplied, and the articles of their faith became more numerous. This took place remarkably among the Greeks in Europe, and the Indians in Asia, the two people in those great divisions of the earth who were most early civilized, and to whom, for that reason, I shall confine all my observations. They believed, that over every movement in the natural world, and over every function in civil or domestic life, even the most common and trivial, a particular deity presided. The manner in which they arranged the stations of these superintending powers, and the offices which they allotted to each, were in many respects the same. What is supposed to be performed by the power of Jupiter, of Neptune, of Æolus, of Mars, of Venus, according to the mythology of the West, is ascribed in the East to the agency of Agnée, the god of fire; Varoon, the god of oceans; Vayoo, the god of wind;* Cama, the god of love; and a variety of other divinities.

The ignorance and credulity of men having thus peopled the heavens with imaginary beings, they ascribed to them such qualities and actions as they deemed suitable to their character and functions. It is one of the benefits derived from

---

* Baghvat-Geeta, p. 94.

true religion, that by setting before men a standard of perfect excellence, which they should have always in their eye, and endeavour to resemble, it may be said to bring down virtue from heaven to earth, and to form the human mind after a divine model. In fabricating systems of false religion, the procedure is directly the reverse. Men ascribe to the beings whom they have deified, such actions as they themselves admire and celebrate. The qualities of the gods who are the objects of adoration, are copied from those of the worshippers who bow down before them; and thus many of the imperfections peculiar to men have found admittance into heaven. By knowing the adventures and attributes of any false deity, we can pronounce, with some degree of certainty, what must have been the state of society and manners when he was elevated to that dignity. The mythology of Greece plainly indicates the character of the age in which it was formed. It must have been in times of the greatest licentiousness, anarchy, and violence, that divinities of the highest rank could be supposed capable of perpetrating actions, or of being influenced by passions, which, in more enlightened periods, would be deemed a disgrace to human nature: It must have been when the earth was still infested with destructive monsters; and mankind, under forms of government too feeble to afford them protection, were exposed to the depredations of lawless robbers, or the cruelty of savage oppressors, that the well known labours of Hercules, by which he was raised from earth to heaven, could have been necessary, or would have been deemed so highly meritorious. The same observation is applicable to the ancient mythology of India. Many of the adventures and exploits of the Indian deities are suited to the rudest ages of turbulence and rapine. It was to check disorder, to redress wrongs, and to clear the earth of powerful oppressors, that Vishnou, a divinity of the highest order, is said to have become successively incarnate, and to have appeared on earth in various forms.*

III. The character and functions of those deities which superstition created to itself as objects of its veneration, having everywhere a near resemblance, the rites of their worship were everywhere extremely similar. Accordingly, as deities were distinguished either by ferocity of character or licentiousness of conduct, it is obvious what services must have been deemed most acceptable to them. In order to conciliate the favour, or to appease the wrath of the former, fasts, mortifications, and penances, all rigid, and many of them excruciating to an extreme degree, were the means employed. Their altars were always bathed in blood; the most costly victims were offered; whole hecatombs were slaughtered; even human sacrifices were not unknown, and were held to be the most powerful expiations. In

---

* Voyage de Sonnerat, tom. i. p. 158, &c.

order to gain the good-will of the deities of the latter description, recourse was had to institutions of a very different kind, to splendid ceremonies, gay festivals, heightened by all the pleasures of poetry, music, and dancing, but often terminating in scenes of indulgence too indecent to be described. Of both these, instances occur in the rites of Greek and Roman worship, which I need not mention to my learned readers.* In the East the ceremonial of superstition is nearly the same. The manners of the Indians, though distinguished from the time when they became known to the people of the West, for mildness, seem, in a more remote period, to have been in a greater degree similar to those of other nations. Several of their deities were fierce and awful in their nature, and were represented in their temples under the most terrific forms. If we did not know the dominion of superstition over the human mind, we should hardly believe, that a ritual of worship suited to the character of such deities could have been established among a gentle people. Every act of religion, performed in honour of some of their gods, seems to have been prescribed by fear. Mortifications and penances so rigorous, so painful, and so long continued, that we read the accounts of them with astonishment and horror, were multiplied. Repugnant as it is to the feelings of an Hindoo to shed the blood of any creature that has life, many different animals, even

---

* Strabo, lib. viii. p. 581. A. Lib. xii. p. 837. C.

the most useful, the horse and the cow, were offered up as victims upon the altars of some of their gods;* and what is still more strange, the Pagodas of the East were polluted with human sacrifices as well as the temples of the West.† But religious institutions and ceremonies of a less severe kind, were more adapted to the genius of a people, formed, by the extreme sensibility both of their mental and corporeal frame, to an immoderate love of pleasure. In no part of the earth was a connexion between the gratification of sensual desire and the rites of public religion, displayed with more avowed indecency than in India. In every Pagoda there was a band of women set apart for the service of the idol honoured there, and devoted from their early years to a life of pleasure; for which the Brahmins prepared them by an education which added so many elegant accomplishments to their natural charms, that what they gained by their profligacy often brought no inconsiderable accession to the revenue of the temple. In every function performed in the Pagodas, as well as in every public procession, it is the office of these women to dance before the idol, and to sing hymns in his praise; and it is difficult to say, whether they trespass most against decency by the gestures they exhibit, or by the verses which they recite. The

---

* Ayeen Akbery, vol. iii. p. 241. Roger, Porte Ouverte, p. 251.

† Heeto-pades, p. 185—322. Asiat. Researches, vol. i. p. 265. Voyage de Sonnerat, vol. i. p. 207. Roger, p. 251.

walls of the Pagoda are covered with paintings in a style no less indelicate;* and in the innermost recess of the temple, for it would be profane to call it the sanctuary, is placed the *Lingam*, an emblem of productive power too gross to be explained.†

IV. How absurd soever the articles of faith may be which superstition has adopted, or how unhallowed the rites which it prescribes, the former are received in every age and country, with unhesitating assent, by the great body of the people, and the latter observed with scrupulous exactness. In our reasonings concerning religious opinions and practices which differ widely from our own, we are extremely apt to err. Having been instructed ourselves in the principles of a religion, worthy in every respect of that divine wisdom by which they were dictated, we frequently express wonder at the credulity of nations in embracing systems of belief which appear to us so directly repugnant to right reason, and sometimes suspect that tenets so wild and extravagant do not really gain credit with them. But experience may satisfy us, that neither our wonder nor suspicions are well founded. No article of the public religion was called in ques-

---

* Voyage de Gentil, vol. i. p. 244. 260. Preface to Code of Gentoo Laws, p. lvii.

† Roger, Porte Ouverte, p. 157. Voyage de Sonnerat, vol. i. p. 41. 175. Sketches, vol. i. p. 203. Hamilton's Trav. vol. i. p. 379.

tion by those people of ancient Europe with whose history we are best acquainted, and no practice which it enjoined appeared improper to them. On the other hand, every opinion that tended to diminish the reverence of men for the gods of their country, or to alienate them from their worship, excited among the Greeks and Romans that indignant zeal which is natural to every people attached to their religion by a firm persuasion of its truth. The attachment of the Indians, both in ancient and modern times, to the tenets and rites of their ancestors, has been, if possible, still greater. In no country, of which we have any account, were precautions taken with so much solicitude to place the great body of the people beyond the reach of any temptation to doubt or disbelief. They not only were prevented, (as I have already observed the great bulk of mankind must always be, in every country), from entering upon any speculative inquiry, by the various occupations of active and laborious life, but any attempt to extend the sphere of their knowledge was expressly prohibited. If one of the Sooder cast, by far the most numerous of the four into which the whole nation was divided, presumed to read any portion of the sacred books, in which all the science known in India is contained, he was severely punished; if he ventured to get it by heart, he was put to death.* To aspire after any higher degree of

---

* Code of Gentoo Laws, chap. 21. § 7.

knowledge than the Brahmins have been pleased to teach, would be deemed not only presumption but impiety. Even the higher casts depended entirely for instruction on the Brahmins, and could acquire no portion of science but what they deigned to communicate. By means of this, a devout reverence was universally maintained for those institutions which were considered as sacred; and though the faith of the Hindoos has been often tried by severe persecutions, excited by the bigotry of their Mahomedan conquerors, no people ever adhered with greater fidelity to the tenets and rites of their ancestors.*

V. We may observe, that when science and philosophy are diffused through any country, the system of superstition is subjected to a scrutiny from which it was formerly exempt, and opinions spread which imperceptibly diminish *its* influence over the minds of men. A free and full examination is always favourable to truth, but fatal to error. What is received with implicit faith in ages of darkness, will excite contempt or indignation in an enlightened period. The history of religion in Greece and Italy, the only countries of Europe which, in ancient times, were distinguished for their attainments in science, confirms the truth of this observation. As soon as science made such progress in Greece as rendered men capable of discerning the wisdom, the

---

* Orme's Fragments, p. 102. Sonnerat, vol. i. p. 194.

foresight, and the goodness displayed in creating, preserving, and governing the world, they must have perceived, that the characters of the divinities which were proposed as the objects of adoration in their temples, could not entitle them to be considered as the presiding powers in nature. A poet might address Jupiter as the father of gods and men, who governed both by eternal laws; but to a philosopher, the son of Saturn, the story of whose life is a series of violent and licentious deeds, which would render any man odious or despicable, must have appeared altogether unworthy of that station. The nature of the religious service celebrated in their temples must have been no less offensive to an enlightened mind, than the character of the deities in honour of whom it was performed. Instead of institutions tending to reclaim men from vice, to form or to strengthen habits of virtue, or to elevate the mind to a sense of its proper dignity, superstition either occupied its votaries in frivolous unmeaning ceremonies, or prescribed rites which operated, with fatal influence, in inflaming the passions, and corrupting the heart.

It is with timidity, however, and caution, that men venture to attack the established religion of their country, or to impugn opinions which have been long held sacred. At first, some philosophers endeavoured, by allegorical interpretations and refined comments, to explain the popular mythology, as if it had been a description of the

s

powers of nature, and of the various events and revolutions which take place in the system of the material world, and endeavoured by this expedient to palliate many of its absurdities. By degrees, bolder theories concerning religion were admitted into the schools of science. Philosophers of enlarged views, sensible of the impiety of the popular superstition, formed ideas concerning the perfections of one Supreme Being, the Creator and Ruler of the universe, as just and rational as have ever been attained by the unassisted powers of the human mind.

If from Europe we now turn to Asia, we shall find, that the observations which I have made upon the history of false religion holds equally true there. In India, as well as in Greece, it was by cultivating science that men were first led to examine and to entertain doubts with respect to the established systems of superstition; and when we consider the great difference between the ecclesiastical constitution (if I may use that expression) of the two countries, we are apt to imagine that the established system lay more open to examination in the latter than in the former. In Greece there was not any distinct race or order of men set apart for performing the functions of religion, or to serve as hereditary and interested guardians of its tenets and institutions. But in India the Brahmins were born the ministers of religion, and they had an exclusive right of presiding in all the numerous rites of worship which superstition prescribed as necessary to avert the wrath of Heaven, or to render it propitious. These distinctions and privileges secured to them a wonderful ascendant over their countrymen; and every consideration that can influence the human mind, the honour, the interest, the power of their order, called upon them to support the tenets, and to maintain the institutions and rites, with which the preservation of this ascendant was so intimately connected.

But as the most eminent persons of the Cast devoted their lives to the cultivation of science, the progress which they made in all the branches of it (of which I have given some account) was great, and enabled them to form such a just idea of the system of nature, and of the power, wisdom, and goodness displayed in the formation and government of it, as elevated their minds above the popular superstition, and led them to acknowledge and reverence one Supreme Being, "the Creator of all things, (to use their own expressions), and from whom all things proceed."*

This is the idea which Abul Fazel, who examined the opinions of the Brahmins with the greatest attention and candour, gives of their theology. "They all," says he, "believe in the unity of the Godhead; and although they hold images in high veneration, it is only because

---

* Baghvat-Geeta, p. 84.

they represent celestial beings, and prevent the thoughts of those who worship them from wandering."* The sentiments of the most intelligent Europeans who have visited India, coincide perfectly with his, in respect to this point. The accounts which M. Bernier received from the Pundits of Benares, both of their external worship, and of one Sovereign Lord being the sole object of their devotion, is precisely the same with that given by Abul Fazel.† Mr Wilkins, better qualified perhaps than any European ever was to judge with respect to this subject, represents the learned Brahmins of the present times as Theists, believers in the unity of God.‡ Of the same opinion is M. Sonnerat, who resided in India seven years, in order to inquire into the manners, sciences, and religion of the Hindoos.§ The Pundits who translated the Code of Gentoo Laws declare, " that it was the Supreme Being, who, by his power, formed all creatures of the animal, vegetable, and material world, from the four elements of fire, water, air, and earth, to be an ornament to the magazine of creation; and whose comprehensive benevolence selected man, the centre of knowledge, to have dominion and authority over the rest; and, having bestowed upon this favourite object judgment and understanding, gave him supremacy over the corners of the world."‖

---

* Ayeen Akbery, vol. iii. p. 3.   † Voyage, tom. ii. p. 159.
‡ Preface to Baghvat-Geeta, p. 24.
§ Voyage, tom. i. p. 198.   ‖ Prelim. Discourse, p. lxxiii.

Nor are these to be regarded as refined sentiments of later times. The Brahmins being considered by the Mahomedan conquerors of India as the guardians of the national religion, have been so studiously depressed by their fanatical zeal, that the modern members of that order are as far inferior to their ancestors in science as in power. It is from the writings of their ancient Pundits that they derive the most liberal sentiments which they entertain at present, and the wisdom for which they are now celebrated has been transmitted to them from ages very remote.

That this assertion is well founded we are enabled to pronounce with certainty, as the most profound mysteries of Hindoo theology, concealed with the greatest care from the body of the people, have been unveiled by the translations from the Sanskreet language lately published. The principal design of the Baghvat-Geeta, an episode in the Mahabarat, a poem of the highest antiquity, and of the greatest authority in India, seems to have been to establish the doctrine of the unity of the Godhead, and from a just view of the divine nature, to deduce an idea of what worship will be most acceptable to a perfect Being. In it, amidst much obscure metaphysical discussion, some ornaments of fancy unsuited to our taste, and some thoughts elevated to a tract of sublimity into which, from our habits of reasoning and judging, we will find it difficult to follow them,* we find descriptions of the Supreme Being entitled to equal praise with those of the Greek philosophers which I have celebrated. Of these I shall now produce one to which I formerly alluded, and refer my readers for others to the work itself: " O mighty Being," says Arjoon, " who art the prime Creator, eternal God of Gods, the World's Mansion! Thou art the incorruptible Being, distinct from all things transient. Thou art before all Gods, the ancient *Pooroosh* [*i. e.* vital soul], and the Supreme Supporter of the universe. Thou knowest all things, and art worthy to be known: Thou art the Supreme Mansion, and by thee, O infinite Form, the universe was spread abroad! Reverence be unto thee before and behind; reverence be unto thee on all sides! O thou who art all in all, infinite is thy power and thy glory. Thou art the Father of all things, animate and inanimate. Thou art the wise Instructor of the whole, worthy to be adored. There is none like unto thee: where, then, in the three worlds, is there one above thee? Wherefore I bow down; and, with my body prostrate upon the ground, crave thy mercy, Lord! worthy to be adored; for thou shouldest bear with me, even as a father with his son, a friend with his friend, a lover with his beloved."† A description of the Supreme Being is given in one of the sacred books of the Hindoos, from

---

* Mr Hastings' Letter, prefixed to the Baghvat-Geeta, p. 7.
† Baghvat-Geeta, p. 94, 95.

which it is evident what were the general sentiments of the learned Brahmins concerning the divine nature and perfections: "As God is immaterial, he is above all conception; as he is invisible, he can have no form; but from what we behold of his works, we may conclude that he is eternal, omnipotent, knowing all things, and present everywhere."*

To men capable of forming such ideas of the Deity, the public service in the Pagodas must have appeared to be an idolatrous worship of images, by a superstitious multiplication of frivolous or immoral rites; and they must have seen, that it was only by sanctity of heart, and purity of manners, men could hope to gain the approbation of a Being perfect in goodness. This truth Veias labours to inculcate in the Mahabarat; but with the prudent reserve and artful precautions natural to a Brahmin, studious neither to offend his countrymen, nor to diminish the influence of his own order. His ideas concerning the mode of worshipping the Deity are explained in many striking passages of the poem; but unwilling to multiply quotations, I satisfy myself with referring to them.†

WHEN we recollect how slowly the mind of man opens to abstract ideas, and how difficult (accord-

---
* Dow's Dissert. p. xl.
† Baghvat-Geeta, p. 55. 67. 75. 97. 119.

ing to an observation in the Mahabarat) an invisible path is to corporeal beings, it is evident that the Hindoos must have attained an high degree of improvement before their sentiments rose so far superior to the popular superstition of their country. The different states of Greece had subsisted long, and had made considerable progress in refinement, before the errors of false religion began to be detected. It was not until the age of Socrates, and in the schools of philosophy established by his disciples, that principles adverse to the tenets of the popular superstition were much propagated.

A LONGER period of time elapsed before the Romans, a nation of warriors and statesmen, were enlightened by science, or ventured upon any free disquisition concerning the objects or the rites of worship authorized by their ancestors. But in India the happy effects of progress in science were much more early conspicuous. Without adopting the wild computations of Indian chronology, according to which, the Mahabarat was composed above four thousand years ago, we must allow that it is a work of very great antiquity, and the author of it discovers an acquaintance with the principles of theology, of morals, and of metaphysics, more just and rational than seems to have been attained, at that period, by any nation whose history is known.

BUT so unable are the limited powers of the human mind to form an adequate idea of the perfections and operations of the Supreme Being, that in all the theories concerning them, of the most eminent philosophers in the most enlightened nations, we find a lamentable mixture of ignorance and error. From these the Brahmins were not more exempt than the sages of other countries. As they held that the system of nature was not only originally arranged by the power and wisdom of God, but that every event which happened was brought about by his immediate interposition; and as they could not comprehend how a being could act in any place unless where it was present, they supposed the Deity to be a vivifying principle diffused through the whole creation, an universal soul that animated each part of it.* Every intelligent nature, particularly the souls of men, they conceived to be portions separated from this great Spirit,† to which, after fulfilling their destiny on earth, and attaining a proper degree of purity, they would be again reunited. In order to efface the stains with which a soul, during its residence on earth, has been defiled, by the indulgence of sensual and corrupt appetites, they taught that it must pass, in a long succession of transmigrations, through the bodies of different animals, until, by what it suffers and what it learns in the various forms of its existence, it shall be so thoroughly refined from all pollution as to be rendered meet

---

* Baghvat-Geeta, p. 65. 78. 85. Bernier, tom. ii. p. 163.
† Dow's Dissert. p. xliii.

for being absorbed into the divine essence, and returns like a drop into that unbounded ocean from which it originally issued.* These doctrines of the Brahmins concerning the Deity, as the soul which pervades all nature, giving activity and vigour to every part of it, as well as the final reunion of all intelligent creatures to their primeval source, coincide perfectly with the tenets of the Stoical School. It is remarkable, that after having observed a near resemblance in the most sublime sentiments of their moral doctrine, we should likewise discover such a similarity in the errors of their theological speculations.†

The human mind, however, when destitute of superior guidance, is apt to fall into a practical error with respect to religion, of a tendency still more dangerous. When philosophers, by their attainments in science, began to acquire such just ideas of the nature and perfections of the Supreme Being, as convinced them that the popular system of superstition was not only absurd but impious, they were fully aware of all the danger which might arise from communicating what they had discovered to the people, incapable of comprehending the force of those reasons

---

* Voy. de. Sonnerat, vol. i. p. 192. 200. Baghvat-Geeta, p. 39. 115. Dow's Dissert. p. xliii.
† Lipsij Physiol. Stoicor. lib. i. dissert. viii. xxi. Seneca, Antoninus, Epictetus, passim.

which had swayed with them, and so zealously attached to established opinions, as to revolt against any attempt to detect their falsehood. Instead, therefore, of allowing any ray of that knowledge which illuminated their own minds to reach them, they formed a theory to justify their own conduct, and to prevent the darkness of that cloud which hung over the minds of their fellow-men from being ever dispelled. The vulgar and unlearned, they contended, had no right to truth. Doomed by their condition to remain in ignorance, they were to be kept in order by delusion, and allured to do what is right, or deterred from venturing upon what is wrong, by the hope of those imaginary rewards which superstition promises, and the dread of those punishments which it threatens. In confirmation of this, I might quote the doctrine of most of the philosophic sects, and produce the words of almost every eminent Greek and Roman writer. It will be sufficient, however, to lay before my readers a remarkable passage in Strabo, to whom I have been so often indebted in the course of my researches, and who was no less qualified to judge with respect to the political opinions of his contemporaries, than to describe the countries which they inhabited. " What is marvellous in fable, is employed," says he, " sometimes to please, and sometimes to inspire terror, and both these are of use, not only with children, but with persons of mature age. To children we propose delightful fictions, in order to encourage them to act well, and such as are terrible, in order to restrain them from evil. Thus when men are united in society, they are incited to what is laudable, by hearing the poets celebrate the splendid actions of fabulous story, such as the labours of Hercules and Theseus, in reward for which they are now honoured as divinities, or by beholding their illustrious deeds exhibited to public view in painting and sculpture. On the other hand, they are deterred from vice, when the punishments inflicted by the gods upon evil doers are related, and threats are denounced against them in awful words, or represented by frightful figures, and when men believe that these threats have been really executed upon the guilty. For it is impossible to conduct women and the gross multitude, and to render them holy, pious, and upright, by the precepts of reason and philosophy; superstition, or the fear of the gods, must be called in aid, the influence of which is founded on fictions and prodigies. For the thunder of Jupiter, the ægis of Minerva, the trident of Neptune, the torches and snakes of the furies, the spears of the gods, adorned with ivy, and the whole ancient theology, are all fables, which the legislators who formed the political constitution of states employ as bugbears to overawe the credulous and simple."*

These ideas of the philosophers of Europe were precisely the same which the Brahmins had

---

* Strabo, lib. i. p. 36. B.

adopted in India, and according to which they regulated their conduct with respect to the great body of the people. As their order had an exclusive right to read the sacred books, to cultivate and to teach science, they could more effectually prevent all who were not members of it from acquiring any portion of information beyond what they were pleased to impart. When the free circulation of knowledge is not circumscribed by such restrictions, the whole community derives benefit from every new acquisition in science, the influence of which, both upon sentiment and conduct, extends insensibly from the few to the many, from the learned to the ignorant. But wherever the dominion of false religion is completely established, the body of the people gain nothing by the greatest improvements in knowledge. Their philosophers conceal from them, with the utmost solicitude, the truths which they have discovered, and labour to support that fabric of superstition which it was their duty to have overturned. They not only enjoin others to respect the religious rites prescribed by the laws of their country, but conform to them in their own practice; and with every external appearance of reverence and devotion, bow down before the altars of deities, who must inwardly be the objects of their contempt. Instead of resembling the teachers of true religion, in the benevolent ardour with which they have always communicated to their fellow-men the knowledge of those important truths with which their own minds were enlightened and rendered happy, the sages of Greece, and the Brahmins of India, carried on, with studied artifice, a scheme of deceit, and, according to an emphatic expression of an inspired writer, they *detained* the truth in unrighteousness.* They knew and approved what was true, but among the rest of mankind they laboured to support and to perpetuate what is false.

Thus I have gone through all the particulars which I originally proposed to examine, and have endeavoured to discover the state of the inhabitants of India with respect to each of them. If I had aimed at nothing else than to describe the civil policy, the arts, the sciences, the religious institutions of one of the most ancient and most numerous races of men, that alone would have led me into inquiries and discussions both curious and instructive. I own, however, that I have all along kept in view an object more interesting, as well as of greater importance; and entertain hopes, that if the account which I have given of the early and high civilization of India, and of the wonderful progress of its inhabitants in elegant arts and useful science, shall be received as just and well established, it may have some influence upon the behaviour of Europeans towards that people. Unfortunately for the human species, in whatever quarter of the globe the people of Europe have acquired dominion, they have

---

* Romans, i. 18.

found the inhabitants not only in a state of society and improvement far inferior to their own, but different in their complexion, and in all their habits of life. Men in every stage of their career are so satisfied with the progress made by the community of which they are members, that it becomes to them a standard of perfection, and they are apt to regard people whose condition is not similar, with contempt, and even aversion. In Africa and America, the dissimilitude is so conspicuous, that, in the pride of their superiority, Europeans thought themselves entitled to reduce the natives of the former to slavery, and to exterminate those of the latter. Even in India, though far advanced beyond the two other quarters of the globe in improvement, the colour of the inhabitants, their effeminate appearance, their unwarlike spirit, the wild extravagance of their religious tenets and ceremonies, and many other circumstances, confirmed Europeans in such an opinion of their own pre-eminence, that they have always viewed and treated them as an inferior race of men. Happy would it be if any of the four European nations, who have successively acquired extensive territories and power in India, could altogether vindicate itself from having acted in this manner. Nothing, however, can have a more direct and powerful tendency to inspire Europeans, proud of their own superior attainments in policy, science, and arts, with proper sentiments concerning the people of India, and to teach them a due regard for their natural rights as men, than their being accustomed, not only to consider the Hindoos of the present times as a knowing and ingenious race of men, but to view them as descended from ancestors who had attained to a very high degree of improvement, many ages before the least step towards civilization had been taken in any part of Europe. It was by an impartial and candid inquiry into their manners, that the Emperor Akber was led to consider the Hindoos as no less entitled to protection and favour than his other subjects, and to govern them with such equity and mildness, as to merit from a grateful people the honourable appellation of " The Guardian of Mankind." It was from a thorough knowledge of their character and acquirements, that his Vizier Abul Fazel, with a liberality of mind unexampled among Mahomedans, pronounces an high encomium on the virtues of the Hindoos, both as individuals and as members of society, and celebrates their attainments in arts and sciences of every kind.* If I might presume to hope that the description which I have given of the manners and institutions of the people of India could contribute in the smallest degree, and with the remotest influence, to render their character more respectable, and their condition more happy, I shall close my literary labours with the satisfaction of thinking, that I have not lived or written in vain.

---

* Ayeen Akbery, vol. iii. p. 2. 81. 95.

NOTES

AND

ILLUSTRATIONS.

Note I. Sect. I. p. 7.

CREDULITY and scepticism are two opposite extremes into which men are apt to run, in examining the events which are said to have happened in the early ages of antiquity. Without incurring any suspicion of a propensity to the latter of these, I may be allowed to entertain doubts concerning the expedition of Sesostris into India, and his conquest of that country.——1. Few facts in ancient history seem to be better established, than that of the early aversion of the Egyptians to a seafaring life. Even the power of despotism cannot at once change the ideas and manners of a nation, especially when they have been confirmed by long habit, and rendered sacred by the sanction of religion. That Sesostris, in the course of a few years, should have so entirely overcome the prejudices of a superstitious people, as to be able to fit out four hundred ships of force in the Arabian Gulf, besides another fleet which he had in the Mediterranean, appears to be extremely improbable. Armaments of such magnitude would require the utmost efforts of a great and long established maritime power.——2. It is remarkable that Herodotus, who inquired with the most persevering diligence into the ancient history of Egypt, and who received all the information concerning it which the priests of Memphis, Heliopolis, and Thebes could communicate, Herodot. Edit. Wesselingij, lib. ii. c. 3. although he relates the history of Sesostris at some length, does not mention his conquest of India; lib. ii. c. 102, &c. That tale, it is probable, was invented in the period between the age of Herodotus and that of Diodorus Siculus, from whom we receive a particular detail of the Indian expedition of Sesostris. His account rests entirely upon the authority of the Egyptian priests; and Diodorus himself not only gives it as his general opinion, " that many things which they related, flowed rather from a desire to promote the honour of their country, than from attention to truth," lib. i. p. 34. Edit. Wesselingij, Amst. 1746; but takes particular notice, that the Egyptian priests, as well as the Greek writers, differ widely from one another in the accounts which they give of the actions of Sesostris, lib. i. p. 62.——3. Though Diodorus asserts, that in relating the history of Sesostris he had studied to select what appeared to him most probable, and most agreeable to the monuments of that monarch still remaining in Egypt, he has admitted into his narrative many marvellous circumstances, which render the whole extremely suspicious. The father of Sesostris, as he relates, collected all the male children who were born in Egypt on the same day with his son, in order that they might be educated together with him, conformable to a mode which he prescribed, with a view of preparing them as proper instruments to carry into execution the great undertakings for which he destined Sesostris. Accordingly, when Sesostris set out upon his Indian expedition, which, from circumstances mentioned by Diodorus, must have been about the fortieth year of his age, one thousand seven hundred of his youthful associates are said to have been still alive, and were intrusted with high command in his army. But if we apply to the examination of this story the certain principles of political arithmetic, it is evident, that if one thousand seven hundred of the male children born on the same day with Sesostris were alive when his great expedition commenced, the number of children born in Egypt on each day of the year must have been at least ten thousand, and the population of the kingdom must have exceeded sixty millions; Goguet, l'Origine des Loix, des Arts, &c. tom. ii. p. 12, &c.; a number far beyond the bounds of credibility, in a kingdom which, from the accurate calculations of M. D'Anville, Memoire sur l'Egypt Anc. et Moderne, p. 23, &c. does not contain more than two thousand one hundred square leagues of habitable country. Decline and Fall of the Rom. Emp. vol. v. p. 348. Another marvellous particular is the description of a ship of cedar, four hundred and ninety feet in length, covered on the outside with gold, and on the inside with silver; which Sesostris consecrated to the Deity who was the chief object of worship at Thebes. Lib. i. p. 67. Such too is the account he gives of the Egyptian army, in which, beside six hundred thousand infantry, and twenty-four thousand cavalry, there were twenty-seven thousand armed chariots. Ibid. p. 64——. These and other particulars appeared so far to exceed the bounds of probability, that the sound understanding of Strabo the geographer rejected, without hesitation, the accounts of the Indian expedition of Sesostris; and he not only asserts, in the most explicit terms, that this monarch never entered India, lib. xv. p. 1007. C. Edit. Casaub. Amst. 1707; but he ranks what has been related concerning his operations in that country with the fabulous exploits of Bacchus and Hercules, p. 1007. D. 1009. B. The philosophical historian of Alexander the Great seems to have entertained the same sentiments with respect to the exploits of Sesostris in

India; Hist. Ind. c. 5. Arrian, Exp. Alex. Edit. Gronov. L. Bat. 1704. What slender information concerning India, or its inhabitants, Herodotus had received, seems to have been derived, not from the Egyptians, but from the Persians, lib. iii. c. 105.; which renders it probable, that in his time there was little intercourse between Egypt and India. If Reland be well founded in his opinion, that many of the words mentioned by ancient authors as Indian are really Persian, we may conclude that there was an early intercourse between Persia and India, of which hardly any trace remains in history. Reland, Dissert. de Veteri Lingua Indic. ap. Dissert. Miscel. vol. i. p. 209.

Note II. Sect. I. p. 8.

When we consider the extent and effects of the Phœnician commerce, the scanty information concerning it which we receive from ancient writers must, on a first view, appear surprising. But when we recollect that all the Greek historians, (Herodotus excepted), who give any account of the Phœnicians, published their works long after the destruction of Tyre by Alexander the Great, we will cease to wonder at their not having entered into minute details with respect to a trade which was then removed to new seats, and carried on in other channels. But the power and opulence of Tyre, in the prosperous age of its commerce, must have attracted general attention. In the Prophecies of Ezekiel, who flourished two hundred and sixty years before the fall of Tyre, there is the most particular account of the nature and variety of its commercial transactions that is to be found in any ancient writer, and which conveys at the same time a magnificent idea of the extensive power of that state. Ch. xxvi. xxvii. xxviii.

Note III. Sect. I. p. 12.

The account given of the revenue of the Persian monarchy by Herodotus is curious, and seems to have been copied from some public record which had been communicated to him. According to it, the Persian empire was divided into twenty satrapys, or governments. The tribute levied from each is specified, amounting in all to 14,560 Euboean talents, which Dr Arbuthnot reckons to be equal to L.2,807,437 sterling money; a sum extremely small for the revenue of the Great King, and which ill accords with many facts concerning the riches, magnificence, and luxury of the East, that occur in ancient authors.

Note IV. Sect. I. p. 13.

Major Rennell, in the second edition of his Memoir, has traced, from very imperfect materials, the routes by which Alexander, Tamerlane, and Nadir Shah penetrated into India, with a degree of accuracy which does honour to his discernment, and displays the superiority of his knowledge in the ancient and modern geography of that country. His researches he has illustrated by an additional map. To these I must refer my readers. Nor are they to consider his laborious investigation merely as an object of curiosity; the geography of that fertile and extensive region of India, distinguished by the name of *Panjab*, with which we are at present little acquainted, may soon become very interesting. If, on the one hand, that firm foundation on which the British empire in India seems to be established, by the successful termination of the late war, remains unshaken;—if, on the other hand, the Seiks, a confederacy of several independent states, shall continue to extend their dominions with the same rapidity that they have advanced since the beginning of the current century, it is highly probable that the enterprizing commercial spirit of the one people, and the martial ardour of the other, who still retain the activity and ardour natural to men in the earliest ages of social union, may give rise to events of the greatest moment. The frontiers of the two states are approaching gradually nearer and nearer to each other, the territories of the Seiks having reached to the western bank of the river Jumnah, while those of the Nabob of Oude stretch along its eastern bank. This Nabob, the ally or tributary of the East India Company, is supported by a brigade of the Bengal army, constantly stationed on his western frontier. Rennell, Mem. Introd. p. cxvi. In a position so contiguous, rivalry for power, interference of interest, and innumerable other causes of jealousy and discord, can hardly fail of terminating, sooner or later, in open hostility. The Seiks possess the whole Soubah of Lahore, the principal part of Moultan, and the western part of Delhi. The dimensions of this tract are about 400 British miles from N. W. to S. E., varying in breadth from 320 to 150 miles. Their capital city is Lahore. Little is known concerning their government and political maxims; but they are represented as mild. In their mode of making war, they are unquestionably savage and cruel. Their army consists almost entirely of horse; of which they can bring at least 100,000 into the field. Maj. Rennell, Mem. 2d edit. Introd. p. cxxi. cxxii. and p. 365. See also Mr Craufurd's Sketches, 2d edit. vol. ii. p. 263, &c.

Note V. Sect I. p. 17.

It is surprising that Alexander did not receive, in the provinces contiguous to India, such an account of the periodical rains in that country, as to shew him the impropriety of carrying on military operations there while these continued. His expedition into India commenced towards the end of spring, Arrian, lib. iv. c. 22. when the rains were already begun in the mountains from which all the rivers in the Panjab flow, and of course they must have been considerably swelled before he arrived on their banks, Rennell, p. 268.—He passed the Hydaspes at midsummer, about the height of the rainy season. In a country through which so many large rivers run, an army on service at this time of the year must have suffered greatly. An accurate description of the nature of the rains and inundations in this part of India, is given by Arrian, lib. v. c. 9.; and one still fuller may be found in Strabo, lib. xv. 1013.—It was of what they suffered by these that Alexander's soldiers complained, Strabo, lib. xv. 1021. D.; and not without reason, as it had rained incessantly during seventy days, Diod. Sicul. xvii. c. 94.—A circumstance which marks the accuracy with which Alexander's officers had attended to every thing in that part of India, deserves notice. Aristobulus, in his Journal, which I have mentioned, observes, that though heavy rains fell in the mountains, and in the country near to them, in the plains below not so much as a shower fell. Strabo, lib. xv. 1013. B. 1015. B. Major Rennell was informed by a person of character, who had resided in this district of India, which is now seldom visited by Europeans, that during great part of the S. W. monsoon, or at least in the months of July, August, and part of September, which is the rainy season in most other parts of India, the atmosphere in the Delta of the Indus is generally clouded, but no rain falls except very near the sea. Indeed, very few showers fall during the whole season. Captain Hamilton relates, that when he visited Tatta, no rain had fallen for three years before. Memoirs, p. 288.—Tamerlane, who, by the vicinity of the seat of his government to India, had the means of being well informed concerning the nature of the country, avoided the error of Alexander, and made his Indian campaign during the dry season. As Nadir Shah, both when he invaded India, A. D. 1738, and in his return next year, marched through the same countries with Alexander, and nearly in the same line of direction, nothing can give a more striking idea of the persevering ardour of the Macedonian conqueror, than the description of the difficulties which Nadir Shah had to surmount, and the hardships which his army endured. Though possessed of absolute power and immense wealth, and distinguished no less by great talents than long experience in the conduct of war, he had the mortification to lose a great part of his troops in crossing the rivers of the Panjab, in penetrating through the mountains to the north of India, and in conflicts with the fierce natives inhabiting the countries which stretch from the banks of the Oxus to the frontiers of Persia. An interesting account of his retreat and sufferings is given in the Memoirs of Khojeh Abdulkurren, a Cashmerian of distinction, who served in his army.

Note VI. Sect. I. p. 19.

THAT a fleet so numerous should have been collected in such a short time, is apt to appear, at first sight, incredible. Arrian, however, assures us, that in specifying this number, he followed Ptolemy, the son of Lagus, whose authority he considered to be of the greatest weight, lib. vi. c. 3. But as the Panjab country is full of navigable rivers, on which all the intercourse among the natives was carried on, it abounded with vessels ready constructed to the conqueror's hands, so that he might easily collect that number. If we could give credit to the account of the invasion of India by Semiramis, no fewer than four thousand vessels were assembled in the Indus to oppose her fleet. Diod. Sicul. lib. ii. c. 74.—It is remarkable, that when Mahmoud of Gazna invaded India, a fleet was collected on the Indus to oppose him, consisting of the same number of vessels. We learn from the Ayeen Akbery, that the inhabitants of this part of India still continue to carry on all their communication with each other by water: the inhabitants of the Circar of Tatta alone have not less than forty thousand vessels of various constructions. Vol. ii. p. 143.

Note VII. Sect. I. p. 21.

ALL these particulars are taken from the Indian History of Arrian, a work different from that already mentioned, and one of the most curious treatises transmitted to us from antiquity. The first part of it consists of extracts from the account given by Nearchus of the climate and soil of India, and the manners of the natives. The second contains that officer's journal of his voyage from the mouth of the Indus to the bottom of the Persian Gulf. The perusal of it gives rise to several observations. —1. It is remarkable that neither Nearchus, nor Ptolemy, nor Aristobulus, nor even Arrian, once mention the voyage of Scylax. This could not proceed from their being unacquainted with it, for Herodotus was a favourite author in the hands of every Greek who had any pretensions to literature. It was probably occasioned by the reasons which they had to distrust the veracity of Scylax, of which I have already taken notice. Accordingly, in a speech which Arrian puts into the mouth of Alexander, he asserts that, except Bacchus, he was the first who had passed the Indus; which implies that he disbelieved what is related concerning Scylax, and was not acquainted with what Darius Hystaspes is said to have done, in order to subject that part of India to the Persian crown. *Arrian,* vii. c. 10. This opinion is confirmed by Megasthenes, who resided a considerable time in India. He asserts that, except Bacchus and Hercules, (to whose fabulous expeditions Strabo is astonished that he should have given any credit, lib. xv. p. 1007. D.) Alexander was the first who had invaded India; *Arrian, Hist. Indic.* c. 5. We are informed by Arrian, that the Assacani, and other people who possessed that country which is now called the kingdom of Candahar, paid tribute, first to the Assyrians, and afterwards to the Medes and Persians; *Hist. Indic.* c. 1. As all the fertile provinces on the north-west of the Indus were anciently reckoned to be part of India, it is probable that what was levied from them is the sum mentioned in the tribute-roll, from which Herodotus drew his account of the annual revenue of the Persian empire, and that none of the provinces to the south of the Indus were ever subject to the Kings of Persia.—2. This voyage of Nearchus affords some striking instances of the imperfect knowledge which the ancients had of any navigation different from that to which they were accustomed in the Mediterranean. Though the enterprising genius and enlarged views of Alexander prompted him to attempt opening an intercourse, by sea, between India and his Persian dominions, yet both he and Nearchus knew so little of the ocean which they wished to explore, as to be apprehensive that it might be found impossible to navigate it, on account of impervious straits, or other obstacles. *Hist. Indic.* c. 20. *Q. Curt.* lib. ix. c. 9. When the fleet arrived near the mouth of the Indus, the astonishment excited by the extraordinary flow and ebb of tide in the Indian Ocean, a phenomenon (according to Arrian) with which Alexander and his soldiers were unacquainted, lib. vi. c. 19. is another proof of their ignorance in maritime science. Nor is there any reason to be surprised at their astonishment, as the tides are hardly perceptible in the Mediterranean, beyond which the knowledge of the Greeks and Macedonians did not extend. For the same reason, when the Romans carried their victorious arms into the countries situated on the Atlantic Ocean, or on the seas that communicate with it, this new phenomenon of the tides was an object of wonder and terror to them. Cæsar describes the amazement of his soldiers at a spring-tide, which greatly damaged the fleet with which he invaded Britain, and acknowledges that it was an appearance with which they were unacquainted; Bell. Gallic. lib. iv. c. 29. The tides on the coast near the mouth of the Indus are remarkably high, and the effects of them very great, especially that sudden and abrupt influx of the tide into the mouths of rivers, or narrow straits, which is known in India by the name of *The Bore*, and is accurately described by Major Rennell, Introd. xxiv. Mem. 278. In the Periplus Maris Erythræi, p. 26. these high tides are mentioned, and the description of them nearly resembles that of the Bore. A very exaggerated account of the tides in the Indian Ocean is given by Pliny, Nat. Hist. lib. xiii. c. 25. Major Rannell seems to think, that Alexander and his followers could not be so entirely unacquainted with the phenomenon of the tides, as Herodotus had informed the Greeks, " that in the Red Sea there was a regular ebb and flow of the tide every day;" lib. ii. c. 11. This is all the explanation of that phenomenon given by Herodotus. But among the ancients there occur instances of inattention to facts, related by respectable authors, which appear surprising in modern times. Though Herodotus, as I have just now observed, gave an account of the voyage performed by Scylax at considerable length, neither Alexander nor his historians take any notice of that event. I shall afterwards have occasion to mention a more remarkable instance of the inattention of later writers to an accurate description which Herodotus had given of the Caspian Sea. From these, and other similar instances which might have been produced, we may conclude, that the slight mention of the regular flow and ebb of tide in the Red Sea, is not a sufficient reason for rejecting, as incredible, Arrian's account of the surprise of Alexander's soldiers when they first beheld the extraordinary effects of the tide at the mouth of the Indus.——3. The course of Nearchus's voyage, the promontories, the creeks, the rivers, the cities, the mountains, which came successively in his view, are so clearly described, and the distances of such as were most worthy of notice are so distinctly marked, that M. D'Anville, by comparing these with the actual position of the country, according to the best accounts of it, ancient as well as modern, has been able to point out most of the places which Nearchus mentions, with a degree of certainty which does as much honour to the veracity of the Grecian navigator, as to the industry, learning, and penetration of the French geographer. Mem. de Litterat. tom. xxx. p. 132, &c.

3 IN modern times, the Red Sea is a name appropriated to the Arabian Gulf, but the ancients denominated the ocean which stretches from that Gulf to India, the Erythræan Sea, from King Erythras, of whom nothing more is known than the name, which in the Greek language signifies *red*. From this casual meaning of the word, it came to be believed that it was of a different colour from other seas, and consequently of more dangerous navigation.

Note VIII. Sect. I. p. 27.

Alexander was so intent on rendering this union of his subjects complete, that after his death there was found in his tablets or commentaries, (among other magnificent schemes which he meditated), a resolution to build several new cities, some in Asia, and some in Europe, and to people those in Asia with Europeans, and those in Europe with Asiatics, " that, (says the historian), by intermarriages, and exchange of good offices, the inhabitants of these two great continents might be gradually moulded into a similarity of sentiments, and become attached to each other with mutual affection." Diod. Sicul. lib. xviii. c. 4.

The Oriental historians have mingled the little that they know concerning the transactions of European nations, particularly concerning the reign of Alexander the Great, and his conquest of Persia, with so many fabulous and incredible circumstances, that hardly any attention is due to them. Though they misrepresented every event in his life, they entertained an high idea of his great power, distinguishing him by the appellation of *Escander Dhûlcarnein*, i. e. the *Two-horned*, in allusion to the extent of his dominions, which, according to them, reached from the western to the eastern extremity of the earth. Herbelot, Bib. Orient. Article *Escander*. Anc. Univ. Hist. vol. v. 8vo. edit. p. 433. Richardson's Dissert. prefixed to his Dictionary of the Persian and Arabic, p. xii. Whether the historians of Indostan have given an account of Alexander's invasion of India with greater accuracy, cannot be known, until some of their works, written in the Sanskreet, are translated. That some traditional knowledge of Alexander's invasion of India is still preserved in the northern provinces of the Peninsula, is manifest from several circumstances. The Rajahs of Chitore, who are esteemed the most ancient establishment of Hindoo Princes, and the noblest of the Rajahpout tribes, boast of their descent from Porus, famous as well in the east as in the west for his gallant opposition to the Macedonian conqueror. Orme's Frag. p. 5. Major Rennell has informed me, by accounts lately received from India, and confirmed by a variety of testimonies, that, in the country of Kuttore, the eastern extreme of the ancient Bactria, a people who claimed to be the descendants of Alexander's followers were existing when Tamerlane invaded that province. In Bijore, a country more to the west in the same district, the Bazira of Alexander, there is a tribe at this day which traces its origin to certain persons left there by the conqueror when he passed through that province. Both Abul Fazel, and Soojah Rae, an eastern historian of good reputation, report this tradition without any material variation. The latter indeed adds, that these Europeans, if we may call them so, continued to preserve that ascendency over their neighbours, which their ancestors may be supposed to have possessed when they first settled here. Although we should reject this pedigree as false, yet the bare claim argues the belief of the natives, for which there must have been some foundation, that Alexander not only conquered Bijore, but also transferred that conquest to some of his own countrymen. Rennell, Mem. 2d edit. p. 162. The people of Bijore had likewise an high idea of Alexander's extensive authority; and they, too, denominated him the *Two-horned*, agreeably to the striking emblem of power in all the eastern languages. Ayeen Akbery, xi. 194. Many instances of this emblem being used, will occur to every person accustomed to read the sacred Scriptures.

Note IX. Sect. I. p. 28.

It seems to be an opinion generally received, that Alexander built only two cities in India, Nicæa, and Bucephalia, situated on the Hydaspes, the modern Chelum, and that Craterus superintended the building of both. But it is evident from Arrian, lib. v. c. ult. that he built a third city on the Acesines, now the Jenaub, under the direction of Hephæstion; and if it was his object to retain the command of the country, a place of strength on some of the rivers to the south of the Hydaspes seems to have been necessary for that purpose. This part of India has been so little visited in modern times, that it is impossible to point out with precision the situation of these cities. If P. Tieffenthaler were well founded in his conjecture, that the river now called Rauvee is the Acesines of Arrian, Bernouilli, vol. i. p. 39. it is probable that this city was built somewhere near Lahore, one of the most important stations in that part of India, and reckoned in the Ayeen Akbery to be a city of very high antiquity. But Major Rennell, in my opinion, gives good reasons for supposing the Jenaub to be the Acesines of the ancients.

Note X. Sect. I. p. 29.

The religious scruples which prevented the Persians from making any voyage by sea, were known to the ancients. Pliny relates of one of the Magi, who was sent on an embassy from Tiridates to the emperor Nero, "Navigare noluerat, quoniam exspuere in Maria, aliisque "mortalium necessitatibus violare naturam eam, fas non "putant;" Nat. Hist. lib. xxx. c. 2. This aversion to the sea they carried so far, that, according to the observation of a well-informed historian, there was not a city of any note in their empire built upon the sea-coast; Ammian. Marcel. lib. xxiii. c. 6. We learn from Dr Hyde, how intimately these ideas were connected with the doctrines of Zoroaster; Rel. Vet. Pers. cap. vi. In all the wars of the Persians with Greece, the fleets of the Great King consisted entirely of ships furnished by the Phœnicians, Syrians, the conquered provinces of the Lesser Asia, and the islands adjacent. Herodotus and Diodorus Siculus mention the quota furnished by each country in order to compose the fleet of twelve hundred ships with which Xerxes invaded Greece, and among these there is not one belonging to Persia. At the same time it is proper to observe, that, according to Herodotus, whose authority is unexceptionable with regard to this point, Ariabigines, a son of Darius, acted as admiral of the Persian fleet, and had several satraps of high rank under his command, and both Persians and Medes served as soldiers on board it; Herod. lib. vii. c. 96, 97. By what motives, or what authority, they were induced to act in this manner, I cannot explain. From some religious scruples, similar to those of the Persians, many of the natives of Indostan, in our own time, refuse to embark on board a ship, and to serve at sea; and yet, on some occasions, the sepoys in the service of the European powers have got the better of these scruples.

Note XI. Sect. I. p. 30.

M. Le Baron de Sainte-Croix, in his ingenious and learned Critique des Historiens d'Alexandre le Grand, p. 96. seems to entertain some doubt with respect to the number of the cities which Alexander is said to have built. Plutarch de Fort. Alex. affirms, that he founded no fewer than seventy. It appears from many passages in ancient authors, that the building of cities, or, what may be considered as the same, the establishment of fortified stations, was the mode of maintaining their authority in the conquered nations, adopted not only by Alexander, but by his successors. Seleucus and Antiochus, to whom the greater part of the Persian empire became subject, were no less remarkable for founding new cities than Alexander, and these cities seemed fully to have answered the purposes of the founders, as they effectually prevented (as I shall afterwards have occasion to observe) the revolt of the conquered provinces. Though the Greeks, animated with the love of liberty and of their native country, refused to settle in the Persian empire while under the dominion of its native monarchs, even when allured by the prospect of great advantage, as M. de Sainte-Croix remarks, the case became perfectly different when that empire was subjected to their own dominion, and they settled there, not as subjects, but as masters. Both Alexander and his successors discovered much discernment in choosing the situation of the cities which they built. Seleucia, which Seleucus founded, is a striking instance of this, and became hardly inferior to Alexandria in number of inhabitants, in wealth, and in importance. Mr Gibbon, vol. i. p. 250. M. D'Anville, Mem. de Litterat. xxx.

Note XII. Sect. I. p. 33.

It is from Justin we receive the slender knowledge we have of the progress which Seleucus made in India, lib. xv. c. 4. But we cannot rely on his evidence, unless when it is confirmed by the testimony of other authors. Plutarch seems to assert, that Seleucus had penetrated far into India; but that respectable writer is more eminent for his discernment of characters, and his happy selection of those circumstances which mark and discriminate them, than for the accuracy of his historical researches. Pliny, whose authority is of greater weight, seems to consider it as certain, that Seleucus had carried his arms into districts of India which Alexander never visited; Plin. Nat. Hist. lib. vi. c. 17. The passage in which this is mentioned is somewhat obscure, but it seems to imply, that Seleucus had marched from the Hyphasis to the Hysudrus, from thence to Palibothra, and from that to the mouth of the Ganges. The distances of the principal stations in this march are marked, the whole amounting to 2244 Roman miles. In this sense M. Bayer understands the words of Pliny; Histor. Regni Græcorum Bactrini, p. 37. But to me it appears highly improbable, that the Indian expedition of Seleucus could have continued so long as to allow time for operations of such extent. If Seleucus had advanced as far into India as the mouth of the Ganges, the ancients must have had a more accurate knowledge of that part of the country than they seem ever to have possessed.

Note XIII. Sect. I. p. 34.

MAJOR RENNELL gives a magnificent idea of this, by informing us, that " the Ganges, after it has escaped from the mountainous tract in which it had wandered above eight hundred miles," Mem. p. 233. " receives in its course through the plains eleven rivers, some of them as large as the Rhine, and none smaller than the Thames, besides as many more of lesser note;" p. 257.

NOTE XIV. SECT. I. p. 34.

In fixing the position of Palibothra, I have ventured to differ from Major Rennell, and I venture to do so with diffidence. According to Strabo, Palibothra was situated at the junction of the Ganges and another river; lib. xv. p. 1028. A. Arrian is still more explicit. He places Palibothra at the confluence of the Ganges and Erranaboas, the last of which he describes as less than the Ganges or Indus, but greater than any other known river;' Hist. Ind. c. 10. This description of its situation corresponds exactly with that of Allahabad. P. Boudier, to whose observations the geography of India is much indebted, says, that the Jumna, at its junction with the Ganges, appeared to him not inferior in magnitude to that river; D'Anville, Antiq. de l'Inde, p. 53. Allahabad is the name which was given to that city by the Emperor Akbar, who erected a strong fortress there; an elegant delineation of which is published by Mr Hodges, No. IV. of his Select Views in India. Its ancient name, by which it is still known among the Hindoos, is *Praeg*, or *Piyag*, and the people of the district are called *Praegi*, which bears a near resemblance to Prasij, the ancient appellation of the kingdom of which Palibothra was the capital; P. Tiessenthaler, Bernouilli, tom. i. p. 223. D'Anville, p. 56. Allahabad is such a noted seat of Hindoo devotion, that it is denominated *The King of Worshipped Places*; Ayeen Akbery, vol. ii. p. 35. "The territory around it, to the extent of forty miles, is deemed holy ground. The Hindoos believe, that when a man dies in this place, whatever he wishes for he will obtain in his next regeneration. Although they teach that suicide in general will be punished with torments hereafter, yet they consider it as meritorious for a man to kill himself at Allahabad:" Ayeen Akbery, iii. 256. P.

Tiessenthaler describes the various objects of veneration at Allahabad, which are still visited with great devotion by an immense number of pilgrims; Bernouilli, tom. i. 224. From all these circumstances, we may conclude it to be a place of great antiquity, and in the same situation with the Palibothra of antiquity.

MAJOR RENNELL has been induced to place Palibothra on the same site with Patna, chiefly by two considerations.——1. From having learned that on or near the site of Patna stood anciently a very large city named *Patelpoother* or *Patalipputra*, which nearly resembles the ancient name of Palibothra. Although there is not now a confluence of two rivers at Patna, he was informed that the junction of the Soane with the Ganges, now twenty-two miles above Patna, was formerly under the walls of that city. The rivers of India sometimes change their course in a singular manner, and he produces some remarkable instances of it. But even should it be allowed, that the accounts which the natives give of this variation in the course of the Soane were perfectly accurate, I question whether Arrian's description of the magnitude of Erranaboas be applicable to that river, certainly not so justly as to the Jumna.——2. He seems to have been influenced, in some degree, by Pliny's Itinerary, or Table of Distances from Taxila (the modern Attock) to the mouth of the Ganges; Nat. Hist. lib. vi. c. 17. But the distances in that Itinerary are marked so inaccurately, and in some instances are so palpably erroneous, that one cannot found upon them with much security. According to it, Palibothra is situated four hundred and twenty-five miles below the confluence of the Jumna and Ganges. The actual distance, however, between Allahabad and Patna, is not more than two hundred British miles. A disagreement so considerable cannot be accounted for, without supposing some extraordinary error in the Itinerary, or that the point of conflux of the Jumna with the Ganges has undergone a change. For the former of these suppositions there is no authority (as far as I know) from any manuscript, or for the latter from any tradition. Major Rennell has produced the reasons which led him to suppose the site of Palibothra to be the same with that of Patna; Memoirs, p. 49—54. Some of the objections which might be made to this supposition he has foreseen, and endeavoured to obviate; and after all that I have added to them, I shall not be surprised, if, in a geographical discussion, my readers are disposed to prefer his decision to mine.

Note XV. Sect. I. p. 36.

I do not mention a short inroad into India by Antiochus the Great, about one hundred and ninety-seven years posterior to the invasion of his ancestor Seleucus. We know nothing more of this transaction, than that the Syrian monarch, after finishing the war he carried on against the two revolted provinces of Parthia and Bactria, entered India, and concluding a peace with Sophagasenus, a King of the country, received from him a number of elephants, and a sum of money; Polyb. lib. x. p. 597, &c. lib. xi. p. 651; edit. Casaub. Justin. lib. xv. c. 4. Bayer's Hist. Regn. Græcor. Pactr. p. 69, &c.

Note XVI. Sect. I. p. 38.

A fact cursorily related by Strabo, and which has escaped the inquisitive industry of M. de Guignes, coincides remarkably with the narrative of the Chinese writers, and confirms it. The Greeks, he says, were deprived of Bactria by tribes or hordes of Scythian Nomades, who came from the country beyond the Jaxartes, and are known by the names of Asij, Parsiani, Tachari, and Sacarauli; Strab. lib. xi. p. 779. A. The Nomades of the ancients were nations who, like the Tartars, subsisted entirely, or almost entirely, as shepherds, without agriculture.

NOTE XVII. SECT. I. p. 40.

As the distance of Arsinoe, the modern Suez, from the Nile, is considerably less than that between Berenice and Coptos, it was by this route that all the commodities imported into the Arabian Gulf might have been conveyed with most expedition and least expense into Egypt. But the navigation of the Arabian Gulf, which even in the present improved state of nautical science is slow and difficult, was in ancient times considered by the nations around it to be so extremely perilous, that it led them to give such names to several of its promontories, bays, and harbours, as convey a striking idea of the impression which the dread of this danger had made upon their imagination. The entry into the Gulf they called *Babelmandeb*, the gate or port of affliction. To a harbour not far distant, they gave the name of *Mete*, i. e. Death. A headland adjacent they called *Gardafan*, the Cape of Burial. Other denominations of similar import are mentioned by the author to whom I am indebted for this information; Bruce's Travels, vol. i. p. 442, &c. It is not surprising then, that the staple of Indian trade should have been transferred from the northern extremity of the Arabian Gulf to Berenice, as by this change a dangerous navigation was greatly shortened. This seems to have been the chief reason that induced Ptolemy to establish the port of communication with India at Berenice, as there were other harbours on the Arabian Gulf which were considerably nearer than it to the Nile. At a later period, after the ruin of Coptos by the Emperor Diocletian, we are informed by Abulfeda, Descript. Egypt, edit. Michaelis, p. 77. that Indian commodities were conveyed from the Red Sea to the Nile, by the shortest route, viz. from Cosseir, probably the Philoteras Portus of Ptolemy, to Cous, the Vicus Apollinis, a journey of four days. The same account of the distance was given by the natives to Dr Pococke; Travels, vol. i. p. 87. In consequence of this, Cous, from a small village, became the city in Upper Egypt next in magnitude to Fostat, or Old Cairo. In process of time, from causes which I cannot explain, the trade from the Red Sea by Cosseir removed to Kene, farther down the river than Cous; Abulfeda, p. 13. 77. D'Anville, Egypte, 196—200. In modern times, all the commodities of India, imported into Egypt, are either brought by sea from Gidda to Suez, and thence carried on camels to Cairo, or are conveyed by land-carriage by the caravan returning from the pilgrimage to Mecca; Niebuhr Voyage, tom. i. p. 224. Volney, i. 188, &c. This, as far as I have been able to trace it, is a complete account of all the different routes by which the productions of the East have been conveyed to the Nile, from the first opening of that communication. It is singular that P. Sicard, Mem. des Missions dans le Levant, tom. ii. p. 157. and some other respectable writers, should suppose Cosseir to be the Berenice founded by Ptolemy, although Ptolemy has laid down its latitude at 23° 50', and Strabo has described it as nearly under the same parallel with that of Syené, lib. ii. p. 195. D. In consequence of this mistake, Pliny's computation of the distance between Berenice and Coptos at two hundred and fifty-eight miles, has been deemed erroneous; Pococke, p. 87. But as Pliny not only mentions the total distance, but names the different stations in the journey, and specifies the number of miles between each; and as the Itinerary of Antonius coincides exactly with his account, D'Anville, Egypte, p. 21. there is no reason to call in question the accuracy of it.

Note XVIII. Sect. I. p. 42.

MAJOR RENNELL is of opinion, " that under the Ptolemies, the Egyptians extended their navigation to the extreme point of the Indian Continent, and even sailed up the Ganges to Palibothra," on the same site (according to him) with the modern Patna; Introd. p. xxxvi. But had it been usual to sail up the Ganges as high as Patna, the interior parts of India must have been better known to the ancients than they ever were; and they would not have continued to derive their information concerning them from Megasthenes alone. Strabo begins his description of India in a very remarkable manner. He requests his readers to peruse with indulgence the account which he gives of it, as it was a country very remote, and few persons had visited it; and of these, many having seen only a small part of the country, related things either from hearsay, or, at the best, what they had hastily remarked while they passed through it in the course of military service, or on a journey; Strabo, lib. xv. p. 1005. B. He takes notice that few of the traders from the Arabian Gulf ever reached the Ganges; ibid. 1006. C. He asserts, that the Ganges enters the sea by one mouth, ibid. 1011. C.; an error into which he could not have fallen if the navigation of that river had been common in his time. He mentions indeed the sailing up the Ganges, ibid. 1010, but it is cursorily in a single sentence; whereas, if such a considerable inland voyage of above four hundred miles, through a populous and rich country, had been customary, or even if it had ever been performed by the Roman, or Greek, or Egyptian traders, it must have merited a particular description, and must have been mentioned by Pliny and other writers, as there was nothing similar to it in the practice of navigation among the ancients. It is observed by Arrian, (or whoever is the author of the Periplus Maris Erythræi,) that previous to the discovery of a new route to India, which shall be mentioned afterwards, the commerce with that country was carried on in small vessels which sailed round every bay, p. 32. Ap. Huds. Geogr. Min. Vessels of such light construction, and which followed this mode of sailing, were ill fitted for a voyage so distant as that round Cape Comorin, and up the Bay of Bengal, to Patna. It is not improbable, that the merchants, whom Strabo mentions as having reached the Ganges, may have travelled thither by land, either from the countries towards the mouth of the Indus, or from some part of the Malabar coast, and that the navigation up the Ganges, of which he casually takes notice, was performed by the natives in vessels of the country. This opinion derives some confirmation from his remarks upon the bad structure of the vessels which frequented that part of the Indian Ocean. From his description of them, p. 1012. C. it is evident that they were vessels of the country.

Note XIX. Sect. I. p. 44.

THE erroneous ideas of many intelligent writers of antiquity with respect to the Caspian Sea, though well known to every man of letters, are so remarkable, and afford such a striking example of the imperfection of their geographical knowledge, that a more full account of them may not only be acceptable to some of my readers, but in endeavouring to trace the various routes by which the commodities of the East were conveyed to the nations of Europe, it becomes necessary to enter into some detail concerning their various sentiments with respect to this matter.—1. According to Strabo, the Caspian is a bay that communicates with the great Northern Ocean, from which it issues at first by a narrow strait, and then expands into a sea extending in breadth five hundred stadia; lib. xi. p. 773. A. With him Pomponius Mela agrees, and describes the strait by which the Caspian is connected with the ocean, as of considerable length, and so narrow that it had the appearance of a river; lib. iii. c. 5. edit. Pliny likewise gives a similar description of it; Nat. Hist. lib. vi. c. 13. In the age of Justinian, this opinion, concerning the communication of the Caspian Sea with the ocean, was still prevalent; Cosm. Indicopl. Topog. Christ. lib. ii. p. 138. C.— 2. Some early writers, by a mistake still more singular, have supposed the Caspian Sea to be connected with the Euxine. Quintus Curtius, whose ignorance of geography is notorious, has adopted this error; lib. vii. c. 7. edit. —3. Arrian, though a much more judicious writer, and who, by residing for some time in the Roman province of Cappadocia, of which he was governor, might have obtained more accurate information, declares in one place the origin of the Caspian Sea to be still unknown; and it is doubtful whether it was connected with the Euxine, or with the great Eastern Ocean which surrounds India; lib. vii. c. 16. In another place he asserts, that there was a communication between the Caspian and the Eastern Ocean; lib. v. c. 26. These errors appear more extraordinary, as a just description had been given of the Caspian by Herodotus, near five hundred years before the age of Strabo. " The Caspian (says he) is a sea by itself, unconnected with any other. Its length is as much as a vessel with oars can sail in fifteen days; its greatest breadth as much as it can sail in eight days;" lib. 1. c. 203. Aristotle describes it in the same manner, and with his usual precision contends that it ought to be called a great lake, not a sea; Meteorolog. lib. ii. Diodorus Siculus concurs with them in opinion, vol. ii. lib. xviii. p. 261. None of those authors determine whether the greatest length of the Caspian was from north to south, or from east to west. In the ancient maps which illustrate the geography of Ptolemy, it is delineated as if its greatest length extended from east to west. In modern times, the first information concerning the true form of the Caspian which the people of Europe received, was given by Anthony Jenkinson, an English merchant, who with a caravan from Russia travelled along a considerable part of its coast in the year 1558; Hakluyt Collect. vol. i. p. 334. The accuracy of Jenkinson's description was confirmed by an actual survey of that sea made by order of Peter the Great, A. D. 1718; and it is now ascertained, not only that the Caspian is unconnected with any other sea, but that its length from north to south is considerably more than its greatest breadth from east to west. The length of the Caspian from north to south is about six hundred and eighty miles, and in no part more than two hundred and sixty miles in breadth from east to west; Cox's Travels, vol. ii. p. 257. The proportional difference of its length and breadth accords nearly with that mentioned by Herodotus. From this detail, however, we learn how the ill founded ideas concerning it, which were generally adopted, gave rise to various wild schemes of conveying Indian commodities to Europe by means of its supposed communication with the Euxine Sea, or with the Northern Ocean. It is an additional proof of the attention of Alexander the Great to every thing conducive to the improvement of commerce, that a short time before his death he gave directions to fit out a squadron in the Caspian, in order to survey that sea, and to discover whether it was connected either with the Euxine or Indian Ocean; Arrian, lib. vii. c. 16.

Note XX. Sect. II. p. 54.

From this curious detail we learn how imperfect ancient navigation was, even in its most improved state. The voyage from Berenice to Ocelis could not have taken thirty days, if any other course had been held than that of servilely following the windings of the coast. The voyage from Ocelis to Musiris would be (according to Major Rennell) fifteen days' run for an European ship in the modern style of navigation, being about seventeen hundred and fifty marine miles, on a straight course; Introd. p. xxxvii. It is remarkable, that though the Periplus Maris Erythræi was written after the voyage of Hippalus, the chief object of the author of it is to describe the ancient course along the coast of Arabia and Persia, to the mouth of the Indus, and from thence down the western shore of the continent to Musiris. I can account for this only by supposing, that from the unwillingness of mankind to abandon old habits, the greater part of the traders from Berenice still continued to follow that route to which they were accustomed. To go from Alexandria to Musiris, required (according to Pliny) ninety-four days. In the year 1788, the Boddam, a ship belonging to the English East-India Company of a thousand tons burden, took only fourteen days more to complete her voyage from Portsmouth to Madras. Such are the improvements which have been made in navigation.

Note XXI. Sect. II. p. 55.

It was the opinion of Plato, that in a well regulated commonwealth the citizens should not engage in commerce, nor the state aim at obtaining maritime power. Commerce, he contends, would corrupt the purity of their morals, and by entering into the sea-service, they would be accustomed to find pretexts for justifying conduct so inconsistent with what was manly and becoming, as would gradually relax the strictness of military discipline. It had been better for the Athenians, he asserts, to have continued to send annually the sons of seven of their principal citizens to be devoured by the Minotaur, than to have changed their ancient manners, and to have become a maritime power. In that perfect republic of which he delineates the form, he ordains that the capital should be situated at least ten miles from the sea; De Legibus, lib. iv. ab initio. These ideas of Plato were adopted by other philosophers. Aristotle enters into a formal discussion of the question, Whether a state rightly constituted should be commercial or not? and though abundantly disposed to espouse sentiments opposite to those of Plato, he does not venture to decide explicitly with respect to it; De Repub. lib. vii. c. 6. In ages when such opinions prevail, little information concerning commerce can be expected.

Note XXII. Sect. II. p. 59.

Pliny, lib. ix. c. 35. Principium ergo culmenque omnium rerum prætij Margaritæ tenent. In lib. xxxvii. c. 4. he affirms, Maximum in rebus humanis prætium, non solum inter gemmas, habet Adamas. These two passages stand in such direct contradiction to one another, that it is impossible to reconcile them, or to determine which is the most conformable to truth. I have adhered to the former, because we have many instances of the exorbitant price of pearls, but none, as far as I know, of diamonds having been purchased at a rate so high. In this opinion I am confirmed by a passage in Pliny, lib. xix. c. 1.: having mentioned the exorbitant price of *Asbestos*, he says, " æquat prætia excellentium Margaritarum;" which implies, that he considered pearls to be of higher price than any other commodity.

NOTE XXIII. SECT. II. p. 59.

PLINY has devoted two entire books of his Natural History, lib. xii. and xiii. to the enumeration and description of the spices, aromatics, ointments, and perfumes, the use of which luxury had introduced among his countrymen. As many of these were the productions of India, or of the countries beyond it, and as the trade with the East was carried on to a great extent in the age of Pliny, we may form some idea of the immense demand for them, from the high price at which they continued to be sold in Rome. To compare the prices of the same commodities in ancient Rome, with those now paid in our own country, is not a gratification of curiosity merely, but affords a standard by which we may estimate the different degree of success with which the Indian trade has been conducted in ancient and modern times. Many remarkable passages in ancient authors, concerning the extravagant price of precious stones and pearls among the Romans, as well as the general use of them by persons of all ranks, are collected by Meursius de Lux. Romanorum, cap. 5.; and by Stanislaus Robierzyckius, in his treatise on the same subject, lib. ii.

c. 1. The English reader will receive sufficient information from Dr Arbuthnot, in his valuable Tables of ancient coins, weights, and measures, p. 172, &c.

NOTE XXIV. SECT. II. p. 61.

M. MAHUDEL, in a memoir read in the academy of inscriptions and belles lettres in the year 1719, has collected the various opinions of the ancients concerning the nature and origin of silk, which tend all to prove their ignorance with regard to it. Since the publication of M. Mahudel's memoir, P. du Halde has described a species of silk, of which I believe he communicated the first notice to the moderns. " This is produced by small insects nearly resembling snails. They do not form cocoons either round or oval like the silk-worm, but spin very long threads, which fasten themselves to trees and bushes as they are driven by the wind. These are gathered and wrought into silk stuffs, coarser than those produced by domestic silk-worms. The insects which produce this coarse silk are wild." Description de l'Empire de la Chine, tom. ii. fol. p. 207. This nearly resembles Virgil's description,

Velleraque ut foliis depectant tenuia Seres.
GEORG. II. 121.

An attentive reader of Virgil will find, that, besides all the other qualities of a great descriptive poet, he possessed an extensive knowledge of natural history. The nature and productions of the wild silk-worms are illustrated at greater length in the large collection of Memoires concernant l'Histoire, les Sciences, les Arts, &c. des Chinois, tom. ii. p. 575, &c.; and by Pere de Mailla, in his voluminous History of China, tom. xiii.

p. 434. It is a singular circumstance in the history of silk, that on account of its being an excretion of a worm, the Mahomedans consider it as an unclean dress; and it has been decided, with the unanimous assent of all the doctors, that a person wearing a garment made entirely of silk, cannot lawfully offer up the daily prayers enjoined by the Koran. Herbal. Bibl. Orient. artic. *Harir*.

Note XXV. Sect. II. p. 62.

If the use of the cotton manufactures of India had been common among the Romans, the various kinds of them would have been enumerated in the Law de Publicanis et Vectigalibus, in the same manner as the different kinds of spices and precious stones. Such a specification would have been equally necessary for the direction both of the merchant and of the tax-gatherer.

Note XXVI. Sect. II. p. 62.

This part of Arrian's Periplus has been examined with great accuracy and learning by Lieutenant Wilford; and from his investigation it is evident, that the Plithana of Arrian is the modern Pultanah, on the southern banks of the river Godavery, two hundred and seventeen British miles south from Baroach; that the position of Tagara is the same with that of the modern Dowlatabad, and the high grounds across which the goods were conveyed to Baroach, are the Ballagaut mountains. The bearings and distances of these different places, as specified by Arrian, afford an additional proof (were that necessary) of the exact information which he had received concerning this district of India; Asiatic Researches, vol. i. p. 369, &c.

Note XXVII. Sect. II. p. 70.

Strabo acknowledges his neglect of the improvements in geography which Hipparchus had deduced from astronomical observations, and justifies it by one of those logical subtleties which the ancients were apt to introduce into all their writings. "A geographer," says he, (*i. e.* a describer of the earth,) "is to pay no attention to what is out of the earth; nor will men, engaged in conducting the affairs of that part of the earth which is inhabited, deem the distinctions and divisions of Hipparchus worthy of notice;" lib. ii. 194. C.

Note XXVIII. Sect. II. p. 70.

What an high opinion the ancients had of Ptolemy we learn from Agathemerus, who flourished not long after him. "Ptolemy," says he, "who reduced geography into a regular system, treats of every thing relating to it, not carelessly, or merely according to ideas of his own, but, attending to what had been delivered by more ancient authors, he adopted from them whatever he found consonant to truth;" Epitome Geogr. lib. i. c. 6. edit. Hudson. From the same admiration of his work, Agathodæmon, an artist of Alexandria, prepared a series of maps for the illustration of it, in which the position of all the places mentioned by Ptolemy, with their longitude and latitude, is laid down precisely according to his ideas; Fabric. Biblioth. Græc. iii. 412.

x

Note XXIX. Sect. II. p. 71.

As these public Surveys and Itineraries furnished the ancient geographers with the best information concerning the position and distances of many places, it may be proper to point out the manner in which they were completed by the Romans. The idea of a general survey of the whole empire was first formed by Julius Cæsar; and having been begun by him under authority of a decree of the senate, was finished by Augustus. As Rome was still far inferior to Greece in science, the execution of this great undertaking was committed to three Greeks, men of great abilities, and skilled in every part of philosophy. The survey of the eastern division of the empire was finished by Zenodoxus in fourteen years five months and nine days. That of the northern division was finished by Theodorus in twenty years eight months and ten days. The southern division was finished in twenty-five years one month and ten days; Æthici Cosmographia apud Geographos, editos à Hen. Stephano, 1577, p. 107. This undertaking was worthy of those illustrious persons who planned it, and suited to the magnificence of a great people. Besides this general survey, every new war produced a new delineation and measurement of the countries which were the seat of it. We may conclude from Vegetius, Instit. Rei Militaris, lib. iii. c. 6. that every governor of a Roman province was furnished with a description of it; in which were specified the distance of places in miles, the nature of the roads, the bye-roads, the short cuts, the mountains, the rivers, &c.; all these, says he, were not only described in words, but were delineated in a map, that, in deliberating concerning his military movements, the eyes of a general might aid the decisions of his mind.

Note XXX. Sect. II. p. 72.

The consequence of this mistake is remarkable. Ptolemy, lib. vii. c. i. computes the latitude of Barrygaza, or Baroach, to be 17° 20′; and that of Cory, or Cape Comorin, to be 13° 20′, which is the difference of four degrees precisely; whereas the real difference between these two places is nearly fourteen degrees.

Note XXXI. Sect. II. p. 72.

Ramusio, the publisher of the most ancient and perhaps the most valuable Collection of Voyages, is the first person, as far as I know, who takes notice of this strange error of Ptolemy; Viaggi, vol. i. p. 181. He justly observes, that the author of the circumnavigation of the Erythræan Sea had been more accurate, and had described the peninsula of India as extending from north to south; Peripl. p. 24. 29.

Note XXXII. Sect. II. p. 75.

This error of Ptolemy justly merits the name of *enormous*, which I have given to it; and it will appear more surprising when we recollect, that he must have been acquainted, not only with what Herodotus relates concerning the circumnavigation of Africa by order of one of the Egyptian Kings, lib. iv. c. 4. but with the opinion of Eratosthenes, who held that the great extent of the Atlantic Ocean was the only thing which prevented a communication between Europe and India by sea; Strab. Geogr. lib. i. p. 113. A. This error, however, must not be imputed wholly to Ptolemy. Hipparchus, whom we may consider as his guide, had taught that the earth is not surrounded by one continuous ocean, but that it is separated by different isthmuses, which divide it into several large basins; Strabo, lib. i. p. 11. B. Ptolemy having adopted this opinion, was induced to maintain that an unknown country extended from Cattigara to Prassum on the south-east coast of Africa; Geogr. lib. vii. c. 3. and 5. As Ptolemy's system of geography was universally received, this error spread along with it. In conformity to it the Arabian geographer Edrissi, who wrote in the twelfth century, taught that a continued tract of land stretched eastward from Sofala on the African coast, until it united with some part of the Indian continent; D'Anville, Antiq. p. 187. Annexed to the first volume of Gesta Dei per Francos, there is an ancient and very rude map of the habitable globe, delineated according to this idea of Ptolemy. M. Gossellin, in his map entitled Ptolemæi Systema Geographicum, has exhibited this imaginary tract of land which Ptolemy supposes to have connected Africa with Asia; Geographie des Grecs analysée.

Note XXXIII. Sect. II. p. 76.

In this part of the Disquisition, as well as in the map prepared for illustrating it, the geographical ideas of M. D'Anville, to which Major Rennell has given the sanction of his approbation, Introd. p. xxxix. have been generally adopted. But M. Gossellin has lately published " The Geography of the Greeks analyzed; or, the Systems of Eratosthenes, Strabo, and Ptolemy, compared with each other, and with the Knowledge which the Moderns have acquired;" a learned and ingenious work, in which he differs from his countryman with respect to many of his determinations. According to M. Gossellin, the Magnum Promontorium, which M. D'Anville concludes to be Cape Romania, at the southern extremity of the peninsula of Malacca, is the point of Bragu, at the mouth of the great river Ava; near to which he places Zaba, supposed by M. D'Anville, and by Barros, Decad. ii. liv. vi. c. 1. to be situated on the Strait of Sincapura or Malacca. The Magnus Sinus of Ptolemy he holds to be the same with the Gulf of Martaban, not the Gulf of Siam, according to M. D'Anville's decision. The position of Cattigara, as he endeavours to prove, corresponds to that of Mergui, a considerable port on the west coast of the kingdom of Siam; and that Thinæ, or Sinæ Metropolis, which M. D'Anville removes as far as Sin-hoa in the kingdom of Cochin China, is situated on the same river with Mergui, and now bears the name of Tanaserim. The Ibadij Insula of Ptolemy, which M. D'Anville determines to be Sumatra, he contends is one of that cluster of small isles which lie off this part of the coast of Siam; p. 137—148. According to M. Gossellin's system, the ancients never sailed through the Straits of Malacca, had no knowledge of the Island of Sumatra, and were altogether unacquainted with the Eastern Ocean. If to any of my readers these opinions appear to be well founded, the navigation and commerce of the ancients in India must be circumscribed within limits still more confined than those which I have allotted to them. From the Ayeen Akbery, vol. ii. p. 7. we learn that Cheen was an ancient name of the kingdom of Pegu: As that country borders upon Ava, where M. Gossellin places the Great Promontory, this near resemblance of names may appear, perhaps, to confirm his opinion that Sinæ Metropolis was situated on this coast, and not so far east as M. D'Anville has placed it.

As Ptolemy's geography of this eastern division of Asia is more erroneous, obscure, and contradictory, than any other part of his work, and as all the manuscripts of it, both Greek and Latin, are remarkably incorrect in the two chapters which contain the description of the countries beyond the Ganges, M. D'Anville, in his Memoir concerning the limits of the world known to the ancients beyond the Ganges, has admitted into it a larger portion of conjecture than we find in the other researches of that cautious geographer. He likewise builds more than usual upon the resemblances between the ancient and modern names of places, though at all times he discovers a propensity, perhaps too great, to trace these, and to rest upon them. These resemblances are often, indeed, very striking, and have led him to many happy discoveries. But in perusing his works, it is impossible, I should think, not to perceive that some which he mentions are far-fetched and fanciful. Whenever I follow him, I have adopted only such conclusions as seem to be established with his accustomed accuracy.

Note XXXIV. Sect. II. p. 86.

The author of the Circumnavigation of the Erythræan Sea has marked the distances of many of the places which he mentions with such accuracy, as renders it a nearer approach than what is to be found in any writer of antiquity, to a complete survey of the coast from Myos-Hormus, on the west side of the Arabian Gulf, along the shores of Ethiopia, Arabia, Persia, and Caramania, to the mouth of the Indus, and thence down the west coast of the Indian Peninsula to Musiris and Barace. This adds to the value of this short treatise, which, in every other respect, possesses great merit. It may be considered as a remarkable proof of the extent and accuracy of this author's intelligence concerning India, that he is the only ancient writer who appears in any degree to have been acquainted with the great division of that country, which still subsists, viz. Indostan Proper, comprehending the northern provinces of the Peninsula, and the Deccan, comprehending the southern provinces. " From Barygaza (says he) the continent stretches to the south; hence that district is called Dachinabades, for, in the language of the country, the south is called Dachanos;" Peripl. p. 29. As the Greeks and Romans, when they adopted any foreign name, always gave it a termination peculiar to their own language, which the grammatical structure of both tongues rendered in some degree necessary, it is evident that Dachanos is the same with Deccan, which word has still the same signification, and is still the name of that division of the Peninsula. The northern limit of the Deccan at present is the river Narbudda, where our author likewise fixes it. Peripl. ibid.

Note XXXV. Sect. II. p. 89.

Though, in deducing the latitudes of places from observations of the sun or stars, the ancient astronomers neglected several corrections which ought to have been applied, their results were sometimes exact to a few minutes, but at other times they appear to have been erroneous to the extent of two or even three degrees, and may perhaps be reckoned, one with another, to have come within half a degree of the truth. This part of the ancient geography would therefore have been tolerably accurate, if there had been a sufficient number of such determinations. These, however, were far from being numerous, and appear to have been confined to some of the more remarkable places in the countries which surround the Mediterranean Sea.

When, from want of more accurate observations, the latitude was inferred from the length of the longest or shortest day, no great degree of precision was, in any case, to be expected, and least of all in the vicinity of the Equator. An error of a quarter of an hour, which, without some mode of measuring time more accurate than ancient observers could employ, was not easily avoided, might produce, in such situations, an error of four degrees in the determination of the latitude.

With respect to places in the torrid zone, there was another resource for determining the latitude. This was by observing the time of the year when the sun was vertical to any place, or when bodies that stood perpendicular to the horizon had no shadow at noon-day: the sun's distance from the Equator at that time, which was known from the principles of astronomy, was equal to the latitude of the place. We have instances of the application of this method in the determination of the parallels of Syene and Meroe. The accuracy which this method would admit of, seems to be limited to about half a degree, and this only on the supposition that the observer was stationary; for if he was travelling from one place to another, and had not an opportunity of correcting the observation of one day by that of the day following, he was likely to deviate much more considerably from the truth.

With respect to the longitude of places, as eclipses of the moon are not frequent, and could seldom be of use for determining it, and only when there were astronomers to observe them with accuracy, they may be left out of the account altogether when we are examining the geography of remote countries. The differences of the meridians of places were therefore anciently ascertained entirely by the bearings and distances of one place from another; and of consequence, all the errors of reckonings, surveys, and itineraries, fell chiefly upon the longitude, in the same manner as happens at present in a ship which has no method of determining its longitude, but by comparing the dead-reckoning with the observations of the latitude; though with this difference, that the errors to which the most skilful of the ancient navigators was liable, were far greater than what the most ignorant shipmaster of modern times, provided with a compass, can well commit. The length of the Mediterranean, measured, in degrees of longitude, from the Pillars of Hercules to the Bay of Issus, is less than forty degrees; but in Ptolemy's maps it is more than sixty, and, in general, its longitudes, counting from the meridian of Alexandria, especially toward the East, are erroneous nearly in the same proportion. It appears, indeed, that in remote seas the coasts were often delineated from an imperfect account of the distances sailed, without the least knowledge of the bearings or direction of the ship's course. Ptolemy, it is true, used to make an allowance of about one-third for the winding of a ship's course. Geogr. lib. i. c. 12.; but it is plain, that the application of this general rule could seldom lead to an accurate conclusion. Of this there is a striking instance in the form which that geographer has given to the Peninsula of India. From the Barygazenum Promontorium to the place marked Locus unde solvunt in Chrysen navigantes, that is, from Surat on the Malabar coast, to about Narsapour on the Coromandel coast, the distance measured along the sea-shore is nearly the same with what it is in reality; that is, about five hundred and twenty leagues. But the mistake in the direction is astonishing, for the Malabar and Coromandel coast, instead of stretching to the south, and intersecting one another at Cape Comorin in a very acute angle, are extended by Ptolemy almost in the same straight line from west to east, declining a little to the south. This coast is, at the same time, marked with several bays and promontories, nearly resembling, in their position, those which actually exist on it. All these circumstances compared together, point out very clearly what were the materials from which the ancient map of India was composed. The ships which had visited the coast of that country, had kept an account of the time which they took to sail from one place to another, and had marked, as they stood along shore, on what hand the land lay, when they shaped their course across a bay or doubled a promontory. This imperfect journal, with an inaccurate account, perhaps, of the latitude of one or two places, was probably all the information concerning the coast of India which Ptolemy was able to procure. That he should have been able to procure no better information from merchants who sailed with no particular view of exploring the coast, will not appear wonderful, if we consider that even the celebrated Periplus of Hanno would not enable a geographer to lay down the coast of Africa with more precision than Ptolemy has delineated that of India.

NOTE XXXVI. SECT. II. p. 98.

THE introduction of the silk-worm into Europe, and the effects which this produced, came under the view of Mr Gibbon, in writing the History of the Emperor Justinian; and though it was an incident of subordinate importance only, amidst the multiplicity of great transactions which must have occupied his attention, he has examined this event with an accuracy, and related it with a precision, which would have done honour to an author who had no higher object of research; vol. iv. p. 71, &c. Nor is it here only that I am called upon to ascribe to him this merit. The subject of my inquiries has led me several times upon ground which he had gone over, and I have uniformly received information from the industry and discernment with which he has surveyed it.

Note XXXVII. Sect. III. p. 102.

This voyage, together with the observations of Abu Zeid al Hasan of Siraf, was published by M. Renaudot, A. D. 1718, under the title of " Anciennes Relations des Indes, et de la Chine, de deux Voyageurs Mahometans, qui y allèrent dans le Neuvieme Siècle; traduites de Arabe, avec des remarques sur les principaux endroits de ces Relations." As M. Renaudot, in his remarks, represents the literature and police of the Chinese in colours very different from those of the splendid descriptions which a blind admiration had prompted the Jesuits to publish, two zealous missionaries have called in question the authenticity of these relations, and have asserted that the authors of them had never been in China. P. Premare Lettr. edifiantes et curieuses, tom. xix. p. 420, &c. P. Parennin, ibid. tom. xxi. p. 158, &c. Some doubts concerning their authenticity were entertained likewise by several learned men in England, on account of M. Renaudot's having given no notice of the manuscript which he translated, but that he found it in the library of M. le Comte de Seignelay. As no person had seen the manuscript since that time, the doubts increased, and M. Renaudot was charged with the crime of imposing upon the public. But the Colbert Manuscripts having been deposited in the King's Library, as (fortunately for literature) most private collections are in France, M. de Guignes, after a long search, discovered the identical manuscript to which M. Renaudot refers. It appears to have been written in the 12th century; Journal des

Sçavans, Dec. 1764, p. 815, &c. As I had not the French edition of M. Renaudot's book, my references are made to the English translation. The relation of the two Arabian travellers is confirmed in many points by their countryman Massoudi, who published his treatise on universal history, to which he gives the fantastical title of " Meadows of Gold, and Mines of Jewels," a hundred and sixty years after their time. From him, likewise, we receive such an account of India in the tenth century, as renders it evident that the Arabians had then acquired an extensive knowledge of that country. According to his description, the Peninsula of India was divided into four kingdoms. The first was composed of the provinces situated on the Indus, and the rivers which fall into it; the capital of which was Moultan. The capital of the second kingdom was Canoge, which, from the ruins of it still remaining, appears to have been a very large city; Rennell's Memoirs, p. 54. In order to give an idea of its populousness, the Indian historians assert, that it contained thirty thousand shops in which betelnut was sold, and sixty thousand sets of musicians and singers, who paid a tax to government; Ferishta, translated by Dow, vol. i. p. 32. The third kingdom was Cachemire. Massoudi, as far as I know, is the first author who mentions this paradise of India, of which he gives a short but just description. The fourth is the kingdom of Guzerate, which he represents as the greatest and most powerful; and he concurs with the two Arabian travellers, in giving the sovereigns of it the appellation of Belhara. What Massoudi relates concerning India is more worthy of notice, as he himself had visited that country; Notices et Extraits des Manuscrits de la Bibliotheque du Roi, tom. i. p. 9, 10. Massoudi confirms what the two Arabian travellers relate, concerning the extraordinary progress of the Indians in astronomical science. According to his account, a temple was built during the reign of Brahmin, the first monarch of India, with twelve towers, representing the twelve signs of the zodiac; and in which was delineated a view of all the stars as they appear in the heavens. In the same reign was composed the famous Sind-Hind, which seems to be the standard treatise of Indian astronomy; Notices, &c. tom. i. p. 7. Another Arabian author, who wrote about the middle of the fourteenth century, divides India into three parts. The northern, comprehending all the provinces on the Indus: The middle, extending from Guzerate to the Ganges: The southern, which he denominates Comar, from Cape Comorin; Notices, &c. tom. ii. p. 46.

Note XXXVIII. Sect. III. p. 103.

THE naval skill of the Chinese seems not to have been superior to that of the Greeks, the Romans, or Arabians. The course which they held from Canton to Siraf, near the mouth of the Persian Gulf, is described by their own authors. They kept as near as possible to the shore until they reached the island of Ceylon, and then doubling Cape Comorin, they sailed along the west side of the Peninsula, as far as the mouth of the Indus, and thence steered along the coast to the place of their destination; Mem. de Litterat. tom. xxxii. p. 367. Some authors have contended, that both the Arabians and Chinese were well acquainted with the mariner's compass, and the use of it in navigation; but it is remarkable that in the Arabic, Turkish, and Persian languages, there is no original name for the compass. They commonly call it *Bosola*, the Italian name, which shews that the knowledge of this useful instrument was communicated to them by the Europeans. There is not one single observation, of ancient date, made by the Arabians on the variation of the needle, or any instruction deduced from it, for the assistance of navigators. Sir John Chardin, one of the most learned and best informed travellers who has visited the East, having been consulted upon this point, returns for answer, " I boldly assert, that the Asiatics are beholden to us for this wonderful instrument, which they had from Europe a long time before the Portuguese conquests. For, first, their compasses are exactly like ours, and they buy them of Europeans as much as they can, scarce daring to meddle with their needles themselves. Secondly, it is certain that the old navigators only coasted it along, which I impute to their want of this instrument to guide and instruct them in the middle of the ocean. We cannot pretend to say that they were afraid of venturing far from home, for the Arabians, the first navigators in the world in my opinion, at least for the eastern seas, have, time out of mind, sailed from the bottom of the Red Sea all along the coast of Africa; and the Chinese have always traded with Java and Sumatra, which is a very considerable voyage. So many islands uninhabited and yet productive, so many lands unknown to the people I speak of, are a proof that the old navigators had not the art of sailing on the main sea. I have nothing but argument to offer touching this matter, having never met with any person in Persia or the Indies to inform me when the compass was first known among them, though I made inquiry of the most learned men in both countries. I have sailed from the Indies to Persia in Indian ships, when no European has been on board but myself. The pilots were all Indians, and they used the fore-staff and quadrant for their observations. These instruments they have from us, and made by our artists, and they do not in the least vary from ours, except that the characters are Arabic. The Arabians are the most skilful navigators of all the Asiatics or Africans; but neither they nor the Indians make use of charts, and they do not much want them: some they have, but they are copied from ours, for they are altogether ignorant of perspective;" Inquiry when the Mahomedans first entered China, p. 141, &c. When M. Niebuhr was at Cairo, he found a magnetic needle in the possession of a Mahomedan, which served to point out the Kaaba, and he gave it the name of *El Magnatis*, a clear proof of its European origin; Voyage en Arabie, tom. ii. p. 169.

Note XXXIX. Sect. III. p. 104.

Some learned men, Cardan, Scaliger, &c. have imagined that the Vasa Murrhina, particularly described by Pliny, Nat. Hist. lib. xxxvii. and occasionally mentioned by several ancient authors both Greek and Roman, were the true porcelain of China. M. l'Abbé Le Bland and M. Larcher have examined this opinion, with full as much industry and erudition as the subject merited, in two Dissertations published in Mem. de Litterat. tom. xliii. From them it is evident that the Vasa Murrhina were formed of a transparent stone dug out of the earth in some of the eastern provinces of Asia. These were imitated in vessels of coloured glass. As both were beautiful and rare, they were sold at a very high price to the luxurious citizens of Rome.

Note XL. Sect. III. p. 106.

The progress of Christianity and of Mahomedanism, both in China and India, is attested by such evidence as leaves no doubt with respect to it. This evidence is collected by Assemanus, Biblioth. Orient. vol. iv. p. 437, &c. 521, &c.; and by M. Renaudot, in two Dissertations annexed to Anciennes Relations; and by M. de la Croze, Histoire de Christianisme des Indes. In our own age, however, we know that the number of proselytes to either of these religions is extremely small, especially in India. A Gentoo considers all the distinctions and privileges of his cast, as belonging to him by an exclusive and incommunicable right. To convert, or to be converted, are ideas equally repugnant to the principles most deeply rooted in his mind; nor can either the Catholic or Protestant missionaries in India boast of having overcome these prejudices, except among a few in the lowest casts, or of such as have lost their cast altogether. This last circumstance is a great obstacle to the progress of Christianity in India. As Europeans eat the flesh of that animal which the Hindoos deem sacred, and drink intoxicating liquors, in which practices they are imitated by the converts to Christianity, this sinks them to a level with the Pariars, the most contemptible and odious race of men. Some Catholic missionaries were so sensible of this, that they affected to imitate the dress and manner of living of Brahmins, and refused to associate with the Pariars, or to admit them to the participation of the sacraments. But this was condemned by the apostolic legate Tournon, as inconsistent with the spirit and precepts of the Christian religion; Voyage aux Indes Orientales, par M. Sonnerat, tom. i. p. 58. note. Notwithstanding the labours of missionaries for upwards of two hundred years, (says a late ingenious writer), and the establishments of different Christian nations, who support and protect them, out of, perhaps, one hundred millions of Hindoos, there are not twelve thousand Christians, and these almost entirely *Chancalas*, or outcasts: Sketches relating to the history, religion, learning, and manners of the Hindoos, p. 48. The number of Mahomedans, or Moors, now in Indostan is supposed to be near ten millions; but they are not the original inhabitants of the country, but the descendants of adventurers who have been pouring in from Tartary, Persia, and Arabia, ever since the invasion of Mahmoud of Gazna, A. D. 1002, the first Mahomedan conqueror of India; Orme, Hist. of Military Transact. in Indostan, vol. i. p. 24. Herbelot, Biblioth. Orient. artic. *Gaznaviah*. As the manners of the Indians in ancient times seem to have been, in every respect, the same with those of the present age, it is probable that the Christians and Mahomedans, said to be so numerous in India and China, were chiefly foreigners, allured thither by a lucrative commerce, or their descendants. The number of Mahomedans in China has been considerably increased by a practice, common among them, of buying children in years of famine, whom they educate in the Mahomedan religion; Hist. Gener. des Voyages, tom. vi. p. 357.

Note XLI. Sect. III. p. 110.

From the Chronicle of Andrew Dandulo, Doge of Venice, who was elevated to that high station at a time when his countrymen had established a regular trade with Alexandria, and imported from it all the productions of the East, it was natural to expect some information concerning their early trade with that country; but, except an idle tale concerning some Venetian ships which had sailed to Alexandria about the year 828, contrary to a decree of the State, and which stole thence the body of St. Mark, (Murat. Script. Rer. Ital. vol. xii. lib. 8. c. 2. p. 170), I find no other hint concerning the communication between the two countries. On the contrary, circumstances occur which shew that the resort of Europeans to Egypt had ceased, almost entirely, for some time. Prior to the seventh and eighth centuries, the greater part of the public deeds in Italy and in other countries of Europe, were written upon paper fabricated of the Egyptian papyrus; but after that period, as Europeans seldom ventured to trade in Alexandria, almost all charters and other deeds are written upon parchment; Murat. Antiq. Ital. Medii Ævi, vol. iii. p. 832. I have been induced, both in the text and in this note, to state these particulars concerning the interruption of trade between the Christians and Mahomedans so fully, in order to correct an error into which several modern authors have fallen, by supposing, that soon after the first conquests of the Caliphs, the trade with India returned into its ancient channels, and the merchants of Europe resorted with the same freedom as formerly to the ports of Egypt and Syria.

Note XLII. Sect. III. p. 115.

It is proper to remark (says Mr Stewart) that the Indians have an admirable method of rendering their religion lucrative, it being usual for the Faquirs to carry with them, in their pilgrimages from the sea-coasts to the interior parts, pearls, corals, spices, and other precious articles of small bulk, which they exchange, on their return, for gold dust, musk, and other things of a similar nature, concealing them easily in their hair, and in the cloths round their middle, carrying on, in proportion to their numbers, no inconsiderable traffic by these means; Account of the kingdom of Thibet, Philosoph. Transact. vol. lxvii. part ii. p. 483.

Note XLIII. Sect. III. p. 123.

Caffa is the most commodious station for trade in the Black Sea. While in the hands of the Genoese, who kept possession of it above two centuries, they rendered it the seat of an extensive and flourishing commerce. Even under all the disadvantages of its subjection, at present, to the Turkish government, it continues to be a place of considerable trade. Sir John Chardin, who visited it A. D. 1672, relates, that during his residence of forty days there, above four hundred ships arrived at Caffa, or sailed from it; Voyages, i. 48. He observed there several remains of Genoese magnificence. The number of its inhabitants, according to M. Peysonel, amounts still to eighty thousand; Commerce de la Mer Noire, tom. i. p. 15. He describes its trade as very great.

Note XLIV. Sect. III. p. 124.

The rapacity and insolence of the Genoese settled in Constantinople, are painted by Nicephorus Gregoras, an eye-witness of their conduct, in very striking colours. "They," says he, "now, *i. e.* about the year 1340, dreamed that they had acquired the dominion of the sea, and claimed an exclusive right to the trade of the Euxine, prohibiting the Greeks to sail to the Mæotis, the Chersonesus, or any part of the coast beyond the mouth of the Danube, without a license from them. This exclusion they extended likewise to the Venetians, and their arrogance proceeded so far as to form a scheme of imposing a toll upon every vessel passing through the Bosphorus;" Lib. xviii. c. 2. § 1.

Note XLV. Sect. III. p. 125.

A PERMISSION from the Pope was deemed so necessary to authorize a commercial intercourse with infidels, that long after this period, in the year 1454, Nicholas V. in his famous bull in favour of Prince Henry of Portugal, among other privileges, grants him a license to trade with Mahomedans, and refers to similar concessions from Pope Martin V. and Eugenius, to the Kings of Portugal; Leibnitz, Codex Jur. Gent. Diplomat. Pars I. p. 489.

Note XLVI. Sect. III. p. 127.

NEITHER Jovius, the professed panegyrist of the Medici, nor Jo. M. Brutus, their detractor, though both mention the exorbitant wealth of the family, explain the nature of the trade by which it was acquired. Even Machiavel, whose genius delighted in the investigation of every circumstance which contributed to aggrandize or depress nations, seems not to have viewed the commerce of his country as a subject that merited any elucidation. Denina, who has entitled the first chapter of his eighteenth book, " The Origin of the Medici, and the Commencement of their Power and Grandeur," furnishes little information with regard to the trade carried on by them. This silence of so many authors is a proof that historians had not yet begun to view commerce as an object of such importance in the political state of nations, as to enter into any detail concerning its nature and effects. From the references of different writers to Scipio Ammirato, Istorie Fiorentine; to Pagnini, Della Decima ed altri gravezze della Mercatura di Fiorentini, and to Balducci, Practica della Mercatura, I should imagine that something more satisfactory might be learned concerning the trade both of the republic and the family of Medici; but I could not find any of these books either in Edinburgh or in London.

Note XLVII. Sect. III. p. 128.

Leibnitz has preserved a curious paper, containing the instructions of the republic of Florence to the two ambassadors sent to the Soldan of Egypt, in order to negociate this treaty with him, together with the report of these ambassadors on their return. The great object of the republic was to obtain liberty of trading in all parts of the Soldan's dominions, upon the same terms with the Venetians. The chief privileges which they solicited were, 1. A perfect freedom of admission into every port belonging to the Soldan, protection while they continued in it, and liberty of departure at what time they chose. 2. Permission to have a consul, with the same rights and jurisdiction as those of the Venetians; and liberty to build a church, a warehouse, and a bath, in every place where they settled. 3. That they should not pay for goods imported or exported higher duties than were paid by the Venetians. 4. That the effects of any Florentine who died in the dominions of the Soldan should be consigned to the consul. 5. That the gold and silver coin of Florence should be received in payments. All these privileges (which shew on what equal and liberal terms Christians and Mahomedans now carried on trade) the Florentines obtained; but from the causes mentioned in the text, they seem never to have acquired any considerable share in the commerce with India; Leibnitz, Mantissa Cod. Jur. Gent. Diplom. Pars altera, p. 163.

Note XLVIII. Sect. III. p. 133.

The eastern parts of Asia are now so completely explored, that the first imperfect accounts of them, by Marco Polo, attract little of that attention which was originally excited by the publication of his travels; and some circumstances in his narrative have induced different authors to justify this neglect, by calling in question the truth of what he relates, and even to assert that he had never visited those countries which he pretends to describe. He does not, say they, ascertain the position of any one place by specifying its longitude or latitude. He gives names to provinces and cities, particularly in his description of Cathay, which have no resemblance to those which they now bear. We may observe, however, that as Marco Polo seems to have been, in no degree, a man of science, it was not to be expected that he should fix the position of places with geographical accuracy. As he travelled through China, either in the suite of the great Khan, or in execution of his orders, it is probable that the names which he gives *to* different provinces and cities, are those by which they were known to the Tartars in whose service he was, not their original Chinese names. Some inaccuracies which have been observed in the relation of his travels may be accounted for, by attending to one circumstance, that it was not published from a regular journal, which, perhaps, the vicissitudes in his situation, during such a long series of adventures, did not permit him to keep, or to preserve. It was composed after his return to his native country, and chiefly from recollection. But notwithstanding this disadvantage, his account of those regions of the East, towards which my inquiries have been directed, contains information with respect to several particulars altogether unknown in Europe at that time, the accuracy of which is now fully confirmed. Mr Marsden, whose accuracy and discernment are well known, traces his description of the island which he calls Java Minor, evidently Sumatra; from which it is apparent, that as Marco Polo had resided a considerable time in that island, he had examined some parts with care, and had inquired with diligence concerning others; Hist. of Sumatra, p. 281. I shall mention some other particulars with respect to India, which, though they relate to matters of no great consequence, afford the best proof of his having visited these countries, and of his having observed the manners and customs of the people with attention. He gives a distinct account of the nature and preparation of Sago, the principal article of subsistence among all the nations of Malayan race, and he brought the first specimen of this singular production to Venice; Ramus. lib. iii. c. 16. He takes notice, likewise, of the general custom of chewing Betel, and his description of the mode of preparing it is the same with that still in use; Ramus. Viaggi, i. p. 55. D. p. 56. B. He even descends into such detail as to mention the peculiar manner of feeding horses in India, which still continues; Ramus. p. 53. F. What is of greater importance, we learn from him that the trade with Alexandria continued, when he travelled through India, to be carried on in the same manner as I conjectured it to have been in ancient times. The commodities of the East were still brought to the Malabar coast by vessels of the country, and conveyed thence, together with pepper and other productions peculiar to that part of India, by ships which arrived from the Red Sea; Lib. iii. c. 27. This, perhaps, may account for the superior quality which Sanudo ascribes to the goods brought to the coast of Syria from the Persian Gulf, above those imported into Egypt by the Red Sea. The former were chosen and purchased in the places where they grew or where they were manufactured, by the merchants of Persia, who still continued their voyages to every part of the East; while the Egyptian merchants, in making up their cargoes, depended upon the assortment of goods brought to the Malabar coast by the natives. To some persons in his own age, what Marco Polo related concerning the numerous armies and immense revenues of the Eastern Princes, appeared so extravagant, (though perfectly consonant to what we now know concerning the population of China, and the wealth of Indostan), that they gave him the name of *Messer Marco Milioni;* Prefat. de Ramus. p. 4. But among persons better informed, the reception he met with was very different. Columbus, as well as the men of science with whom he corresponded, placed such confidence in the veracity of his relations, that upon them the speculations and theories which led to the discovery of the New World, were in a great measure founded; Life of Columbus by his Son, c. 7, 8.

Note XLIX. Sect. III. p. 140.

In the year 1301, Joanna of Navarre, the wife of Philip le Bel King of France, having been some days in Bruges, was so much struck with the grandeur and wealth of that city, and particularly with the splendid appearance of the citizens' wives, that she was moved (says Guicciardini) by female envy to exclaim with indignation, " I thought that I had been the only Queen here, but I find there are many hundreds more;" Descrit. de Paesi Bassi, p. 408.

Note L. Sect. III. p. 141.

In the History of the reign of Charles V. vol. i. p. 162, I observe, that, during the war excited by the famous League of Cambray, while Charles VIII. of France could not procure money at a less premium than forty-two per cent. the Venetians raised what sums they pleased at five per cent. But this, I imagine, is not to be considered as the usual commercial rate of interest at that period, but as a voluntary and public-spirited effort of the citizens, in order to support their country at a dangerous crisis. Of such laudable exertions, there are several striking instances in the history of the republic. In the year 1379, when the Genoese, after obtaining a great naval victory over the Venetians, were ready to attack their capital, the citizens, by a voluntary contribution, enabled the senate to fit out such a powerful armament as saved their country; Sabellicus, Hist. Rer. Venet. dec. ii. lib. vi. p. 385. 390. In the war with Ferrara, which began in the year 1472, the senate, relying upon the attachment of the citizens to their country, required them to bring all their gold and silver plate, and jewels, into the public treasury, upon promise of paying the value of them at the conclusion of the war, with five per cent. of interest; and this requisition was complied with cheerfully; Petr. Cyrnæus de Bello Ferrar. ap. Murat. Script. Rer. Ital. vol. xxi. p. 1016.

Note LI. Sect. III. p. 142.

Two facts may be mentioned as proofs of an extraordinary extension of the Venetian trade at this period:—
1. There is in Rymer's Great Collection, a series of

grants from the Kings of England, of various privileges and immunities to Venetian merchants trading in England, as well as several commercial treaties with the republic, which plainly indicate a considerable increase of their transactions in that country. These are mentioned in their order by Mr Anderson, to whose patient industry and sound understanding every person engaged in any commercial research must have felt himself greatly indebted on many occasions.——2. The establishment of a Bank by public authority, the credit of which was founded on that of the State. In an age and nation so well acquainted with the advantages which commerce derives from the institution of banks, it is unnecessary to enumerate them. Mercantile transactions must have been numerous and extensive before the utility of such an institution could be fully perceived, or the principles of trade could be so fully understood as to form the regulations proper for conducting it with success. Venice may boast of having given the first example to Europe, of an establishment altogether unknown to the ancients, and which is the pride of the modern commercial system. The constitution of the Bank of Venice was originally founded on such just principles, that it has served as a model in the establishment of banks in other countries, and the administration of its affairs has been conducted with so much integrity, that its credit has never been shaken. I cannot specify the precise year in which the Bank of Venice was established by a law of the State. Anderson supposes it to have been A. D. 1157; Chron. Deduct. vol. i. p. 84. Sandi Stor. Civil. Venes. Part II. vol. ii. p. 768. Part. III. vol. ii. p. 892.

Note LII. Sect. III. p. 143.

An Italian author of good credit, and a diligent inquirer into the ancient history of its different governments, affirms, that if the several States which traded in the Mediterranean had united together, Venice alone would have been superior to them all, in naval power and in extent of commerce; Denina, Revolutions d'Italie traduits par l'Abbe Jardin, lib. xviii. c. 6. tom. vi. p. 339. About the year 1420, the Doge Mocenigo gives a view of the naval force of the republic, which confirms this decision of Denina. At that time it consisted of three thousand trading vessels, of various dimensions, on board which were employed seventeen thousand sailors; of three hundred ships of greater force, manned by eight thousand sailors; and of forty-five large galeasses, or carracks, navigated by eleven thousand sailors. In public and private arsenals sixteen thousand carpenters were employed; Mar. Sanuto Vite de Duchi di Venezia, ap. Mur. Script. Rer. Ital. vol. xxii. p. 959.

Note LIII. Sect. III. p. 160.

When we take a view of the form and position of the habitable parts of Asia and Africa, we will see good reasons for considering the camel as the most useful of all the animals over which the inhabitants of these great continents have acquired dominion. In both, some of the most fertile districts are separated from each other by such extensive tracts of barren sands, the seats of desolation and drought, as seem to exclude the possibility of communication between them. But as the ocean, which appears, at first view, to be placed as an insuperable barrier between different regions of the earth, has been rendered, by navigation, subservient to their mutual intercourse, so by means of the camel, which the Arabians emphatically call *The ship of the Desert*, the most dreary wastes are traversed, and the nations which they disjoin are enabled to trade with one another. Those painful journeys, impracticable by any other animal, the camel performs with astonishing despatch. Under heavy burdens of six, seven, and eight hundred weight, they can continue their march during a long period of time, with little food or rest, and sometimes without tasting water for eight or nine days. By the wise economy of Providence, the camel seems formed of purpose to be the beast of burden in those regions where he is placed, and where his service is most wanted. In all the districts of Asia and Africa, where deserts are most frequent and extensive, the camel abounds. This is his proper station, and beyond this the sphere of his activity does not extend far. He dreads alike the accesses of heat and of cold, and does not agree even with the mild climate of our temperate zone. As the first trade in Indian commodities, of which we have any authentic account, was carried on by means of camels, Genesis xxxvii. 25. and as it is by employing them that the conveyance of these commodities has been so widely extended over Asia and Africa, the particulars which I have mentioned concerning this singular animal appeared to be necessary towards illustrating this part of my subject. If any of my readers desire more full information, and wish to know how the ingenuity and art of man have seconded the intentions of Nature, in training the camel from his birth for that life of exertion and hardship to which he is destined, he may consult Histoire Naturelle, by M. le Comte de Buffon, artic. *Chameau et Dromedaire*, one of the most eloquent, and, as far as I can judge from examining the authorities which he has quoted, one of the most accurate descriptions given by that celebrated writer. M. Volney, whose accuracy is well known, gives a description of the manner in which the camel performs its journey, which may be agreeable to some of my readers. "In travelling through the desert, camels are chiefly employed because they consume little, and carry a great load. His ordinary burden is about seven hundred and fifty pounds; his food, whatever is given him, straw, thistles, the stones of dates, beans, barley, &c. With a pound of food a-day, and as much water, he will travel for weeks. In the journey from Cairo to Suez, which is forty or forty-six hours, they neither eat nor drink; but these long fasts, if often repeated, wear them out. Their usual rate of travelling is very slow, hardly above two miles an hour; it is vain to push them,— they will not quicken their pace; but, if allowed some short rest, they will travel fifteen or eighteen hours a-day;" Voyage, tom. ii. p. 383.

Note LIV. Sect. III. p. 162.

In order to give an adequate idea of the extensive circulation of Indian commodities by land-carriage, it would be necessary to trace the route, and to estimate the number of the various caravans by which they are conveyed. Could this be executed with accuracy, it would be a curious subject of geographical research, as well as a valuable addition to commercial history. Though it is inconsistent with the brevity which I have uniformly studied in conducting this Disquisition, to enter into a detail of so great length, it may be proper here, for illustrating this part of my subject, to take such a view of two caravans which visit Mecca, as may enable my readers to estimate more justly the magnitude of their commercial transactions. The first is the caravan which takes its departure from Cairo in Egypt, and the other from Damascus in Syria; and I select these, both because they are the most considerable, and because they are described by authors of undoubted credit, who had the best opportunities of receiving full information concerning them. The former is composed not only of pilgrims from every part of Egypt, but of those which arrive from all the small Mahomedan states on the African coast of the Mediterranean, from the empire of Morocco, and even from the Negro kingdoms on the Atlantic. When assembled, the caravan consists at least of fifty thousand persons, and the number of camels employed in carrying water, provisions, and merchandise, is still greater. The journey, which, in going from Cairo and returning thither, is not completed in less than a hundred days, is performed wholly by land; and as the route lies mostly through sandy deserts, or barren uninhabited wilds, which seldom afford any subsistence, and where often no sources of water can be found, the pilgrims always undergo much fatigue, and sometimes must endure incredible hardships. An early and good description of this caravan is published by Hakluyt, vol. ii. p. 202, &c. Maillet has entered into a minute and curious detail with regard to it; Descript. de l'Egypte, part ii. p. 212, &c. Pococke has given a route, together with the length of each day's march, which he received from a person who had been fourteen times at Mecca, vol. i. p. 188. 261, &c.—The caravan from Damascus, composed of pilgrims from almost every province of the Turkish empire, is little inferior to the former in number, and the commerce which it carries on is hardly less valuable; Voyage de Volney, tom. ii. p. 251, &c. Ohsson, Tabl. Gener. de l'Empire Othom. iii. p. 275, &c. This pilgrimage was performed in the year 1741, by Khojeh Abdulkurreem, whom I formerly mentioned, Note V. p. 296. He gives the usual route from Damascus to Mecca, computed by hours, the common mode of reckoning a journey in the East, through countries little frequented. According to the most moderate estimate, the distance between the two cities, by his account, must be above a thousand miles; a great part of the journey is through a desert, and the pilgrims not only endure much fatigue, but are often exposed to great danger from the wild Arabs; Memoirs, p. 114, &c. It is a singular proof of the predatory spirit of the Arabs, that although all their independent tribes are zealous Mahomedans, yet they make no scruple of plundering the caravans of pilgrims while engaged in performing one of the most indispensable duties of their religion. A remarkable instance of this occurred in the year 1757; Travels through Cyprus, Syria, &c. by Abbé Mariti, vol. ii. p. 117, &c. Engl. Translation. Great as these caravans are, we must not suppose that all the pilgrims who visit Mecca belong to them; such considerable additions are received from the extensive dominions of Persia, from every province of Indostan, and the countries to the east of it, from Abyssinia, from various states on the southern coast of Africa, and from all parts of Arabia, that when the whole are assembled they have been computed to amount to two hundred thousand. In some years the number is farther increased by small bands of pilgrims from several interior provinces of Africa, the names and situations of which are just beginning to be known in Europe. For this last fact we are indebted to the Association for promoting the Discovery of the Interior Parts of Africa, formed by some British Gentlemen, upon principles so liberal, and with views so public-spirited, as do honour to themselves and to their country; Proceedings, &c. p. 174.

In the Report of the Committee of the Privy-Council on the Slave Trade, other particulars are contained; and it appears that the commerce carried on by caravans in the interior parts of Africa is not only widely extended, but of considerable value. Besides the great caravan which proceeds to Cairo, and is joined by Mahomedan pilgrims from every part of Africa, there are caravans which have no object but commerce, which set out from Fez, Algiers, Tunis, Tripoli, and other states on the sea-coast, and penetrate far into the interior country. Some of them take no less than fifty days to reach the place of their destination; and, as the medium of their rate of travelling may be estimated at about eighteen miles a-day, the extent of their journey may be easily computed. As both the time of their outset, and their route, are known, they are met by the people of all the countries through which they travel, who trade with them. Indian goods of every kind form a considerable article in this traffic, in exchange for which the chief commodity they can give is slaves. Part vi.

As the journeys of the caravans, which are purely commercial, do not commence at stated seasons, and their routes vary according to the convenience or fancy of the merchants of whom they are composed, a description cannot be given of them with the same degree of accuracy as of the great caravans which visit Mecca. But by attending to the accounts of some authors, and the occasional hints of others, sufficient information may be gathered to satisfy us, that the circulation of eastern goods by these caravans is very extensive. The same intercourse which was anciently kept up by the provinces in the north-east of Asia with Indostan and China, and which I formerly described, still subsists. Among all the numerous tribes of Tartars, even of those which retain their pastoral manners in greatest purity, the demand for the productions of these two countries is very considerable; Voyages de Pallas, tom. i. p. 357. &c. tom. ii. p. 422. In order to supply them with these, caravans set out annually from Boghar, (Hakluyt, vol. i. p. 332.) Samarcand, Thibet, and several other places, and return with large cargoes of Indian and Chinese goods. But the trade carried on between Russia and China in this part of Asia is by far the most extensive and best known. Some connexion of this kind, it is probable, was kept up between them from the earliest period, but it increased greatly after the interior parts of Russia were rendered more accessible by the conquests of Zingis Khan and Tamerlane. The commercial nations of Europe were so well acquainted with the mode of carrying on this trade, that soon after the Portuguese had opened the communication with the East by the Cape of Good Hope, an attempt was made, in order to diminish the advantages which they derived from this discovery, to prevail on the Russians to convey Indian and Chinese commodities through the whole extent of their empire, partly by land-carriage and partly by means of navigable rivers, to some port on the Baltic, from which they might be distributed through every part of Europe; Ramusio, Raccolto da Viaggi, vol. i. p. 374. B. Hist. du Commerce de la Russie, par M. Schreder, tom. i. p. 13, 14. This scheme, too great for the monarch then on the throne of Russia to carry into execution, was rendered practicable by the conquests of Ivan Basilowitz, and the genius of Peter the Great. Though the capitals of the two empires were situated at the immense distance of six thousand three hundred and seventy-eight miles from each other, and the route lay for above four hundred miles through an uninhabited desert, (Bell's Travels, vol. ii. p. 167.) caravans travelled from the one to the other. But though it had been stipulated, when this intercourse was established, that the number of persons in each caravan should not exceed two hundred, and though they were shut up within the walls of a Caravanserai during the short time they were suffered to remain in Pekin, and were allowed to deal only with a few merchants, to whom a monopoly of the trade with them had been granted; yet, notwithstanding all these restraints and precautions, the jealous vigilance with which the Chinese government excludes foreigners from a free intercourse with its subjects, was alarmed, and the admission of the Russian caravans into the empire was soon prohibited. After various negociations an expedient was at length devised, by which the advantages of mutual commerce were secured, without infringing the cautious arrangements of Chinese policy. On the boundary of the two empires, two small towns were built almost contiguous, Kiachta inhabited by Russians, and Maimatschin by Chinese. To these all the marketable productions of their respective countries are brought by the subjects of each empire; and the furs, the linen and woollen cloth, the leather, the glass, &c. of Russia, are exchanged for the silk, the cotton, the tea, the rice, the toys, &c. of China. By some well-judged concessions of the sovereign now seated on the throne of Russia, whose enlarged mind is superior to the illiberal maxims of many of her predecessors, this trade is rendered so flourishing, that its amount annually is not less than eight hundred thousand pounds sterling, and it is the only trade which China carries on almost entirely by barter. Mr Coxe, in his account of the Russian discoveries, has collected, with his usual attention and discernment, every thing relative to this branch of trade, the nature and extent of which were little known in Europe; Part ii. chap. ii. iii. iv. Nor is Kiachta the only place where Russia receives Chinese and Indian commodities. A considerable supply of both is brought by caravans of independent Tartars to Orenburg, on the river Jaik, (Voyage de Pallas, tom. i. p. 355, &c.) to Troitzkaia, on the river Oui, and to other places which I might mention. I have entered into this long detail concerning the mode in which the productions in India and China are circulated through Russia, as it affords the most striking instance I know, of the great extent to which valuable commodities may be conveyed by land-carriage.

Note LV. Sect. IV. p. 166.

The only voyage of discovery in the Atlantic Ocean towards the south, by any of the ancient commercial states in the Mediterranean, is that of Hanno, undertaken by order of the republic of Carthage. As the situation of that city, so much nearer the Straits than Tyre, Alexandria, and the other seats of ancient trade which have been mentioned, gave it more immediate access to the ocean; that circumstance, together with the various settlements which the Carthaginians had made in different provinces of Spain, naturally suggested to them this enterprise, and afforded them the prospect of considerable advantages from its success. The voyage of Hanno, instead of invalidating, seems to confirm the justness of the reasons which have been given, why no similar attempt was made by the other commercial states in the Mediterranean.

Note LVI. Sect. IV. p. 167.

Though the intelligent authors whom I have quoted considered this voyage of the Phœnicians as fabulous, Herodotus mentions a circumstance concerning it which seems to prove that it had really been performed. "The Phœnicians," says he, "affirmed that, in sailing round Africa, they had the sun on their right hand, which to me appears not to be credible, though it may be deemed so by others;" Lib. iv. c. 42. This, it is certain, must have happened, if they really accomplished such a voyage. The science of astronomy, however, was in that early period so imperfect, that it was by expérience only that the Phœnicians could come at the knowledge of this fact; they durst not, without this, have ventured to assert what would have appeared to be an improbable fiction. Even after what they related, Herodotus disbelieved it.

Note LVII. Sect. IV. p. 176.

NOTWITHSTANDING this increasing demand for the productions of India, it is remarkable, that during the sixteenth century some commodities which are now the chief articles of importation from the East, were either altogether unknown, or of little account. Tea, the importation of which, at present, far exceeds that of any other production of the East, has not been in general use in any country of Europe a full century; and yet, during that short period, from some singular caprice of taste, or power of fashion, the infusion of a leaf brought from the farthest extremity of the earth, of which it is perhaps the highest praise to say that it is innoxious, has become almost a necessary of life in several parts of Europe, and the passion for it descends from the most elevated to the lowest orders in society. In 1785 it was computed, that the whole quantity of tea imported into Europe from China was about nineteen millions of pounds, of which it is conjectured that twelve millions were consumed in Great Britain and the dominions depending upon it; Dodsley's Annual Register for 1784 and 1785, page 156. In 1789 twenty-one millions of pounds were imported. The porcelain of China, now as common in many parts of Europe as if it were of domestic manufacture, was not known to the ancients. Marco Polo is the first among the moderns who mentions it. The Portuguese began to import it not long after their first voyage to China, A. D. 1517; but it was a considerable time before the use of it became extensive.

Note LVIII. p. 200.

According to all the writers of antiquity, the Indians are said to be divided into seven tribes or casts; Strabo, lib. xv. p. 1029. C. &c. Diod. Sicul. lib. ii. p. 153, &c. Arrian, Indic. c. 10. They were led into this error, it is probable, by considering some of the subdivisions of the casts, as if they had been a distinct independent order. But that there were no more than four original casts, we learn from the concurring testimony of the best informed modern travellers. A most distinct account of these we have in "La Porte Ouverte, ou la vraie Representation de la Vie, des Mœurs, de la Religion, et du Service des Brahmines, qui demeurent sur les Costes de Choromandel," &c. This was compiled before the middle of last century, by Abraham Roger, chaplain of the Dutch factory at Pullicate. By gaining the confidence of an intelligent Brahmin, he acquired information concerning the manners and religion of the Indians, more authentic and extensive than was known to Europeans prior to the late translations from the Sanscreet language. I mention this book, because it seems to be less known than it deserves to be. There remains now no doubt with respect either to the number or the functions of the casts, as both are ascertained from the most ancient and sacred books of the Hindoos, and confirmed by the accounts of their own institutions, given by Brahmins eminent for their learning. According to them, the different casts proceeded from Brahma, the immediate agent of the creation under the Supreme Power, in the following manner, which establishes both the rank which they were to hold, and the office which they were required to perform.

The *Brahmin*, from the mouth (wisdom): To pray, to read, to instruct.

The *Chehetree*, from the arms (strength): To draw the bow, to fight, to govern.

The *Bice*, from the belly or thighs (nourishment): To provide the necessaries of life by agriculture and traffic.

The *Sooder*, from the feet (subjection): To labour, to serve.

THE prescribed occupations of all these classes are essential in a well regulated state. Subordinate to them is a fifth, or adventitious class, denominated *Burrun Sunkur*, supposed to be the offspring of an unlawful union between persons of different casts. These are mostly dealers in petty articles of retail trade; Preface to the Code of Gentoo Laws, p. xlvi. and xcix. This adventitious class is not mentioned, as far as I know, by any European author. The distinction was too nice to be observed by them, and they seem to consider the members of this cast as belonging to the Sooder. Besides these acknowledged casts, there is a race of unhappy men, denominated, on the Coromandel coast, *Pariars*, and in other parts of India, *Chandalas*. These are outcasts from their original order, who by their misconduct have forfeited all the privileges of it. Their condition is, undoubtedly, the lowest degradation of human nature.

No person of any cast will have the least communication with them; Sonnerat, tom. i. p. 55, 56. If a Pariar approach a *Nayr*, *i. e.* a warrior of high cast, on the Malabar coast, he may put him to death with impunity. Water or milk are considered as defiled even by their shadow passing over them, and cannot be used until they are purified; Ayeen Akbery, vol. iii. p. 243. It is almost impossible for words to express the sensation of vileness that the name of Pariar or Chándala conveys to the mind of a Hindoo. Every Hindoo who violates the rules or institutions of his cast, sinks into this degraded situation. This it is which renders Hindoos so resolute in adhering to the institutions of their tribe, because the loss of cast is, to them, the loss of all human comfort and respectability; and is a punishment, beyond comparison, more severe than excommunication in the most triumphant period of papal power.

THE four original casts are named, and their functions described in the Máhabarat, the most ancient book of the Hindoos, and of higher authority than any with which Europeans are hitherto acquainted; Baghvat-Geeta, p. 130. The same distinction of casts was known to the author of Heeto-pades, another work of considerable antiquity, translated from the Sanskreet, p. 251.

THE mention of one circumstance respecting the distinction of casts has been omitted in the text. Though the line of separation be so drawn, as to render the ascent from an inferior to a higher cast absolutely impossible, and it would be regarded as a most enormous impiety if one in a lower order should presume to perform any function belonging to those of a superior cast; yet in certain cases, the Pundits declare it to be lawful for persons of a high class to exercise some of the occupations allotted to a class below their own, without losing their cast by doing so; Pref. of Pundits to the Code of Gentoo Laws, p. 100. Accordingly we find Brahmins employed in the service of their Princes, not only as ministers of state, Orme's Fragments, p. 207. but in subordinate stations. Most of the officers of high rank in the army of Sevagi, the founder of the Mahratta state, were Brahmins; and some of them Pundits or learned Brahmins; Ibid. p. 97. Hurry Punt and Purseram Bhow, who commanded the Mahratta forces, which acted in conjunction with the army of Lord Cornwallis against Tippoo Saib, were Brahmins. Many Sepoys in the service of the East-India Company, particularly in the Bengal presidency, are of the Brahmin cast.

ANOTHER fact concerning the casts deserves notice. An immense number of pilgrims, amounting in some years to more than 150,000, visit the Pagoda of Jaggernaut in Orissa, (one of the most ancient and most revered places of Hindoo worship), at the time of the annual festival in honour of the deity to whom the temple is consecrated. The members of all the four casts are allowed promiscuously to approach the altar of the idol, and seating themselves without distinction, eat indiscriminately of the same food. This seems to indicate some remembrance of a state prior to the institutions of casts, when all men were considered as equal. I have not such information as enables me to account for a practice so repugnant to the first ideas and principles of the Hindoos, either sacred or civil; Bernier, tom. ii. p. 102. Tavernier, book ii. c. 9. Anquetil, Disc. Prelim. p. 81. Sketches, p. 96.

SOME of my readers must have observed, that I have not mentioned the numerous orders of Indian devotees, to all of whom European writers gave the appellation of *Faquirs;* a name by which the Mahomedans distinguish fanatical monks of their own religion. The light in which I have viewed the religious institutions of the Hindoos, did not render it necessary that I should consider the Indian Faquirs particularly. Their number, the rigour of their mortifications, the excruciating penances which they voluntarily undergo, and the high opinion which the people entertain of their sanctity, have struck all travellers who had visited India, and their descriptions of them are well known. The powerful influence of enthusiasm, the love of distinction, and the desire of obtaining some portion of that reverence and those honours which the Brahmins are born to enjoy, may account for all the extraordinary things which they do and suffer. One particular concerning them merits notice. This order of devotees appears to have been very ancient in India. The description of the *Germani*, which Strabo takes from Megasthenes, applies almost in every circumstance to the modern Faquirs; Lib. xv. p. 1040. B.

Note LIX. p. 202.

WHAT I have asserted in the text is in general well-founded. It is the opinion, however, of gentlemen who have seen much of India, and who observed all they saw with a discerning eye, that the conquests both of the Mahomedans and of the Europeans have had some effect upon the manners and customs of the natives. They imagine that the dress which the Hindoos now wear, the turban, the jummah, and long drawers, is an imitation of that worn by their Mahomedan conquerors. The ancient dress of the Indians, as described by Arrian, Hist. Indic. c. 16. was a muslin cloth thrown loosely about their shoulders, a muslin shirt reaching to the middle of the leg, and their beards were dyed various colours; which is not the same with that used at present.

The custom of secluding women, and the strictness with which they are confined, is likewise supposed to have been introduced by the Mahomedans. This supposition is in some measure confirmed by the drama of Sacontala, translated from the Sanskreet. In that play several female characters are introduced, who mingle in society, and converse as freely with men, as women are accustomed to do in Europe. The author, we may presume, describes the manners, and adheres to the customs of his own age. But while I mention this remark, it is proper likewise to observe, that from a passage in Strabo there is reason to think, that in the age of Alexander the Great women in India were guarded with the same jealous attention as at present. "When their Princes" (says he, copying Megasthenes), "set out upon a *public hunt*, they are accompanied by a number of their women, but along the road in which they travel ropes are stretched on each side, and if any man approach near to them, he is instantly put to death;" Lib. xv. p. 1037. A. In some parts of India, where the original manners of the people may be supposed to subsist in greatest purity, particularly in the high country towards the sources of the Indus, women of rank reside in private apartments, secluded from society; Forster's Travels, vol. i. p. 228. Women even of the Brahmin cast appear in the streets without a veil; and it is only, as I am informed, in the houses of persons of high rank or great opulence, that a distinct quarter or haram is allotted to the women. The influence of European manners begins to be apparent among the Hindoos who reside in the town of Calcutta. Some of them drive about in English chariots, sit upon chairs, and furnish their houses with mirrors. Many circumstances might be mentioned, were this the proper place, which, it is probable, will contribute to the progress of this spirit of imitation.

Note LX. p. 203.

It is amusing to observe how exactly the ideas of an intelligent Asiatic coincide with those of the Europeans on this subject. "In reflecting," says he, "upon the poverty of Turan (the countries beyond the Oxus) and Arabia, I was at first at a loss to assign a reason why these countries have never been able to retain wealth, whilst, on the contrary, it is daily increasing in Indostan. Timour carried into Turan the riches of Turkey, Persia, and Indostan, but they are all dissipated; and, during the reigns of the four first Caliphs, Turkey, Persia, part of Arabia, Ethiopia, Egypt, and Spain, were their tributaries; but still they were not rich. It is evident, then, that this dissipation of the riches of a state, must have happened either from extraordinary drains, or from some defect in the government. Indostan has been frequently plundered by foreign invaders, and not one of its Kings ever gained for it any acquisition of wealth; neither has the country many mines of gold and silver, and yet Indostan abounds in money and every other kind of wealth. The abundance of specie is undoubtedly owing to the large importation of gold and silver in the ships of Europe, and other nations, many of whom bring ready money in exchange for the manufactures and natural productions of the country. If this is not the cause of the prosperous state of Indostan, it must be owing to the peculiar blessing of God;" Memoirs of Kojeh Abdulkureem, a Cashmerian of distinction, p. 42.

Note LXI. p. 209.

That the monarchs of India were the sole proprietors of land, is asserted in most explicit terms by the ancients.

The people (say they) pay a land-tax to their Kings, because the whole kingdom is regal property; Strabo, lib. xv. p. 1030. A. Diod. Sicul. lib. ii. p. 153. This was not peculiar to India. In all the great monarchies of the East, the sole property of land seems to be vested in the sovereign as lord paramount. According to Chardin, this is the state of property in Persia, and lands were let by the monarch to the farmers who cultivated them, on conditions nearly resembling those granted to the Indian Ryots; Voyages, tom. iii. p. 339. &c. 4to. M. Volney gives a similar account of the tenure by which lands are held in one of the great provinces of the Turkish empire; Voyage en Syrie, &c. tom. ii. p. 369, &c. The precise mode, however, *in* which the Ryots of Indostan held their possessions, is a circumstance in its ancient political constitution, with respect to which gentlemen of superior discernment, who have resided long in the country, and filled some of the highest stations in government, have formed very different opinions. Some have imagined that grants of land were made by the sovereign to villages or small communities, the inhabitants of which, under the direction of their own chiefs or heads-men, laboured it in common, and divided the produce of it among them in certain proportions; Descript. de l'Ind. par M. Bernouilli, tom. ii. 223, &c. Others maintain, that the property of land has been transferred from the crown to hereditary officers of great eminence and power, denominated *Zemindars*, who collect the rents from the Ryots, and parcel out the lands among them. Others contend, that the office of the Zemindars is temporary and ministerial, that they are merely collectors of revenue, removeable at pleasure, and the tenure by which the Ryots hold their possessions is derived immediately from the sovereign. This last opinion is supported with great ability by Mr Grant, in an Inquiry into the nature of Zemindary Tenures in the landed property of Bengal, &c. This question still continues to be agitated in Bengal, and such plausible arguments have been produced in support of the different opinions, that although it be a point extremely interesting, as the future system of British finance in India appears likely to hinge, in an essential degree, upon it, persons well acquainted with the state of India have not been able to form a final and satisfactory opinion on this subject; Captain Kirkpatrick's Introd. to the Institutes of Ghazan Khan, New Asiatic Miscel. N0. II. p. 130. Though the sentiments of the Committee of Revenue, composed of persons eminent for their abilities, lean to a conclusion against the hereditary right of the Zemindars in the soil, yet the Supreme Council, in the year 1786, declined, for good reasons, to give any decisive judgment on a subject of such magnitude.—This note was sent to the press before I had it in my power to peruse Mr Rouse's ingenious and instructive dissertation concerning the landed property of Bengal. In it he adopts an opinion contrary to that of Mr Grant, and maintains, with that candour and liberality of sentiment which are always conspicuous where there is no other object in view but the discovery of truth, that the Zemindars of Bengal possessed their landed property by hereditary right. Were I possessed of such knowledge, either of the state of India, or of the system of administration established there, as would be requisite for comparing these different theories, and determining which of them merits the preference, the subject of my researches does not render it necessary to enter into such a disquisition. I imagine, however, that the state of landed property in India might be greatly illustrated by an accurate comparison of it with the nature of feudal tenures; and I apprehend that there might be traced there a succession of changes, taking place in much the same order as has been observed in Europe, from which it might appear;

that the possession of land was granted at first during pleasure, afterwards for life, and at length became perpetual and hereditary property. But even under this last form, when land is acquired either by purchase or inheritance, the manner in which the right of property is confirmed and rendered complete, in Europe by a Charter, in India by a *Sunnud* from the sovereign, seems to point out what was its original state. According to each of the theories which I have mentioned, the tenure and condition of the Ryots nearly resemble the description which I have given of them. Their state, we learn from the accounts of intelligent observers, is as happy and independent as falls to the lot of any race of men employed in the cultivation of the earth. The ancient Greek and Roman writers, whose acquaintance with the interior parts of India was very imperfect, represent the fourth part of the annual produce of land as the general average of rent paid to the sovereign. Upon the authority of a popular author who flourished in India prior to the Christian era, we may conclude that the sixth part of the people's income was, in his time, the usual portion of the sovereign; Sacontala, Act v. p. 53. It is now known, that what the sovereign receives from land varies greatly in different parts of the country, and is regulated by the fertility or barrenness of the soil, the nature of the climate, the abundance or scarcity of water, and many other obvious circumstances. By the account given of it, I should imagine that, in some districts, it has been raised beyond its due proportion. One circumstance with respect to the administration of revenue in Bengal merits notice, as it redounds to the honour of the Emperor Akber, the wisdom of whose government I have often had occasion to celebrate. A general and regular assessment of revenue in Bengal was formed in his reign. All the lands were then valued, and the rent of each inhabitant and of each village ascertained. A regular gradation of accounts was established. The rents of the different inhabitants who lived in one neighbourhood being collected together, formed the account of a village; the rents of several villages being next collected into one view, formed the accounts of a larger portion of land: The aggregate of these accounts exhibited the rent of a district; and the sum total of the rents of all the districts in Bengal, formed the account of the revenue of the whole province. From the reign of Akber to the government of Jaffeer Ali Cawn, A. D. 1757, the annual amount of revenue, and the modes of levying it, continued with little variation. But in order to raise the sum which he had stipulated to pay the English on his elevation, he departed from the wise arrangements of Akber; many new modes of assessment were introduced, and exactions multiplied.

Note LXII. p. 211.

I shall mention only one instance of their attention to this useful regulation of police. Lahore, in the Panjab, is distant from Agra, the ancient capital of Indostan, five hundred miles. Along each side of the road between these two great cities, there is planted a continued row of shady trees, forming an avenue, to which (whether we consider its extent, its beauty, or utility in a hot climate,) there is nothing similar in any country; Rennell's Memoir, p. 69.

Note LXIII. p. 215.

We cannot place the equitable and mild government of Akber in a point of view more advantageous, than by contrasting it with the conduct of other Mahomedan princes. In no country did this contrast ever appear more striking than in India. In the thousandth year of the Christian era, Mahmud of Ghazna, to whose dominion were subjected the same countries which formed the ancient kingdom of Bactria, invaded Indostan. Every step of his progress in it was marked with blood and desolation. The most celebrated Pagodas, the ancient monuments of Hindoo devotion and magnificence, were destroyed, the ministers of religion were massacred, and with undistinguishing ferocity the country was laid waste, and the cities were plundered and burnt. About four hundred years after Mahmud, Timur, or Tamerlane, a conqueror of higher fame, turned his irresistible arms against Indostan; and though born in an age more improved, he not only equalled, but often so far surpassed the cruel deeds of Mahmud, as to be justly branded with the odious name of the " Destroying Prince," which was given to him by the Hindoos, the undeserving victims of his rage. A rapid but striking description of their devastations may be found in Mr Orme's Dissertation on the Establishments made by the Mahomedan conquerors in Indostan. A more full account of them is given by Mr Gibbon, vol. v. p. 646. vol. vi. p. 389, &c. The arrogant contempt with which bigotted Mahomedans view all the nations who have not embraced the religion of the Prophet, will account for the unrelenting rigour of Mahmud and Timur towards the Hindoos, and greatly enhances the merit of the tolerant spirit and moderation with which Akber governed his subjects. What impression the mild administration of Akber made upon the Hindoos, we learn from a beautiful letter of Jesswant Sing, Rajah of Joudpore, to Aurengzebe, his fanatical and persecuting successor. " Your royal ancestor, Akber, whose throne is now in heaven, conducted the affairs of this empire in equity and firm security for the space of fifty-two years, preserving every tribe of men in ease and happiness; whether they were followers of Jesus or of Moses, of David or of Mahomed; were they Brahmins; were they of the sect of Dharians, which denies the eternity of matter, or of that which ascribes the existence of the world to chance,—they all equally enjoyed his countenance and favour; insomuch that his people, in gratitude for the indiscriminate protection which he afforded them, distinguished him by the appellation of *Juggot Grow*, Guardian of Mankind.—If your Majesty places any faith in any of those books, by distinction called divine, you will there be instructed that God is the God of all mankind, not the God of Mahomedans alone. The Pagan and the Mussulman are equally in his presence. Distinctions of colours are of his ordination. It is He who gives existence. In your temples, to his Name the voice is raised in prayer; in a house of images, where the bell is shaken, still He is the object of adoration. To vilify the religion and customs of other men, is to set at naught the pleasure of the Almighty. When we deface a picture, we naturally incur the resentment of the painter; and justly has the poet said, ' Presume not to arraign or to scrutinize the various works of Power Divine.'" For this valuable communication we are indebted to Mr Orme; Fragments, notes, p. xcvii. I have been assured by a gentleman who has read this letter in the original, that the translation is not only faithful but elegant.

Note LXIV. p. 226.

I HAVE not attempted a description of any subterraneous excavations but those of Elephanta, because none of them have been so often visited, or so carefully inspected. In several parts of India there are, however, stupendous works of a similar nature. The extent and magnificence of the excavations in the island of Salsetta are such, that the artist employed by Governor Boon to make drawings of them asserted, that it would require the labour of forty thousand men for forty years to finish them; Archæologia, vol. vii. p. 336. Loose as this mode of estimation may be, it conveys an idea of the impression which the view of them made upon his mind. The Pagodas of Ellore, eighteen miles from Aurungabad, are likewise hewn out of the solid rock, and if they do not equal those of Elephanta and Salsetta in magnitude, they surpass them far in their extent and number. M. Thevenot, who first gave any description of these singular mansions, asserts, that for above two leagues all around the mountain, nothing is to be seen but Pagodas; Voy. part iii. chap. 44. They were examined at greater leisure and with more attention by M. Anquetil du Perron; but as his long description of them is not accompanied with any plan or drawing, I cannot convey a distinct idea of the whole. It is evident, however, that they are the works of a powerful people; and among the innumerable figures in sculpture with which the walls are covered, all the present objects of *Hindoo worship* may be distinguished. Zend-avesta; Disc. Prelim. p. 223. There are remarkable excavations in a mountain at Mavalipuram near Sadras. This mountain is well known on the Coromandel coast by the name of the *Seven Pagodas*. A good description of the works there, which are magnificent and of high antiquity, is given; Asiat. Researches, vol. i. p. 145, &c. Many other instances of similar works might be produced if it were necessary. What I have asserted, p. 225. concerning the elegance of some of the ornaments in Indian buildings, is confirmed by Colonel Call, chief engineer at Madras, who urges this as a proof of the early and high civilization of the Indians. " It may safely be pronounced," says he, " that no part of the world has more marks of antiquity for arts, sciences, and civilization, than the Peninsula of India, from the Ganges to Cape Comorin. I think the carvings on some of the Pagodas and Choultries, as well as the grandeur of the work, exceeds any thing executed now-a-days, not only for the delicacy of the chisel, but the expense or construction, considering, in many instances, to what distances the component parts were carried, and to what heights raised;" Philosophical Transactions, vol. lxii. p. 354. I am happy to find my idea, that the first temples erected by the Hindoos were formed upon the model of those caverns in which the rites of religion were originally celebrated, confirmed and more fully unfolded by Mr Hodges. In a short dissertation on the primitive standard, or prototype, of the different styles of architecture, viz. the Egyptian, Hindoo, Moorish, Gothic, and Chinese, he has examined and illustrated that curious subject with great ingenuity; Travels in India, p. 63—77.

NOTE LXV. p. 230.

INDIA, says Strabo, produces a variety of substances which dye the most admirable colours. That the *Indicum* which produced the beautiful blue colour, is the same with the *Indigo* of the moderns, we may conclude, not only from the resemblance of the name, and the similarity of the effects, but from the description given by Pliny in the passage which I have quoted in the text. He knew that it was a preparation of a vegetable substance, though he was ill informed both concerning the plant itself, and the process by which it was fitted for use; which will not appear surprising, when we recollect the account formerly given of the strange ignorance of the ancients with respect to the origin and preparation of silk. From the colour of Indigo, in the form in which it was imported, it is denominated by some authors, *Atramentum Indicum*, and *Indicum Nigrum*, Salmas. Exercit. p. 180; and is mentioned under the last of these names, among the articles of importation from India; Peripl. Mar. Erythr. p. 22. The colour of the modern Indigo, when undiluted, resembles that of the ancient Indicum, being so intensely coloured as to appear black; Delaval's Experim. Inquiry into the Cause of the Changes of Colours, Pref. p. xxiii. Indigo is the principal dye-stuff used by the natives of Sumatra, and is much cultivated in that island; but the mode of preparing it differs from that which is common among the people of Indostan; Marsden, Hist. of Sumatra, p. 77. There has been lately found in the Circar of Rajamundry a new species of Indigo, denominated the *Tree Indigo*, which, as it grows wild and in great abundance, promises to be a discovery of considerable use; Oriental Repertory, No. I. p. 39, &c. The *Gum-lacca*, used in dyeing a red colour, was likewise known to the ancients, and by the same name which it now bears; Salmas. Exercit. p. 810. This valuable substance, of such extensive utility in painting, dyeing, japanning, varnishing, and in the manufacture of sealing-wax, is the production of a very minute insect. These insects fix themselves upon the succulent extremities of the branches of certain trees, and are soon glued to the place on which they settle, by a thick pellucid liquid which exudes from their bodies, the gradual accumulation of which forms a complete cell for each insect, which is the tomb of the parent, and the birth-place of its offspring. This glutinous substance, with which the branches of trees are entirely covered, is the Gum-lacca. An account of its formation, nature, and use, is given in the Philos. Trans. vol. lxxi. part ii. p. 374. in a concise, accurate, and satisfactory manner. Some curious observations upon this insect are published by Mr Roxburgh, who cultivates the study of Natural History in India with great assiduity and success; Asiatic Researches, vol. iii. p. 361. It is remarkable that Ctesias seems to have received an account tolerably distinct of the insect by which the Gum-lacca is produced, and celebrates the beauty of the colour which it dyes; Excerpta ex Indic. ad calc. Herodot. edit. Wesseling. p. 830. *Indian Dyers* was the ancient name of those who dyed either the fine blue or the fine red, which points out the country whence the materials they used were brought; Salmas. ib. p. 810. From their dyeing cotton-stuffs with different colours, it is evident that the ancient Indians must have made some considerable proficiency in chemical knowledge. Pliny, lib. xxxv. c. ii. § 42. gives an account of this art as far as it was known anciently. It is precisely the same with that now practised in calico-printing.

Note LXVI. p. 240.

As Sanskreet literature is altogether a new acquisition to Europe, Baghvat-Geeta, the first translation from that language, having been published so late as A. D. 1785, it is intimately connected with the subject of my inquiries, and may afford entertainment to some of my readers, after having reviewed in the text, with a greater degree of critical attention, the two Sanskreet works most worthy of notice, to give here a succinct account of other compositions in that tongue with which we have been made acquainted. The extensive use of the Sanskreet language is a circumstance which merits particular attention. " The grand source of Indian literature," (says Mr Halhed, the first Englishman who acquired the knowledge of Sanskreet), " the parent of almost every dialect from the Persian Gulf to the China Seas, is the Sanskreet, a language of the most venerable and unfathomable antiquity; which, although at present shut up in the libraries of Brahmins, and appropriated solely to the records of their religion, appears to have been current over most of the Oriental world; and traces of its original extent may still be discovered in almost every district of Asia. I have been often astonished to find the similitude of Sanskreet words with those of Persian and Arabic, and even of Latin and Greek; and those not in technical and metaphorical terms, which the mutation of refined arts and improved manners might have occasionally introduced, but in the ground-work of language, in monosyllables, in the names of numbers, and the appellations of such things as would be first discriminated on the immediate dawn of civilization. The resemblance which may be observed in the characters on the medals and signets of various districts of Asia, the light which they reciprocally reflect upon each other, and the general analogy which they all bear to the same grand prototype, afford another ample field for curiosity. The coins of Assam, Napaul, Cashmeere, and many other kingdoms, are all stamped with Sanskreet characters, and mostly contain allusions to the old Sanskreet mythology. The same conformity I have observed on the impression of seals from Bootan and Thibet. A collateral inference may likewise be deduced from the peculiar arrangement of the Sanskreet alphabet, so very different from that of any other quarter of the world. This extraordinary mode of combination still exists in the greatest part of the East, from the Indus to Pegu, in dialects now apparently unconnected, and in characters completely dissimilar; and it is a forcible argument that they are all derived from the same source. Another channel of speculation presents itself in the names of persons and places, of titles and dignities, which are open to general notice, and in which, to the farthest limits of Asia, may be found manifest traces of the Sanskreet;" Preface to the Grammar of the Bengal Language, p. 3. After this curious account of the Sanskreet tongue, I proceed to enumerate the works which have been translated from it, besides the two mentioned in the text.—1. To Mr Wilkins we are indebted for *Heeto-pades* or *Amicable Instruction*, in a series of connected fables, interspersed with moral, prudential, and political maxims. This work is in such high esteem throughout the East, that it has been translated into every language spoken there. It did not escape the notice of the emperor Akber, attentive to every thing that could contribute to promote useful knowledge. He directed his Vizier, Abul Fazel, to put it into a style suited to all capacities, and to illustrate the obscure passages in it, which he accordingly did, and gave it the title of, *The Criterion of Wisdom*. At length these fables made their way into Europe, and have been circulated there with additions and alterations, under the names of Pilpay and Æsop. Many of the Sanskreet apologues are ingenious and beautiful, and have been copied or imitated by the fabulists of other nations. But in some of them the characters of the animals introduced are very ill sustained: To describe a tyger as extremely devout, and practising charity, and other religious duties, p. 16; or an old mouse well read in the *Neetee Sastras*, i. e. Systems of morality and policy, p. 24; a cat reading religious books, p. 35, &c. discovers a want of taste, and an inattention to propriety. Many of the moral sayings, if considered as detached maxims, are founded upon a thorough knowledge of life and manners, and convey instruction with elegant simplicity. But the attempt of the author to form his work into a connected series of fables, and his mode of interweaving with them such a number of moral reflections in prose and in verse, renders the structure of the whole so artificial, that the perusal of it becomes often unpleasant. Akber was so sensible of this, that, among other instructions, he advises his Vizier to abridge the long digressions in that work. By these strictures it is far from my intention to detract in the smallest degree from the merit of Mr Wilkins. His country is much indebted to him for having opened a new source of science and taste. The celebrity of the Heeto-pades, as well as its intrinsic merit, notwithstanding the defects which I have mentioned, justify his choice of it, as a work worthy of being made known to Europe in its original form. From reading this and his other translations, no man will refuse him the praise, to which he modestly confines his pretensions, " of having drawn a picture which we suppose to be a true likeness, although we are unacquainted with the original;" Pref. p. xiv.—2. In the first number of the New Asiatic Miscellany, we have a translation of a celebrated composition in the East, known by the title of the *Five Gems*. It consists of stanzas by five poets who attended the court of Abissura, King of Bengal. Some of these stanzas are simple and elegant.—3. An ode translated from Wulli; in which that extravagance of fancy, and those far-fetched and unnatural conceits which so often disgust Europeans with the poetical compositions of the East, abound too much. The editor has not informed us to whose knowledge of the Sanskreet we are indebted for these two translations.—4. Some original grants of land, of very ancient dates, translated by Mr Wilkins. It may seem odd, that a charter or legal conveyance of property should be ranked among the literary compositions of any people. But so widely do the manners of the Hindoos differ from those of Europe, that as our lawyers multiply words and clauses, in order to render a grant complete, and to guard against every thing that may invalidate it, the *Pundits* seem to despatch the legal part of the deed with brevity, but, in a long preamble and conclusion, make an extraordinary display of their own learning, eloquence, and powers of composition, both in prose and verse. The preamble to one of these deeds is an encomium of the monarch who grants the land, in a bold strain of Eastern exaggeration: " When his innumerable army marched, the heavens were so filled with the dust of their feet that the birds of the air could rest upon it."—" His elephants moved like walking mountains, and the earth oppressed by their weight mouldered into dust." It concludes with denouncing vengeance against those who should venture to infringe this grant: " Riches and the life of man are as transient as drops of water upon the leaf of the lotus. Learning this truth, O man! do not attempt to deprive another of his property;" Asiatic Researches, vol. i. p. 123, &c. The other grant, which appears to be still more ancient, is not less remarkable. Both were found engraved on plates of copper; Ib. p. 357, &c.—5. The translation of part of the Shaster, published by Colonel Dow, in the year 1768, ought perhaps to have been first mentioned. But as this translation was not made by him from the Sanskreet, but taken from the mouth of a Brahmin, who explained the Shaster in Persian, or in the vulgar language of Bengal, it will fall more properly under notice when we come to inquire into the state of science among the Hindoos, than in this place, where we are endeavouring to give some idea of their taste and composition.

Note LXVII. p. 250.

As many of my readers may be unacquainted with the extravagant length of the four eras or periods of Indian chronology, it may be proper to give an account of them from Mr Halhed's Preface to the Code of Gentoo Laws, p. xxxvi.

1. THE *Suttée Jogue* (or age of purity) is said to have lasted three million two hundred thousand years; and

they hold that the life of man was extended in that age to one hundred thousand years; and that his stature was twenty-one cubits.

2. THE *Tirtah Jogue* (in which one-third of mankind was corrupted) they suppose to have consisted of two million four hundred thousand years, and that men lived to the age of ten thousand years.

3. THE *Dwapaar Jogue* (in which half of the human race became depraved) endured one million six hundred thousand years; and the life of man was then reduced to a thousand years.

4. THE *Collee Jogue* (in which all mankind are corrupted, or rather lessened, for that is the true meaning of *Collee*) is the present era, which they suppose ordained to subsist four hundred thousand years, of which near five thousand are already past; and the life of man in that period is limited to one hundred years.

IF we suppose the computation of time in the Indian chronology to be made by solar or even by lunar years, nothing can be more extravagant in itself, or more repugnant to our mode of calculating the duration of the world, founded on sacred and infallible authority. Some attempts have been made by learned men, particularly by M. Bailly, in a very ingenious dissertation on that subject, to bring the chronology of the Hindoos to accord somewhat better with that of the Old Testament; but as I could not explain the principles upon which he founds his conclusions, without entering into long and intricate discussions foreign from the subject of this Dissertation, and as I cannot assent to some of his opinions, I shall rest satisfied with referring to his Astron. Indienne, Disc. Prelim. p. lxxvii. and leave my readers to judge for themselves. I am happy to observe that a memoir on the Chronology of the Hindoos will be published in the Second Volume of the Transactions of the Society of Bengal, and I hope that some learned member of that body will be able, from his acquaintance with the languages and history of the country, to throw light upon a subject which its connection with religion and science renders extremely interesting. From one circumstance, however, which merits attention, we may conclude, that the information which we have hitherto received concerning the chronology of the Hindóos is very incorrect. We have, as far as I know, only five original accounts of the different Jogues or eras of the Hindoos. The first is given by M. Roger, who received it from the Brahmins on the Coromandel coast. According to it, the Suttee Jogue is a period of one million seven hundred and twenty-eight thousand years; the Tirtah Jogue is one million two hundred and ninety-six thousand years; the Dwapaar Jogue is eight hundred and sixty-four thousand years. The duration of the Collee Jogue he does not specify; Porte Ouverte, p. 179. The next is that of M. Bernier, who received it from the Brahmins of Benares. According to him, the duration of the Suttee Jogue was two million five hundred thousand years; that of Tirtah Jogue one million two hundred thousand years; that of the Dwapaar Jogue is eight hundred and sixty-four thousand years. Concerning the period of the Collee Jogue, he likewise is silent; Voyages, tom. ii. p. 160. The third is that of Colonel Dow, according to which the Suttee Jogue is a period of fourteen million of years; the Tirtah Jogue one million eighty thousand; the Dwapaar Jogue seventy-two thousand, and the Collee Jogue thirty-six thousand years; Hist. of Hindost. vol. i. p. 2. The fourth account is that of M. de Gentil, who received it from the Brahmins of the Coromandel coast; and as his information was acquired in the same part of India, and derived from the same source with that of M. Roger, it agrees with his in every particular; Mem. de l'Academ. des Sciences pour 1772, tom. ii. part i. p. 176. The fifth is the account of Mr Halhed, which I have already given. From this discrepancy, not only of the total numbers, but of many of the articles in the different accounts, it is manifest that our information concerning Indian chronology is hitherto as uncertain as the whole system of it is wild and fabulous. To me it appears highly probable, that when we understand more thoroughly the principles upon which the factitious eras or Jogues of the Hindoos have been formed, that we may be more able to reconcile their chronology to the true mode of computing time, founded on the authority of the Old Testament; and may likewise find reason to conclude, that the account given by their astronomers of the situation of the heavenly bodies at the beginning of the Collee Jogue, is not established by actual observation, but the result of a retrospective calculation. Whoever undertakes to investigate farther the chronology of the Hindoos, will derive great assistance from a Memoir of Mr Marsden on that subject, in which he has explained the nature of their year, and the several eras in use among them, with much ingenuity and precision; Philos. Transact. vol. lxxx. part ii. p. 560.

Note LXVIII. p. 259.

In the public buildings of India, we find proofs and monuments of the proficiency of the Brahmins in science, particularly of their attention to astronomical observation. Their religion enjoins, that the four sides of a Pagoda should face the four cardinal points. In order to execute this with accuracy, they take a method described by M. le Gentil, which discovers a considerable degree of science. He carefully examined the position of one of their Pagodas, and found it to be perfectly exact; Voy. tom. i. p. 133. As some of their Pagodas are very ancient, they must have early attained such a portion of knowledge as was requisite for placing them properly. On the ceilings of Choultries, and other ancient edifices, the twelve-signs of the zodiac are often delineated; and from their resemblance to those which are now universally used, it is highly probable that the knowledge of these arbitrary symbols was derived from the East. Colonel Call has published a drawing of the signs of the zodiac, which he found on the ceiling of a Choultry at Verdapettah, in the Madura country; Phil. Transact. vol. lxii. p. 353. I have a drawing of them in my possession, differing from his in some of the figures, but I cannot say in what particular place it was found. Sir Robert Barker describes an observatory at Benares which he visited A. D. 1772. In it he found instruments for astronomical observation, of very large dimensions, and constructed with great skill and ingenuity. Of all these he has published drawings; Phil. Trans. vol. lxvii. p. 598. According to traditionary account, this observatory was built by the Emperor Akber. The view which Sir Robert took of it was an hasty one. It merits a more attentive inspection, in order to determine whether it was constructed by Akber, or erected in some more early period. Sir Robert intimates, that none but Brahmins, who understood the Sanskreet, and could consult the astronomical tables written in that language, were capable of calculating eclipses. P. Tiessenthaler describes, in a very cursory manner, two observatories furnished with instruments of extraordinary magnitude, at Jepour and Ougein, in the country of Malwa; Bernouilli, tom. i. p. 316. 347. But these are modern structures.

Since the first edition of the Historical Disquisition was published, the Souriak Seddantam, or, according to a more correct orthography, the Súrya Siddhánta, on the principles of which I had observed that all the Indian astronomy is founded, has been discovered at Benares by Sir Robert Chambers. He immediately communicated this valuable work to Samuel Davis, Esq. who has favoured the world with a translation of several considerable extracts from it.

The Súrya Siddhánta is composed in the Sanskreet language, and professes to be a divine revelation, (as Abul Fazel had related, Ayeen Akbery, III. p. 8.) communicated to mankind more than two millions of years ago, towards the close of the Sutty or Satya Jogue, the first of the four fabulous ages into which the Hindoo Mythologists divide the period during which they suppose the world to have existed. But when this accompaniment of fiction and extravagance is removed, there is left behind a very rational and elaborate system of astronomical calculation. From this Mr Davis has selected what relates to the calculation of eclipses, and has illustrated it with great ingenuity. The manner in which that subject is treated, has so close an affinity to the methods formerly brought from India, and of which I have given some account, as to confirm strongly the opinion that the Súrya Siddhánta is the source from which all the others are derived. How far the real date of this work may be ascertained from the rules and tables which it contains, will be more clearly established when a translation of the whole is published. In the mean time it is evident, that what is already known with respect to these rules and tables, is extremely favourable to the hypothesis which ascribes a very high antiquity to the astronomy of the Brahmins.

THE circumstance, perhaps, most worthy of attention, in the Extracts now referred to, is the system of Trigonometry included in the Astronomical Rules of the Súrya Siddhánta; Asiat. Research. ii. p. 245. 249. It may be shewn that this system is founded on certain Geometrical Theorems, which though modern Mathematicians be well acquainted with, were certainly unknown to Ptolemy and the Greek Geometricians.

IT is with pleasure, too, we observe, that Mr Davis has in his possession several other ancient books of Hindoo astronomy, and that there is reason to expect from him a translation of the whole Súrya Siddhánta.

IT must be added, that we also learn from the second volume of the Asiatic Researches, that some vestiges of Algebraical calculation have been discovered among the Brahmins; particularly Rules for the solution of certain Arithmetical questions, with which it would seem that nothing but Algebra could have furnished them; Asiat. Research. ii. p. 468. note, 487. 495.

MY friend, Mr Professor Playfair, has examined that Extract from the Súrya Siddhánta which gives an account of the ancient Hindoo System of Trigonometry, and has discovered the principles on which it is founded. It is with pleasure I announce, that the result of this examination will be communicated soon to the Public, and will afford an additional proof of the extraordinary progress which the natives of India had early made in the most abstruse sciences.

INDEX

TO THE

DISQUISITION CONCERNING ANCIENT INDIA.

A

Abul Fazel, minister to Akber, sovereign of Indostan, publishes the Ayeen Akbery, 215; and Heeto-Pades, 375.

Acesines, a city built on that river by Alexander the Great, 303.

Æras of *Indian Chronology*, explained, 377. Remarks on, 378.

Africa, general idea of the continent of, and of its trade, 158. Origin of the slave-trade, 181.

Agathemerus, his account of the island of Taprobane, 84. His character of Ptolemy the geographer, 321.

Agathodæmon illustrates the geography of Ptolemy, by maps, 321.

Akber, sovereign of Indostan, his character, 214. 368.

Albuquerque, Alphonso, the Portuguese admiral, seizes the island of Ormus, 152. His operations on the Red Sea, 153.

Alexander the Great, his extensive views respecting India, 13. His expedition to India, 14. His war with Porus, 16. How obliged to relinquish his enterprise, 17. His measures for opening a maritime communication with India, 19. His account of India confirmed by modern observations, 22. His political views in exploring that country, 24. His measures to unite his European and Asiatic subjects, 26. Consequences of his death, 31. The sufferings of his army from the periodical rains, 295. His surprise at the tides of the Indian Ocean, 299. Cities built by him in India, 304. Intended a survey of the Caspian Sea, 315.

Alexandria, long the chief seat of commerce with India, 13. The light-house on the Pharos erected by Ptolemy Lagus,

39. Mode of conducting the silk trade at that port, 61. The Venetians trade there for silk, 124. And the Florentines, 127. Is subjected to the Turks, 155.

Algebra, a mode of calculation not unknown to the Brahmins, 383.

Allahabad, the modern name of the ancient city of Palibothra, 34. Account of this city by Megasthenes, 35. Remarks of Major Rennell on this subject, 307.

America, discovered by Christopher Columbus, 144. The East India trade a continual drain from its silver mines, 180. Origin of the slave-trade, 181. Contrast between the natives of America and of India, when first discovered, 183. The trade of Europe with each compared, 186. Was obliged to be colonized in order to be improved, 187. Supplies Europe with its products, in return for manufactures, *ib*.

Antiochus the Great, his inroad into India, 309.

Antoninus, Marcus, Emperor, notices of an embassy sent by him to the Emperor of China, 78.

Antwerp, greatly enriched by becoming the staple of the Hanseatic League, 140.

Arabians, anciently great dealers in spices from the East, 57. Great alterations effected in their manners by the religion of Mahomet, 99. They conquer Egypt and Persia, 100. A view of their commercial navigation, 101. Are the first who mention porcelain and tea, 104. Derived the knowledge of the mariner's compass from Europe, 383. Make no scruple to plunder the caravans travelling to Mecca, 351.

Aristotle, his political advice to Alexander the Great, 26. His just description of the Caspian Sea, 315. Doubted the expediency of encouraging commerce in a well regulated state, 317.

Aromatics, why much used by the ancients, 56.

Arrian, character of his history of the Indian expedition of Alexander the Great, 21. His account of the commerce of the ancients, 62. Inquiry into his geographical knowledge of India, 65. Is the first ancient writer who had any knowledge of the eastern coast of the great peninsula of India, 67. His account of Alexander's Indian fleet corroborated, 297. Character of his Indian history, *ib*. His account of the Caspian Sea, 314. The places mentioned in his Periplus compared with modern situations and names, 320. 326.

Arts and Sciences, where first cultivated, 2.

Asbestos, its extravagant price among the Romans, 318.

Astronomy, testimonies of the great proficiency of the Indostans in, 249.

Augsburg, greatly enriched by becoming a mart for Indian commodities, 140.
Augustus, Emperor, reduces Egypt to a Roman province, 45.
Ayeen Akbery, account of the mutual intercourse of the East Indians by water, from, 297. See *Sanskreet* literature.

B

Babelmandeb, derivation of the name, 310.
Bactria, rise of the kingdom of, and its acquisitions in India, 37. Is overwhelmed by the Tartars, 37. 310.
Baghvat-Geeta, the pure theology taught in that poem, 276.
Bailly, M. his examination into the antiquity of astronomy in India, 254.
Bank of Venice, the first establishment of that kind formed in Europe, 346.
Barygaza, a considerable emporium on the coast of ancient India, its situation ascertained, 62.
Bassora, the city of, founded by the Caliph Omar, 101.
Benares, the peculiar seat of Indostan science and literature, 257. Account of the observatory there, 381.
Berenice, the city of, founded to facilitate the trade between Alexandria and India, 40.
Bernier, M. his account of the Indian chronology, 379.
Bijore, inhabited by a tribe descended from a colony left there by Alexander the Great, 302.
Boddam, East India ship, remarkable speedy voyage of, from Portsmouth to Madras, 316.
Brahmins, in India, their sacred rites and high privileges, 206. Inquiry into the state of scientific knowledge among them, 241. Their religious hierarchy and worship, 259. Their great learning taught them a theology superior to the popular superstition, 275. Their doctrines coincide with the tenets of the Stoical school, 282. Studiously concealed religious truths from the people, 285.
Bruce, the information his travels afford concerning the maritime expeditions of King Solomon, 10.
Bruges made the staple of the trade of the Hanseatic League, 130. Is greatly enriched, 139.
Burrun Sunker, a class among the Hindoos, described, 358.
Byzantine historians, a character of, 105.

C

Caffa, the great trade carried on there, 339.
Cairo, account of the caravan that travels from thence to Mecca, 349.

Calicut, reception of Vasco de Gama in that country, 146.

Call, Colonel, his general opinion of the antiquity of arts and sciences in India, 370.

Camel, the valuable properties of that animal, 3. Is peculiarly formed for traversing sandy deserts, 347.

Candahar, under what name known to Alexander the Great, 16.

Canton, in China, a factory settled there by the early Arabs, 103.

Cape of Good Hope, circumstances that led to the discovery of a passage to India that way, 145. Is said by Herodotus to have been passed by some Phœnician ships, 167. Importance of the discovery of this passage by the Portuguese, 189.

Caravans, the origin of, 3. Were protected and encouraged under the Roman dominion, 78. Great commercial use of, in the East, 161. Account of the caravans which visit Mecca, 349. A considerable slave-trade carried on by the African caravans, 351.

Caspian Sea, erroneous opinion of the ancient geographers concerning, 44. 314. By whom first described in modern times, 315. Its dimensions, *ib.*

Casts, or orders of society among the native Gentoos described, 199. Remarks on the policy and tendency of this arrangement, 200. Their peculiar names, ranks, and offices described, 358.

Cathay, the ancient name of China, 132.

Ceylon, supposed to be the island described by ancient geographers under the name of Taprobane, 84. Christian churches planted there by Persian missionaries, 105. Is visited by Marco Polo, the Venetian, 133.

Chardin, Sir John, his testimony that the Orientals derived the use of the mariner's compass from the Europeans, 334. His account of the trade of Caffa, 339.

Chillambrum, description of the Pagoda there, 226.

China, the only country whence the Romans obtained silk, 60. Through what medium they received it, 65. How the silk-worm was conveyed from thence to Europe, 98. Is traded to by the Arabians, 102. First mention of porcelain and tea, 104. The Christian religion propagated there by Persian missionaries, 105. How the silk of, was conveyed to Constantinople, after the Greeks were excluded from the port of Alexandria, 107. Estimate of the Chinese practice of navigation, 333. How the number of Mahometans increase in China, 337. A commercial intercourse, by land, opened between that country and Russia, 352. Amazing exportation of tea from, to Europe, 356.

Chitore, the high descent claimed by the Rajahs of, 302.
Chronology, Indian, the four eras of, 377. Remarks on, 378.
Cleopatra, value of her famous pearl ear-rings, 59.
Colchos, the ancient pearl fishery there, still carried on by the Dutch, 66.
Colours, Indian, for dyeing, account of, 371.
Columbus, his views in that voyage by which he discovered America, 144. His reliance on the authority of Marco Polo, the Venetian traveller, 344. See *Gama*.
Commerce, the extension of, abated the hostile sentiments which actuated one nation against another, 130. Unfavourable opinion of Plato concerning, 317.
Common law, the origin of, traced, 213.
Comorin, Cape, is accurately described by Arrian, 66.
Compass, mariner's, was unknown by the ancient Chinese and Arabs, 333.
Constantinople taken and plundered by the crusaders, 119. Subversion of the Latin empire there, 121. Is conquered by the Turks, and made the seat of their government, 134.
Conveyancing, specimen of the ancient Indian style of, 376.
Coromandel Coast, the inhabitants of, always great traders, 91.
Cosmas Indicopleustes, some account of, and of his Christian topography, 93. His account of the island of Taprobane, 94.
Cotton manufactures, evidence of their not being common among the Romans, 320.
Crusades to the Holy Land, the origin of, traced, and their commercial effects, 113. The crusaders acquired the policy and arts of the people whom they subdued, 116. Brought different nations acquainted with each other, 130.

D.

Damascus, account of the caravan that travels from thence to Mecca, 350.
Damask, the name of that species of silk manufacture, whence derived, 138.
Dandulo, Andrew, the character of his Venetian Chronicle, 337.
D'Anville, M. his opinion as to the course pursued in the trading voyages of King Solomon's ships, 10. His corrections of Ptolemy's geography of India, 73. Corroborates Nearchus's account of India, 300. His geography of India controverted by M. Gossellin, 324.
Darius, the son of Hystaspes, King of Persia, his researches into and conquests in India, 13.
Deccan, the ancient Dachanos of Arrian, 327.

Delta of the Indus, the general state of the weather there, 296.
Diamonds, not so highly esteemed by the Romans as pearls, 318.
Diodorus Siculus, his history of the Indian expedition of Sesostris examined, 290.
Dow, Colonel, account of his translation of the Shaster, 244. 377. His account of the Indian Chronology, 379.
Doulatabad, the same with the ancient Tagara, 320.
Du Halde, his description of a peculiar species of silk, 319.
Dutch States, became the first rivals of the Portuguese in the trade to India, 179.
Dyes, Indian, the excellence of, 371.

E

East, the regions of, where arts and sciences were first cultivated, 2. The intercourse between different countries how first carried on, *ib*. The first maritime communication with, from the West, 5. See *India*.
Eclipses, how calculated by the Brahmins of India, 251.
Egypt, ancient prejudice of the inhabitants against any intercourse with foreigners, 5. How the Egyptians became a commercial people, 6. The city of Alexandria built, 13. The seat of government fixed there by Ptolemy Lagus, 39. Intercourse between the city of Berenice and India, 40. Its opulence derived from its commerce with the East, 42. Is reduced to a Roman province, 45. Manner of conducting the silk trade at the port of Alexandria, 61. Conquest of, by the Arabs, 100. The Venetians resort to Alexandria for silk, 124. And the Florentines, 127. Commercial view of the countries, 137. Is subdued by the Turks, 155. How the Indian trade has been conducted through that country at different times, 310.
Elagabulus, the first Roman Emperor who wore silk, 60.
Elephanta, island, account of the ancient pagoda there, 221.
Ellore, general account of the pagodas there, 370.
Æsop's Fables, the origin of, traced, 375.
Ethics, state of, in India, 245.
Europe, a review of the state of, at the time of the subversion of the Greek empire, 135. Extensive operation of the commercial genius of, 183. The Europeans receive the products of America, and supply it with manufactures, 187. The exportation of silver to India, how beneficial to Europe, 189. Importance of the discovery of the passage to India round the Cape of Good Hope, *ib*.

F

Faquirs of India unite trade with devotion in their pilgrimages, 114. 338. Brief account of, 361.
Figures, arithmetical, originally derived from India, 248.
Five Gems, an ancient Sanskreet poem, account of, 376.
Florence, rise of the state of, by manufactures and the banking business, 126. A commercial treaty concluded with Egypt, 127. Summary of the instructions to their ambassadors to the Soldan, 341.

G

Gama, Vasco de, his voyage from Lisbon to India, 146.
Ganges, account of that river by Major Rennell, 307.
Genoa, motives that stimulated the Genoese to assist in subverting the Latin empire at Constantinople, 122. The great advantages they derived from this measure, 123. Character of the Genoese government, *ib.* The Genoese expelled from all their Grecian settlements by the Turks, 134. Character of, by Nicephorus Gregoras, 339.
Gentile, M. le, his account of the Indian Chronology, 379.
Gentoos, see *Brahmins* and *Hindoos*.
Gibbon, Mr, the Roman historian, testimony in favour of his accuracy, 330.
Gossellin, M. character of his geography of the Greeks analyzed, 324.
Greeks, their national pride at the time of Alexander the Great, 25. How they attained the breeding of silk-worms under the Emperor Justinian, 97. Are shut out from the port of Alexandria by the Mahomedan Arabs, 100. The Greek empire conquered by Mahomet II. 134. How they were deprived of Bactria, 309. Origin of the ancient mythology of, 266.
Gum Lacca, natural history of, and its uses in manufacture, 372.

H

Halhed, Mr, his account of the Sanskreet literature, 374.
Hanno commanded the only voyage for discovery undertaken by any of the ancient states in the Mediterranean, 355.
Hanseatic League formed, and the staple fixed at Bruges, 130.
Hastings, Mr, Governor-general of Bengal, his attention to forming a code of Hindoo laws, 215.

Hecto-Pades, or Amicable Instruction, an ancient Sanskreet composition, account and character of, 375.

Herodotus affirms the Cape of Good Hope to have been passed by some Phœnician vessels, 167. His history of Sesostris examined, 290. His unsatisfactory account of the tides in the Red Sea, 299. His just description of the Caspian Sea, 314.

Hindoos, that people exactly described in the account of the Indian expedition of Alexander the Great, 23. Their inflexible adherence to their religion, and casts, 336. Their four orders, or casts, described, 199. Remarks on the policy and tendency of this popular arrangement, 200. Their high antiquity, and nature of their institutions, 216. Character of their judicial code, 217. State of sciences among them, 242. Their religious tenets and practices, 259. Their names, ranks, and offices of their several casts described, 358. Their temples, 371.

Hiram, King of Tyre, assists King Solomon in his naval undertakings, 9.

Hippalus, captain of an Egyptian vessel, avails himself of the monsoons, in sailing from the Arabian Gulf to the Malabar Coast, 52.

Hipparchus, the first who attempted to make a catalogue of the stars, 69.

History, authentic, the period of, extremely limited, 1. Is minute in the records of blood, but silent as to the progress of useful arts, 51.

Hydaspes, river, a numerous fleet assembled there by Alexander the Great, 18.

Hyphasis, river, the utmost limit of Alexander the Great's progress in India, 17.

I & J

Java Minor of Marco Polo ascertained, 343.

Jenaub, a city built on that river by Alexander the Great, 303.

Jenkinson, Anthony, the first modern traveller who gives a just description of the Caspian Sea, 315.

Jeswont Sing, his letter to Aurengzebe, containing a character of Sultan Akber, 368.

Jewels, their great use and high estimation among the ancients, 58.

Jews, when they effected a commercial intercourse with India, 9. Inquiry into the maritime commerce of King Solomon, 10. Their commercial effort terminated in his reign, *ib.*

India, the first naval communication with, from the West, 5. The trade of the Phœnicians with, how conducted, 7. Naval expedition of the Persians to, 11. Conquests of Darius Hystaspes in, 12. Alexandria, for many centuries, the chief seat of trade with, 13. Expedition of Alexander the Great to, 15. Flourishing state of the country at that time, 17. Alexander's voyage down the Indus, 19. Political state of the country at that time, 21. Alexander's views in this expedition, 24. Expedition of Seleucus, one of the successors of Alexander, 32. Embassy of Megasthenes to, 33. Conquests of the Bactrian Princes in, 37. Remains afterwards undisturbed by Europeans, until the Cape of Good Hope was doubled by the Portuguese, 38. A commercial intercourse established with Egypt, *ib.* How Rome was supplied with eastern commodities, 47. Advantage taken of the monsoons, in sailing from the Gulf of Arabia to the Malabar Coast, 52. Its commodities, articles of luxury, 55. Spices and aromatics, 56. Precious stones, 58. Silk, 59. General view of its exports and imports, 63. Comparison between the ancient and modern trade with India, 65. D'Anville's corrections of Ptolemy's geography of, 73. The trade by caravans protected and encouraged by the Romans, 77. The inhabitants of the Coromandel Coast always great traders, 91. The account given of India by Cosmas Indicopleustes, 93. The Romans rivalled in the Indian trade by the Persians, 94. The Italian states engaged in the Indian trade, 109. Account of the Indian trade by Marino Sanudo, 128. Comparative view of the Indian trade, as carried on by different nations at different times, 136. A direct voyage to India effected by the Portuguese, 146. The staple of the Portuguese trade established at the city of Malacca, 150. A commercial empire established in the East by the Portuguese, 156. How it came to pass that the discovery of a direct navigation to India was reserved for modern times, 164. The conduct of ancient and modern navigators to the East, compared, 168. The prices of Indian commodities greatly reduced by the opening a direct communication with India, 171. The India trade a continual drain of American silver from Europe, 180. Contrast between the state of the natives of India and America, when first discovered, 183. The trade of Europe with each, compared, 186. The silver exported to India contributes to enrich instead of impoverishing Europe, 188. Importance of the discovery of the passage to India round the Cape of Good Hope to Europe, 189. Examination of the improbabilities attending the supposed expedition of Sesostris to India, 289. Remarks on the weather there, 295. Remarks on the naval expedition of Nearchus, 298.

Peculiarities in the Indian tides, 299. Aversion of the natives of the East to the sea, 303. Major Rennell's account of the river Ganges, 306. Endeavours to ascertain the situation of the ancient city of Palibothra, 307. How the Indian trade has been carried on through Egypt at different times, 310. Erroneous descriptions of the Caspian Sea by ancient writers, 313. Deccan, the ancient Dachanos of Arrian, 327. The use of the mariner's compass learned by the Easterns from the Europeans, 333. The Gentoos inflexible in their religion, 336. Computed number of Mahomedans in India, *ib*. Extensive circulation of eastern goods by the caravans, 352. The natives of India the earliest known people who were civilized, 197. Their division into casts, 199. The perfection of Indian manufactures accounted for, 201. The general tenure of land there, 208. Character of the Hindoo code of laws, 217. General account of the Pagodas, 221. Fortresses, 228. Mechanic arts, 229. Literature, 232. Their sciences, 241. Their religious tenets, 259. Origin of superstition, 263. The pure theology of the Brahmins, 274. General reflections formed on the preceding review of the eastern nations, 284. The manners and customs of the natives influenced by the Mahomedan and European intruders, 362. Account of the Sanskreet literature, 374. The Heeto-Pades, 375. The Five Gems, 376. Ode from Wulli, *ib*. Specimen of Indian conveyancing, 377. The four eras of Indian chronology explained, *ib*.

Indicum of the ancients, the same with modern indigo, 371.

Indigo, the several kinds of, mentioned by authors, and its uses, 372.

Indus, river, passed by Alexander the Great, 16. His voyage down that river, 19.

Institutions of India, the permanency of, accounted for, 202.

Interest of money, the most exact standard of commercial profits, 141. Chronological view of, *ib*.

Joanna of Navarre, her exclamation at the wealth of the city of Bruges, 344.

Italy, rise of the commercial states of, 109. They import the productions of India, *ib*. The profits they reaped from the Crusades, 117. See *Venice, Genoa*, &c.

Itineraries of the Roman empire, how formed, 322.

Julius Cæsar, his magnificent present to Servilia, the mother of Brutus, 59. His ignorance of the British tides, 299. A general survey of the whole Roman empire undertaken by him, 322.

Justin, observations on his account of the progress made by Seleucus in India, 305.

Justinian, Emperor, how he introduced the silk-worm into the Greek empire, 97.

L

Land, the general tenures of, in India, 209. 363. Specimen from an ancient grant of, 376.
Latitudes, how ascertained by the ancient geographers, 86. Were more readily determined by them than longitudes, 89. 328.
Lawyers, European, the style of, compared with that of the Eastern Pundits, 376.
Leibnitz, his account of the instructions given to the Florentine ambassadors to the Soldan of Egypt, 341.
Logic and metaphysics, state of, in India, 243.
Longitudes of places, how determined by ancient geographers, 87. 328.

M

Magellan effects a passage for the East Indies westward from America, 177.
Mahabarat, an ancient Indian epic poem, account of, 232. Extracts from, 243. 246. 277.
Mahmoud of Gaznah, the vast fleet that opposed his invasion of India, 207.
Mahomet, rapid spread of his religion, and the great effects produced by it, 99. Contributed greatly to extend the commerce of Asia and Africa, 159.
Mahomet II. Emperor of the Turks, subdues the Grecian empire, 134.
Mahudel, M. his proofs of the ignorance of the ancients as to the nature of silk, 319.
Malabar Coast, probable derivation of its name, 94. How mentioned by the Arabian writers, 104.
Malacca, the city of, rendered the staple of the trade carried on in the East by the Portuguese, 150.
Maldive Islands, probable derivation of their name, 94.
Man, a review of his progress in social life, 204.
Manufactures, Indian, the perfection of, accounted for, 201.
Maps, none prior to those formed to illustrate Ptolemy's geography have reached modern times, 85.
Marco Polo, the Venetian, account of his travels, 132. Objections to his relations, and vindication of them, 342.
Marseilles opens a trade with Constantinople for Indian commodities, 111.

Massoudi, the Arabian, his account of India, 332.

Mecca, the temple there visited as well by commercial as by devout pilgrims, 114. The pilgrimages to, contributed greatly to facilitate trade, 159. Account of the caravans which visit the temple there, 349.

Medici, Cosmo di, a Florentine merchant, negociates a commercial treaty with Egypt in favour of his countrymen, 127.

Mediterranean Sea, the chief seat of ancient commerce, 166.

Magasthenes, his embassy from Seleucus King of Syria, to India, 33. His account of India, 34.

Mocenigo, Doge of Venice in the fifteenth century, his account of the naval strength of that republic, 347.

Monkish annalists, a character of, 110.

Monsoons, the first application of them in voyages to India, 52.

Moses, the books of, the most ancient and genuine record of the early ages of the world, 1.

Musiris, a port on the coast of Malabar, frequented by ancient navigators in the Indian trade, 52.

Mythology of the Greeks, the natural origin of, 266.

N

Nadir Shah, general review of his Indian expedition, 296.

Nagara of Ptolemy, its latitude according to D'Anville, 80.

Navigation, origin of, traced, 4. Where first cultivated, 5. How introduced among the Egyptians, 6.

Nearchus commands the naval expedition of Alexander the Great down the Indus, 19. Remarks on, 298.

Nicephorus Gregoras, his character of the Genoese at Constantinople, 339.

Niebuhr, his evidence in favour of the European origin of the mariner's compass, 335.

O

Omar, Caliph, founds the city of Bassora, 101.

Ormus, the island of, seized by the Portuguese, 152. Description of, *ib.*

Oude, Nabob of, the great probability of disputes between him and the Seiks, 294.

P

Pagodas of India, general account of, 221. 370. Are placed with astronomical precision, 380.

Palibothra, endeavours to ascertain the situation of that city, 307.

Palmyra, by whom, and on what occasion built, 48. Its stupendous ruins, 50. Its present state, 51.

Panjab, progress of Alexander the Great through that country, 16.

Papyrus, occasion of its being disused for writing on, 338.

Parchment, when first used for the record of charters and deeds, 338.

Pariars, the most contemptible race of men in India, 336. 358.

Patna, evidences of its not being the ancient city of Palibothra, 308.

Pearls, their high estimation among the Romans, 58. Were dearer than diamonds, 318.

Pera, the chief suburb of Constantinople, granted to the Genoese on the subversion of the Latin empire there, 122. The Genoese expelled by the Turks, 134.

Persia, how the commerce between that country and India was conducted, 43. Vigorous cultivation of the India trade, 95. The silk trade engrossed by the Persians, 96. Their extortions introduce the silk-worm to Europe, 97. Is conquered by the Arabs, 100. Nestorian churches planted there, 105. Amount of the revenue of the Persian monarchs from Herodotus, 293. Instances of their ancient aversion to the sea, 304.

Phalanx, Macedonian, how formed by Alexander the Great, 27.

Phœnicians, how they opened a commercial intercourse with India, 7. Are said by Herodotus to have passed the Cape of Good Hope, 167.

Philosophy the cure for superstition, 272.

Pilgrimages to the Holy Land, undertaken as well from commercial as from pious motives, 117. Account of the pilgrimages to Mecca, 349.

Pilpay's fables, the origin of, traced, 375.

Plato, his political objections to commerce in a well regulated commonwealth, 317.

Pliny the elder, his slender knowledge of India, 68. His account of the island of Taprobane, 83. Observations on his account of the progress of Seleucus in India, 306.

Pomponius Mela, his account of the island of Taprobane, 82. And of the Caspian Sea, 314.

Porcelain, the first mention of, by Arabian travellers, 104.

Portugal, circumstances that led the Portuguese to the discovery of the Cape of Good Hope, 145. Vigorous exertions of the Portuguese to cultivate the eastern trade, 149. They aim at a monopoly of the trade to the East, 151. Establish a commercial empire in the East, 156. Their activity in exploring the eastern countries, 169. They drive the Venetians out of the European markets, by reducing the prices of Indian goods, 172. How they remained so long in the exclusive possession of the Indian trade, 176. Are rivalled at length in the Indian Ocean by the Dutch, 178. And by the English, 179. Repulse the efforts of Solyman the Magnificent to drive them from India, 191. Their intercourse with Infidels licensed by a Papal bull, 340.

Porus opposes the progress of Alexander the Great in India, 16. Remains steady to the Macedonian interest, 32.

Potosi, the discovery of the silver mines of, the first permanent source of wealth derived by Spain from America, 185.

Ptolemy, the geographer, estimate of his scientifical knowledge, 69. Established geography upon its proper principles, *ib.* His accounts of the continent of India examined, 72. His geography of India adjusted by that of modern times by M. D'Anville, 73. Instances of his exactness in some positions, 80. His account of the island of Taprobane, 83. His character, by Agathemerus, 321. His geographical errors, 323. From what materials he composed his geography of India, 330.

Ptolemy Lagus establishes the seat of the Egyptian government at Alexandria, and erects the light-house on the Pharos, 39.

Ptolemy Philadelphus projects a grand canal to facilitate the intercourse between Egypt and India, 39. Founds the city of Berenice, 40.

Pultanah, the ancient Plithania of Arrian, 320.

R

Ramusio detects the geographical errors of Ptolemy, 323.

Raynal, Abbé, character of his history of the East and West-Indies, 189.

Red Sea, derivation of the name, and the different applications of it by the ancients and the moderns, 300.

Religion and superstition discriminated, 261.

Renaudot, M. his translation of the eastern voyage of two Mahomedans, from the Arabic, vindicated from the charge of imposition, 331.

Rennell, Major, his illustrations of the Indian expedition of Alexander the Great, 20. 293. 202. His account of the river Ganges, 306. Remarks on his account of the situation of the city of Palibothra, 307. His opinion of the Egyptian navigation examined, 312.

Rhinocolura, the ancient port of communication between Phœnicia and India, 8.

Roger, M. his account of the Indian chronology, 379.

Rome, rise of the power of, 45. How supplied with Indian commodities, 48. Its imports from thence, articles of luxury, 55. Spices, 56. Precious stones, 58. Silk, 59. Remained ignorant of the nature or production of silk, 60. How the breeding silk-worms was introduced into the eastern empire, 97. Consequences of the Roman empire being dissolved by the Barbarians, 129. How the itineraries of the empire were formed, 322.

Russia, a commercial intercourse by land opened between that country and China, 353.

Ryots of Indostan, inquiry into the tenure by which they hold their possessions, 364.

S

Sacontala, an ancient Indian dramatic poem, account of, 235.

Sacotecas, the mines of, in Mexico, importance of the discovery of, to Spain, 185.

Saint Croix, Baron de, observations on his Critique des Historiens d'Alexandre le Grand, 304.

Samarcand, by what name known to Alexander the Great, 14. Its latitude, as ascertained by D'Anville, 80.

Sandracottus, an Indian prince, his revolt against, and treaty with Seleucus, King of Syria, 32.

Sanskreet literature, a new acquisition, 373. Mr Halhed's account of, 374.

Sanudo, Marino, his account of the Venetian trade with India in the fourteenth century, 128.

Sciences and Arts, where first cultivated, 2. A view of the state of, in India, 242.

Scylax, of Caryandra, his naval expedition to India, 11. Gives fabulous accounts of the country, 12. Why his voyage is not mentioned by Arrian, 297.

Sepoys, modern, established upon the same principle with the phalanx of Persians formed by Alexander the Great, 28.

Seiks, of India, probability of disputes between them and the British, 294. Their situation and character, *ib*.

Seleucus, the successor of Alexander, his expedition to India, 32. Observations on, 305.

Selim, Sultan, the conqueror of the Mamelukes, his attention to the advantages of the Indian commerce, 190.

Semiramis, the vast fleet that opposed her invasion of India, 297.

Sera Metropolis, of Ptolemy, its latitude according to D'Anville, 81.

Seringham, description of the pagoda there, 226.

Sesostris, King of Egypt, the first who rendered the Egyptians a commercial people, 6. Improbabilities attending his supposed expedition to and conquest of India, 289.

Shaster, some account of, 244. 377.

Sielediba, account given of this island by Cosmas Indicopleustes, 94.

Silk, its high estimation among the Romans, 59. The trade for, engrossed by the Persians, 96. Silk-worms obtained and cultivated by the Greeks, 97. Account of the Venetian and Florentine trade for silk, 125. Ignorance of the ancients as to its production, 319. Why disliked by the Turks, 320.

Silver is continually drained from Europe to carry on the East India trade, 180. Europe how enriched by this exportation, 188.

Sinæ Metropolis, of Ptolemy, endeavours of M. D'Anville to ascertain its situation, 76.

Slave-trade, modern, the origin of, 181. Is largely carried on by the African caravans, 351.

Solomon, King of Judea, inquiry into his maritime commerce, 9. Builds Tadmor in the Desert, 48.

Solyman the Magnificent, his efforts to drive the Portuguese from India, 191.

Soul, description of, from the Mahabarat, 243.

Spain, how that country happened to have the advantage and honour of discovering America, 144. Gold and silver the only profitable articles they found in America, 185. Are obliged to colonize in order to improve their discoveries, 187.

Spices, and aromatics, why much used by the ancients, 56. Vast modern consumption of them, 175.

Strabo, his obscure knowledge of India, 67. His account of the island of Taprobane, 82. Denies that Sesostris ever entered India, 291. Evidence of his slender knowledge of India, 312. His account of the Caspian Sea, 314. How he justifies his neglect of Hipparchus, 321. His free exposition of ancient theology, 283. His account of the jealous caution with which the Indian women were guarded, 362. His account of the ancient dyes, 371.

Sumatra, the island of, visited by the early Arabians, 103. Was the Java Minor of Marco Polo, 343.
Superstition and religion discriminated, 261. Origin of superstition, 262. Progress of, 267. Picture of Oriental superstition, 268. Philosophy fatal to, 272.
Surya Siddhanta, the scientifical merit of that ancient Oriental composition, 382.
Sylla, vast quantities of spices consumed in his funeral pile, 56.

T

Tadmor in the Desert, by whom built, and for what purpose, 48. Its stupendous ruins, 50. Its present state, 52.
Tamerlane, his judicious choice of the season for his Indian campaign, 296.
Taprobane, Strabo's account of that island, 82. Pliny's account of it, *ib*. Ptolemy's account of it, 83. Appears to be the island of Ceylon, 84. Account given of this island by Cosmas Indicopleustes, 93.
Tatta, great drought there, 296. Vast numbers of vessels for water carriage there, 297.
Tea has, within a century, become a necessary of life in many parts of Europe, 356. Amazing annual importation of, *ib*.
Tea-tree, first mention of, by Arabian travellers, 104.
Tides of the Indian Ocean, peculiarities in, 299.
Trade, how at first conducted between different countries, 3. Between Egypt and India, 38. Exports and imports of India, 55.
Transmigration of souls, the Eastern doctrine of, explained, 281.
Turks, their scruples concerning the wearing of silk, 320.
Tyre, the best account of the commercial transactions of that city to be found in the prophet Ezekiel, 292.

V

Vasa Murrhina, of Pliny, inquiry into the nature and composition of, 335.
Venice, first rise of, as a commercial state, 109. Constantinople taken, in conjunction with the crusaders, 119. The Venetians engage largely in the trade and manufacture of silk, 120. The Latin empire in the East subverted, 121. The Venetians supplanted in the trade with Constantinople by the Genoese, 124. They settle a trade with Alexandria, 125. Account of the Venetian trade with India, in the

fourteenth century, 128. Travels of Marco Polo, 132. Their trade extended by the Turks subduing the Greek empire, 134. Remarks on their trade for Indian goods, 136. Evidences of the great wealth they acquired by this trade, 140. Alarm taken at the direct voyage to East India, by Vasco de Gama, 149. Measures prosecuted by the Venetians to check the progress of the Portuguese in the East, 153. The Portuguese supplant them in the European market, by reducing the prices of Indian goods, 172. The great extent of their trade, 345. The bank of Venice the first formed of any in Europe, 346. Amount of the Venetian naval strength in the fifteenth century, 347.

Ulug Beg, his astronomical tables, 80.

Virgil, a good natural historian, as well as a descriptive poet, 318.

Volney, M. his account of the camel, 349. And of the caravan from Damascus to Mecca, 350.

W

Wilford, Lieutenant, his examination of Arrian's Periplus by modern names and situations, 320.

Wilkins, Mr, account of his translation of the Heeto-Pades, 375.

Women, the jealous seclusion of, in India, whence derived, 362.

Wulli, character of an ode translated from, 376.

Z

Zemindars, their office in the government of Indostan, 364.

THE END.

Printed by Walker and Greig,
Edinburgh.